A Warrior's Quilt of Personal Military History

Also by Brigadier General Albin F. Irzyk (Ret.)

He Rode Up Front for Patton

Gasoline to Patton, A Different War

The 14th Armored Cavalry Regiment During the Berlin Crisis 1961

Unsung Heroes, Saving Saigon

A WARRIOR'S QUILT OF PERSONAL MILITARY HISTORY

BRIGADIER GENERAL ALBIN F. IRZYK (RET.)

Ivy House Publishing Group
Raleigh, NC
WWW.IVYHOUSEBOOKS.COM

PUBLISHED BY IVY HOUSE PUBLISHING GROUP
5122 Bur Oak Circle, Raleigh, NC 27612
United States of America
919.782.0281
www.ivyhousebooks.com

ISBN: 978-1-57197-505-8
Library of Congress Control Number: 2010930350

Printed in The United States of America

DEDICATION

Two weeks after graduating from college in 1940, when Hitler was marching down the Champs-Élysées in Paris, I found myself as a brand new cavalry second lieutenant in command of a platoon of 40 seasoned cavalry troopers. That was my first introduction to the 18-, 19-, 20-, 21-, 22-year-old young Americans who fight and win our country's wars.

It would be my destiny every day for the next 31 years to serve closely and under every possible circumstance with those young men who over those years would number in the many hundreds. Many of those circumstances would sorely test them, and some would be as difficult as an individual can possibly face.

It was gratifying for me, and I was honored and privileged that my life's work would be sharing those challenges and experiences with those young men. We served together at Ft. Myer, VA; Ft. Dix, NJ; Ft. Devens, MA; Ft. Knox, KY; the Occupation of Germany. We trained together at Pine Camp, NY; Camp Bowie, TX; the Mojave Desert; Salisbury Plains, England. We fought together at Chaumont, Belgium; Fresnes-en-Saulnois, France; St. Johatm, Germany; Saigon, Vietnam; the Central Highlands, Vietnam.

To me there is no greater calling than for an individual to put on a military uniform prepared to serve, fight, and even die for his country. For 31 years, I have watched that individual in action. America is uniquely blessed. It has had absolutely superb young men serving it.

It is because of the dedication, selflessness, courage and bravery of those young men that we have retained our blessed freedoms, and our rich and unique way of life.

It is to those young, fine Americans that this book is dedicated.

This book is also dedicated to a group that serves their fellow man. They do it relentlessly, selflessly, with great skill, determination and dedication. In a sense they are soldiers. They fight the good fight. Their battlefield is not the ground outside, but often the floorboards of the ICU (Intensive Care Unit).

They recently had a difficult fight. It was because of that skill, determination, and dedication that they prevailed. They won the battle. Had they not, I would not be writing this today.

I dedicate this book as well to Emory Johns Creek Hospital of Johns Creek, Georgia. That hospital has collected together a group of superb, outstanding individuals—doctors, nurses, staff personnel, aides of all types, personnel who work behind the scenes—to form a most unusual, close, capable team.

That team saved and extended my life.

TABLE OF CONTENTS

VIETNAM WAR

SUPPLEMENTAL

AUTHOR'S NOTE

My long life has spanned all of our country's wars during the 20th and 21st Centuries.

My first exposure and awareness of war was as a youth in patriotic New England. On the important holidays—4th of July, Memorial Day, Armistice Day—I watched spellbound as Veterans (Grand Army of the Republic, many from WWI) marched very proudly in the parades. The spectators watched the Veterans with great admiration, respect, and even reverence. Little did I know then that I, myself, would one day not only become a Veteran, but that service to my country would be my life's work. Because of that I would be deeply involved in my country's critical wars, and I would engage in one of life's greatest endeavors—commanding American troops in combat.

During my long period of service, as time and events permitted, I wrote articles about events and individuals, which I deemed significant, which I wanted "on the record" and important, as I believed them to be, and could easily escape the attention of historians. And that is exactly what has happened.

There appears little in the history books about: 1) **Urmitz,** where a 518-meter bridge teeming with German personnel and equipment was blown sky high by Germans, the last bridge to be blown over the Rhine, 2) **Chaumont, Belgium**, the location of a vicious German counterattack and bloody battle during the "Bulge," 3) **Ohrdruf**, the first concentration camp liberated by Allied soldiers, and an eye opener to the world, 4) **Singling**, an accurate portrayal of the 4th Armored Division's last battle in France, before turning north to the "Battle of the Bulge," 5) **Saigon**, the Tet fight for the U.S. Embassy.

Similarly, events not necessarily of direct combat, but still of significant historical interest, have likewise been overlooked. Two prime examples: 1) An account of the first (and undoubtedly last) time that a tank battalion with light and medium tanks forded a major river, in this case the mighty Moselle in France, 2) The Cold War actions of the 14th Armored Cavalry Regiment along the "Iron Curtain" in Germany, during the Berlin Crisis of 1961, when a stray shot from a Russian or an American weapon could easily have started WWIII.

Also included are articles that could only come from this author: 1) Vivid descriptions of two vastly different close and significant encounters with Gen. George S. Patton, 2) A spirited defense of the Sherman tank, 3) Unraveling some of the "mystery" surrounding the relief of Maj. Gen. John S. Wood of the 4th Armored Division during combat.

It is obvious that much of what is included between these covers is of significant historical interest. Yet it would never make the big headlines or occupy space on book pages, for the actions and experiences described here are at the basic, ground-fighting level. Historians apparently were not aware of them, believed them of little importance, or ignored them. Many years have passed, and much of what is covered here sits under the dust of obscurity. I am in the twilight of my life, and if I do not bring it out "for the record," no one else will. There is much here of historical interest for the student of military history. The great amount of military activity during the 20th Century was absolutely unprecedented.

This book is about history. Thus, it is a history book. Yet, it was not written by an historian. An historian has to resort to and rely on sources.

Yet, what his sources provide is often inaccurate, distorted, exaggerated, or incomplete. So his published work loses some credibility.

This history book has not been written by an historian. It was written by a *Participant*. I was deeply involved in every action described in this book, watched them firsthand. I did not have to go to sources. I am the source. Thus, this history book is as authentic as a history book can possibly be.

CHAPTER ONE

GENERAL PATTON'S HISTORIC SWEEP ACROSS FRANCE AUGUST 15-SEPTEMBER 1, 1944

Written by by Brig. Gen. Albin F. Irzyk. Reprinted from
Gasoline to Patton: A Different War, *Elderberry Press, 2004.*

P atton's reputation as a uniquely bold and successful field commander was quickly established during Operation Torch in North Africa. His performance in Morocco was most impressive, particularly because of his extremely low casualties. After the Kasserine debacle in North Africa, he did a masterful job of turning around the demoralized Second Corps, and leading it to victory. He left that campaign recognized as the United States Army's outstanding combat leader. His reputation was enhanced, and his star shone even more brilliantly, after his campaign in Sicily was acknowledged as an extraordinary operation. Now this same General Patton was pointed and primed to meet yet another challenge—this one his greatest one by far.

It would be a masterful campaign. Historians universally would label it one of the great achievements in military history and another Patton triumph. It would gain for him the fame that he had always sought, a great step toward military immortality, and growth and substance to the ever-growing and developing Patton legend.

He was still busy as elements of his Third Army had reached the lower Seine, crossed it, and were now advancing north alongside it. But he recognized that he was heading for, what would for him be, a dead end, and that the demands, challenges, and opportunities lay elsewhere. So he looked deep to the south over his right shoulder, and like the starter at a track meet, figuratively, fired his pistol. The XIIth and XXth Corps in the runners' starting boxes were unleashed at the sound of the shot to drive in the only direction that mattered—EAST!

The XIIth Corps had a brand-new commander, whose background was completely Infantry, so he would not be able to contribute a great deal. But the XIIth Corps had "P" Wood and his 4th Armored Division, already battle-tested, hardened, proven.

As was to be expected, Patton positioned the tanks of the 4th Armored Division in the forefront—they would lead his Third Army (as they would again and again in the future), and would once again be his spearhead. The 4th Armored was my division, and here is how we made history.

As soon as General Wood received his orders from General Patton to move, he deliberately began exercising loose control over his subordinate tactical commanders. He eased up on the reins, gave them their heads, and, figuratively with a touch of his spurs and a flick of his riding crop, sent them on their way. His tanks were soon on a tear—a hell-for-leather drive. (Secretary of War Henry L. Stimson, a long-time friend of Patton's, would observe in "delighted admiration," that "Patton had set his tanks to run around France like bed-bugs in a Georgetown kitchen.")

To carry out his aggressive philosophy the division would operate like cavalry—slashing, sidestepping, with speed as surprise. The tankers were confident and cocky (they had already proved of what they were capable), and demonstrated a daring, audacious, hard-riding, fast-shooting style. The 4th Armored advanced hard and fast, bypassed strongly held centers of resistance with rapid flanking movements and deep penetrations (the battle cry was "bypass and haul ass.") When towns or strong points could not be bypassed, they were taken in stride with sudden headlong assaults, bruising power, and violent fire, which broke the enemy. We avoided pitched battles, probed for weak spots, and pushed through into the enemy's rear areas. The division had a "restless ardor" for pursuit of a defeated enemy. Its outstanding characteristics were its ability to move and shoot, but above all to move. Movement became its middle name, constant momentum its trademark. A German colonel captured during this period, an officer who had commanded units in Russia, exclaimed, "To know the commander of this Armored Division would explain to me how this army managed to achieve such a speed of advance, which in many instances caught us completely unprepared."

The division was aided immeasurably by extremely favorable operational conditions. It was almost perfect tank weather and ideal tank country. The days were long and the nights short. Thus, there were many hours in the operational day. The fields in the predominantly open country were dry, permitting the tanks to go almost anywhere they chose to go. The water in the creeks, streams, and even small rivers was low, and many of their beds were dry—ideal for fording. If a bridge were blown and the water too deep for fording, the engineers, who stayed closed-up, immediately installed a hasty bridge, enabling the tanks to move ahead with a minimum of delay.

Enemy resistance was disorganized. However, there were many who put up a stiff, even fanatical, defense. Key cities and towns were well defended. The Germans installed hasty mines, blew craters in roads, and fired antitank guns from strategically placed positions. They blew bridges as they withdrew, and often defended the sites. Great numbers fought ferociously. There were many who stopped their retreat and wanted to fight, but we would not let them. Instead of engaging them, we outflanked and swept past them. Once we were around and behind them, even the most fanatical recognized that the "jig was up," and it was futile to continue to fight. By this time we knew, and they knew, that our fire from the rear was more deadly and three times more effective than fire from the front. By using maneuver and surprise, we avoided costly frontal attacks and kept casualties very low.

When we saw fresh tracks, it was like the fox after the stricken hare. We were advancing faster than they could flee. When we caught up with them, we destroyed them. Many of the fleeing enemy had no desire to fight. They were hurrying in the direction of their homeland in the hope that somewhere, before the border was reached, they could organize their forces, and present a stiff, organized defense.

To accelerate its advance and to cover more ground, the 4th Armored, in its advance to the east, operated on a broad front. Up ahead to the left would be Combat Command "A" (CCA) and on the right, Combat Command "B" (CCB). Following behind and always ready for employment, behind one of the forward Combat Commands or independently, was the third Combat Command, Reserve Command (CCR). CC "A" and CC "B" operated virtually independently and moved on parallel axes, usually with considerable distance between them; on occasion they were as much as 45 kilometers apart. Until now, such employment had been unheard of. During my military schooling, it was continually and adamantly stressed that attacking units must be mutually supporting. Operating 45 kilometers apart hardly met that criterion, so the 4th Armored was "throwing away the book." The tactics of the division would be unpredictable, unconventional, and opportunistic, so, they habitually would be guilty of not following "the book."

During the advance across France, Third Army was the south flank of the entire Allied Expeditionary Force; the XII Corps, to which the 4th Armored was assigned, protected the south flank of Third Army, the 4th Armored was the south flank of XII Corps, and my Combat Command "B" was the southernmost element of the 4th. Thus, the right flank of the 4th Armored was wide open—there was absolutely nothing to our right.

Wood never worried about his flanks. He developed a long, amazing, unique, and lasting relationship with the Thunderbolts and Mustangs of the XIX Tactical Air Command, which not only closely supported our operations, but watched our flanks as well. The teamwork between the XIXTAC and the 4th Armored was probably closer in spirit and superior in quality to that of any similar operation in WWII, and would not be equaled during that war.

During this period, we moved too rapidly and were too widely scattered for the conventional gathering of commanders for their instructions and orders, or for the traditional, very detailed operations orders, stressed *ad infinitum* at the service schools. General Wood resorted to simple, oral orders, and "mission-type orders." His own orders from Patton came by radio, or on overlays that were jeeped in or flown in by artillery spotter planes. The normal overlay order was quite simple. It usually consisted merely of a line of departure (usually the most forward positions which we held), a broad directional arrow (axis of advance), a goose egg with the letters OBJ (objective, always way out front), and the terse order, "Get going at first light." That's all we had, that's all we needed. And in many instances we needed no orders; we continued doing what we had been doing. It is reputed that at one point early on, when a senior commander, after seizing an objective earlier than expected requested further instructions from Patton, the answer was, "Go East and go like hell." That was a classic example of a "mission type order."

Our daily output during that sweep was absolutely sensational and unbelievable. Our tanks made daily advances of as much as 37 miles, 51 miles, 30 miles, and 48 miles. Because of lasting daylight, we operated well into the evening. First light came very, very early. There were not too many hours of darkness. During the brief periods we stopped, we utilized the time to refuel our tanks and other vehicles, and to replace our expended ammunition. The only logistical item constantly in short supply was sleep.

During that advance across France, one action best typified the *élan*, spirit, daring, and aggressiveness of the 4th Armored Division. On August 25, a task force from Combat Command "A" consisting of tank and armored infantry mounted in their half-tracks advanced toward the large, important city of Troyes, which was well southeast of Paris, and sat on the Seine River. Troyes was a particularly good example of a German center of resistance that we had been facing. It was also one that could not be bypassed, but had to be taken head-on. Because of its location, holding the city was of vital importance to the Germans. There was no question but that it would be heavily and determinedly defended. As it turned out, the heavily dug-in and waiting garrison numbered many hundreds of men. In the advance thus far, the attacking elements of the 4th Armored had relied heavily on speed. Before Troyes speed was more essential than ever. Now was not the time to begin a slow, methodical, careful, time-consuming attack upon the city, even though the situation called for just such a maneuver.

So the tanks of the task force quickly spread out in a wide formation, and the armored infantry mounted in their half-tracks dispersed in an irregular formation behind the tanks. Without hesitation and with all guns blazing, they made a bold, powerful, fast-moving attack across three and one-half miles of wide-open ground directly at Troyes. It was a dispersed, spread formation, desert-type move reminiscent of an old Cavalry charge, as well as the actions and formations employed during our training exercises in the Mojave Desert. The enemy quickly opened fire, sending artillery and direct fire rounds at the charging attackers, but the mobile units moved so rapidly that most of the hurried rounds landed behind them and were generally ineffective. As the tanks neared the city, they saw tank ditches up ahead directly in their path. Instead of slowing down, they increased their speed and actually leaped across the ditches. What may have appeared to be a totally reckless, foolhardy maneuver was, instead, so bold, so audacious, so unexpected that it stunned, shocked, and completely demoralized the enemy. The defenders were so shaken that they appeared to be in a trance, and the attackers quickly and successfully overran and seized the city, and most importantly, Third Army troops were across the Seine. Defenders later said that they just could not believe what they had seen and experienced. By the next day the elements of CC "A" were clearing up Troyes, holding the high ground northeast of the city, and effecting systematic destruction of the Germans attempting to flee to the east.

Unbelievably, on August 31, Combat Command "A" was sitting on the east bank of the Meuse River, and would be joined by CC "B" the next day. My tank battalion had advanced an absolutely sensational 328 miles in 12 days. Even more remarkable—we had moved from the Atlantic to the Meuse in only 18 days. It was not only astonishing but exciting to realize that we were now merely 63 miles from the German border, and that the great prize, the Rhine River, which could prove to be the ultimate objective, was, amazingly, only 140 direct miles away. One hundred forty miles? Why that was less than half the distance we had advanced in the last 12 days!

In less than a month Patton had thrown a 700-mile right hook across the widest part of France. Our tanks had already put nearly 1,500 miles on their speedometers. They had advanced down the Normandy peninsula and into the heart of Brittany, taken a side trip to the Atlantic, and then led Third Army's drive to the Meuse. Now euphoria gripped us tightly. The possibilities and probabilities to the east were staggering. The roads were clear ahead, and the Moselle River would be undefended. From there the avenues to Germany were wide open. The American forces had by now destroyed the bulk of the enemy needed to man the empty fortifications of the Siegfried Line. The remnants just could not retire fast enough to reach, much less organize, man, and defend, those defensive barriers, which had been constructed inside their homeland. And not too far behind that was the Rhine with, realistically, undefended bridges. The possibility was high that the Germans would collapse when the Rhine River was reached.

On the morning of September 2, we were poised, positioned, ready and eager to continue our push into Germany.

* * *

Author's Note: A brief answer to what happened next is found in Chapter 3, with a more complete answer in my book, *Gasoline to Patton, A Different War,* Elderberry Press, Inc., 2005.

CHAPTER TWO

GALLOPING JUGGERNAUT

Written by Maj. Albin F. Irzyk. Reprinted with permission from
Military Review: *A Monthly Review of Military Literature*
from the Command and General Staff School at Fort Leavenworth, Kansas,
volume XXV, number 1, April 1945.

O n July 25, 1944, prefaced by a huge, stunning air bombard-
ment, an offensive was launched in Normandy. A waiting
world which had been hearing of no progress on the stalemated French front and which had been taking solace in crushing
Russian victories, was stirred with excitement at the initial success of
the Cotentin drive. As each succeeding day brought news of more and
more progress, excitement mounted and estimates on the possibilities
resulting from the breakthrough knew no bounds.

People everywhere began to read of the work of armored columns,
which were starting a headlong drive across France, and which were to
write new pages in the history of the war. Tanks and tank commanders
suddenly gained for themselves new and greater eminence. For many
days, papers wrote of little else. The world had become armor con-
scious, and the work of armored columns was on everyone's lips. The
speed and accomplishments of American armor were compared most
favorably with what the Germans and Russians had done during their
most triumphant days.

This article will describe in some detail the operations of tanks, a
tank battalion, and an armored column. The operations recorded may
or may not have been typical of other and similar units, and the methods

and tactics employed can, no doubt, be improved upon. At any rate, the units whose actions I shall describe met with much success, so the basis upon which they worked must have been sound.

In my opinion, tank and therefore armored warfare in France to date can be divided generally into three phases: (1) "Hedgerow Phase," (2) "Road-March Phase," and (3) "River-Crossing Phase." The fourth phase and perhaps subsequent phases are looming before us. Each of the three phases now behind us will be discussed separately. [The editor of *Military Review*, in which this article originally appeared, omitted the "Hedgerow Phase" from print.]

ROAD-MARCH PHASE

Dawn, after a long, dark, troublesome night, came to hedgerow fighting on July 25. Tanks, supported by infantry who rode the tanks, were massed, and with a violent, thunderous, and desperate effort achieved the breakthrough, which proved to be the turning point of the war. Tanks and armored units jumped into the foreground and gained an enviable position which to date they have not had to relinquish. From that day to this they have spearheaded the effort in France, and their accomplishments and achievements are many. By breaking out of the hedges during the latter part of July, the "Hedgerow Phase" was left behind and the second phase, a much more colorful one, began.

With the crust broken, armored units now formed up into armored columns to begin the push, which was rapidly to become a headlong race. Each column with its cavalry troop [mechanized], armored infantry battalion, armored artillery battalions, tank battalion, tank destroyer company, antiaircraft platoon, engineer company, maintenance company, and medical company now began to move on the road. In single column, vehicle behind vehicle, with at least seventy yards' distance between vehicles and often much more, the column stretched for many miles. Led by an advance guard at first consisting of the cavalry troop in front, followed by an armored infantry company, a platoon of tank destroyers, an armored field artillery battery, and finally by an engineer platoon, the column moved out slowly, and was jerky. Like a young child taking its first few unsteady steps, the column was finding its feet. Short, slow moves followed by long, monotonous halts typified the progress of the column during the first two or three days. Although the enemy had been broken, disorganized, and put to flight, he was still close enough in front to fight, harass, and thus delay.

Initially, the advance guard was under the command of the infantry battalion commander. His unit, less the advance guard company, led the main body. Close behind were the balance of the tank destroyers followed by all the artillery. Interspersed in the column were vehicles of the antiaircraft platoon, combat command headquarters, and artillery group headquarters. Near the end of the column was the tank battalion followed by the miscellaneous service elements.

During the days ahead, the make-up of the advance guard and the main body was to be modified often. As just described, it proved to be highly effective and successful during the first days.

After he was routed, the enemy, with fight still left in him, gathered on the main roads and in villages and towns along the roads. It was the early resistance that the retreating Boche provided that delayed the column and caused the short moves and the long halts. Jerry placed occasional hasty mines and roadblocks, and blew small bridges over creeks. He defended his roadblocks lightly, but he sniped treacherously and tenaciously in the villages.

As a result, the cavalry proceeded slowly and, with the help of the infantry and engineers behind them, cleared the mines and the roadblocks with their handfuls of defenders and cleared the snipers and riflemen out of the villages. The latter often had to be cleared house by house. Resistance as a whole, however, was not heavy, and therefore artillery, tanks, and more infantry were not needed. Rather, it was merely annoying and time-consuming. Meanwhile, power and strength and mobility were halted back along the column.

Despite the disturbances and annoyances, the column moved and miles were consumed. Upon reaching the large cities standing squarely in the path of the column and which were key objectives, resistance was much stronger and better organized. Here the column had to halt, deploy, and do battle. The enemy in such a spot could not be thrust aside merely with the pass of a hand.

Conquest of such cities took time, planning, and coordination as well as hard, bitter, savage, bloody fighting and losses. Artillery had to go into position and blast the town. All available infantry left their half-tracks and advanced on foot. Cavalry and even engineers assisted the doughboys. Tanks deployed and outflanked; and they guarded and defended key places, approaches and exits as well. Resistance consisted again of mines, and of snipers and riflemen in nearly every building. Their resistance was strengthened by heavy and troublesome mortar fire and by antitank guns cleverly placed. The process of cleaning these spots was slow and painstaking. Streets had to be swept for mines. Building after building had to be cleared. Snipers, machine gunners, and mortar crews had to be captured or destroyed. Only then could the column form up and move again.

Movement was once more steady, but only until the next city was reached. The deployment, attack, and conquest had to be repeated. Enemy tanks now were met at road intersections in towns. Defending forces often greatly outnumbered the attackers, and only because the worried Germans were on the run, had inferior organization, and were oppressed by a spirit and morale that had been seriously and severely cracked were the advancing elements able to dislodge them rapidly and capture them by the thousands.

It was at about this time that the tactical air force, of which so many had read so much, really showed its wares. The airmen proved on more than one occasion to be the balance of power, the force that rapidly changed a ding-dong, give-and-take struggle into a glowing victory. From that day on, they ranged far above the column in all its movements and are at this very moment giving the units close, prompt support. The P-47s especially, which are so familiar to members of the column, and the P-51s as well, won an increasing amount of admiration from day to day, until today when they are most deeply respected. Very, very often they bring sunshine to an otherwise gloomy situation, and their presence perceptibly raises morale and often virtually physically raises men from their foxholes.

At about this time, too, tanks were brought up to the advance guard. First it was a platoon and later a company. It was found that the presence of tanks in front speeded progress considerably. Often, the enemy who defended hotly and fought tooth and nail against cavalry and infantry changed their minds quickly when tanks put in an appearance. They either ran away or came in with hands on their heads.

With resistance fairly stiff and with the presence of enemy tanks and antitank guns imminent, a platoon of tanks in front with the cavalry worked well. Two quarter-ton C & Rs and an M-8 reconnaissance vehicle working with and immediately in front of the tanks proved highly satisfactory. The peeps and reconnaissance car picked the route, and poked around corners and around bends in the roads. If all was clear, they kept moving. If something other than tanks or antitank guns lurked ahead, they pulled back beside or behind the tanks until the enemy was blasted by the tanks. If an enemy tank or an antitank gun was ahead, the tanks were sufficiently warned. Without exposing themselves beforehand, they were able to maneuver around the tank or antitank gun lying in ambush and destroy it. A company of tanks directly behind a troop of cavalry, too, was found to be most effective.

Upon reaching Brittany, with key cities in Normandy already entered on the victory ledger, the armored columns picked up speed rapidly and began a trek that gained for itself portentous results. The column rolled unceasingly and then rolled some more.

Opposition now became scattered. The column often caught the enemy in vehicles, in carts, and on bicycles fleeing just in front of it. Capture of these was easy and even fun. Occasionally, towns and villages were briefly and hotly defended by dismounted men.

Bridges were still found blown, but were rarely defended. Each of these necessitated a short delay. They were hardly perceptible, however, when compared to the ground covered.

Delays and resistance notwithstanding, the column now made progress and attained speeds and gained results seldom approached, much less equaled, by similar units on maneuvers. The column reached its peak and reached a state of near-perfection in road marching by accomplishing a feat that, in my mind, has not been equaled in combat or on maneuvers. Facing no resistance whatsoever, the column marched continuously for thirty-six hours and covered a total distance of 258 miles.

Back in hedgerow fighting, when enemy ack-ack was heavy, when Me 109s were apt to appear at any moment, a new star, a new hero was born. The liaison pilots in their grasshopper cubs endeared themselves to everyone. Now they became the darlings of the armored column. Affectionately labeled the "Maytag Messerschmitts," they hovered always over the column like a mother hen caring for her brood. It was a cheering sight to see the planes at the first crack of dawn and to see them continuously until night had completely fallen. Often they were in the air on days with such a low ceiling that it seemed foolhardy, indeed, to fly. In addition to being a strong morale factor, the planes served in a far more important and in an intensely practical manner. They flew ahead of the column and reported back on condition of bridges, on clearness of the route, and on the presence of enemy. Often miles before the column hit opposition, the units had been warned by the grasshoppers of what to expect. Above all, the liaison pilots were ready to adjust artillery fire just as soon as the first battery could leave the roads and "toss" out its first round.

Soon Brittany was cut and portions of France farther and farther east were penetrated. To move faster and to accomplish twice as much, the column was now divided into two columns. Both columns were potent forces all their own. Each had its own objectives, and although both were controlled by the same headquarters, one worked separately from the other.

In one column was a portion of a cavalry troop, the tank battalion with a company of armored infantry attached, one field artillery battalion and often more, a platoon of engineers, a platoon of tank destroyers, and units from the service elements, all under the command of the tank battalion commander. The other column, commanded by the armored infantry battalion commander, consisted of the remainder of the cavalry reconnaissance troop, the infantry battalion, at least one battalion of field artillery, a company less a platoon of tank destroyers, a company of tanks, a platoon of engineers, and service elements. Both columns were kept generally abreast, and in the course of their operations were often brought together into assembly areas for reorganization prior to embarking on new missions.

As in Brittany, much of the advance was against light, scattered, and disorganized resistance. Only in the large cities and towns was resistance stiff. Many of the cities so famous and well known to us were key places in highly important and strategic locations. Railroads and roads in many cases radiated from these cities in all directions. The desperate Huns defended these locations hotly with what they had. A different plan, a different attack, naturally, had to be followed in each case because of varied terrain, type of defense, and strength of resisting elements; but in all cases the armored column was forced to deploy and to use all its forces, which fortunately were usually enough. The capture of such a city took a day, perhaps two or three. Then the race by the buoyant, cocky, and triumphant forces continued to the next defended locality.

Throughout the second phase, progress was so rapid it was exhilarating. The column gained a maximum of results with a minimum of effort and losses. Nevertheless, lessons were learned which will prove valuable in future movements.

An advance guard must have a light force as its point, and, in my opinion, this should consist of a cavalry troop or a platoon. Such a unit carefully checks and follows the designated route and modifies it in the event the one selected proves impractical. Because of its mobility and speed, the cavalry is able to move swiftly when fired upon and at the same time report the nature, strength, and location of the opposition.

Immediately behind must be a striking force consisting of light tanks, tank destroyers, and often better yet, medium tanks, or a combination of all three. If opposition is weak, the armored vehicles can wipe it out without unduly delaying the progress of the column. If heavy, the armor is able to pin down the enemy by fire and test his strength and dispositions while other elements in the column are deploying.

In the advance guard, an infantry unit, preferably a company, is needed to follow the tanks closely on the road and especially in close action when the infantry is then dismounted. Infantry behind tanks is vitally needed to mop up and dispose of stragglers missed by the tanks, to search and clear buildings, to protect tanks from the rear, and to collect and handle prisoners.

An engineer platoon and an artillery battery must be included in the advance guard. Having the engineer platoon near the front of the column makes them available for quick mine probing, for demolishing roadblocks, and for rebuilding small bridges. The artillery is needed near the front so as to be able to go into position rapidly and to register on the enemy immediately. Thus, by the time the artillery battalion has left the road and has moved into position, the advance guard battery will be able to furnish the data necessary to fire the battalion without delay.

The order of march of the above elements is debatable. No hard and fast rule can be laid down. Rather, the order must be adjusted often to suit the terrain over which the column is to move, and the nature of obstacles and opposition anticipated.

There will be instances when the infantry will lead the main body, and occasions will arise when the tanks will go ahead. As in the case of the order of march of the advance guard, the existing situation will be the deciding factor. In all cases, however, the artillery will follow immediately behind the leading unit. When artillery is called for, it can be assumed that a grim situation lurks ahead. It is vital that the artillery be up in front where it can do some good and in a hurry!

It goes without saying that, when called for, the artillery has road priority. Everything moving or stopped gets out of the way. The roads must be opened and cleared so that nothing will delay the passing of the artillery vehicles.

In any discussion of the make-up of a column, the rear guard must not be neglected, especially when the column has no other elements following directly behind. If vehicles packing a good wallop tail the column, it is sure to be in good hands. Small units of tanks and tank destroyers are suggested for the job.

In a marching column, whether in an approach march when contact is imminent or with contact already made, the very same principles and lessons learned in training and on maneuvers apply more strongly than ever. lt might be well to discuss briefly a few of those most abused.

The prime objective of the column commander is to get a column to the designated place in sufficient strength, in good enough condition, and in proper order *to fight it immediately.* Success in this matter will be ever out of reach unless everyone in the column practices strict road discipline. Vehicles must maintain a distance of no greater than seventy yards, but to be careless in this matter is to be burdened with an endlessly long, straggling column.

Units within the column must be alerted prior to stopping and starting. The strictest of control is required. This practice is particularly applicable to organizations within units. Everything must stop and start together. To violate this procedure is to cause many vehicles in the column to speed continuously at a breakneck speed in a hopeless effort to catch the vehicle in front. When such a situation exists, it is an easy matter for a vehicle to take a wrong turn and to carry much of the column with it. A disaster of no mean proportions could easily result.

Once the column is moving, nothing except a light wheeled vehicle, or artillery vehicles as previously mentioned, may pass. Only vehicles used for column control and those needed up ahead should be permitted to double the column. Track vehicles and tanks must never pass a moving column. Double banking, however, is permissible when the column is halted.

On a long march, vehicles fall out frequently for maintenance, and a knotty problem is the result. As soon as repairs are completed on a vehicle, the natural tendency for the crew is to race frantically in a reckless effort to catch their organization. Such an effort endangers lives both in the vehicle and in the column and breaks and confuses the column as well. Such a practice can be efficiently solved. It was found highly satisfactory for the unit maintenance officer to collect all repaired vehicles into a column of his own and to march them as a unit until the march was completed. It was discovered, too, that often a vehicle that had fallen out for maintenance caused an unnecessary halt all the way behind it. Two instances of carelessness were responsible. Had the vehicle immediately posted a guide to wave by all vehicles behind it, or had someone in the vehicle behind immediately gone forward to investigate the cause of the halt, no unnecessary delay would have resulted.

On long marches at a steady, rapid pace, especially on very hot days, tanks became heated, bogey wheels suffered, and rubber tracks took severe punishment. To save wear and tear on vehicles and on crews, an extended halt during the hottest part of the day was deemed most advisable.

Night marching could be very profitable, and conversely it could prove exceedingly unprofitable. If distance had to be covered rapidly at almost any cost, great gains could be made on a night that was clear and bright, and especially with a moon. Marching in the cool of the evening with the dust settled by atmospheric conditions often brought highly satisfactory results. To march on a dark night, however, was of little proportionate value, dangerous, and foolhardy. In fact, it was an invitation to disaster. Much could happen. Vehicles could become lost easily and take dozens of other vehicles with them. Sudden stops meant numerous accidents. Above all, vehicular crews became exhausted by the time daylight came. At best, progress had to be slow. All in all, unless assured of a clear, bright night, it would definitely be most wise to go into a bivouac as night descended, and to get on the road again at first light.

The pace of the column must always be set by the slowest-moving vehicle in the column. Otherwise, over an extended march many vehicles would never catch up.

A column the size of the initial one described and subjected to many of the violations just discussed has been known to stretch for the unheard-of length of seventy-six miles on a forced march. That is, indeed, something of which to beware.

The galloping juggernaut, which for many days had been rolling in nothing but high gear, suddenly came to a screeching halt. The glamor of war and unstinted success tumbled suddenly on crumbling walls and quickly gasped its last. The first of the rivers was reached, and the road-march phase faded quickly away. Progress from here on was to become costly and slow. The third phase was in the offing.

RIVER-CROSSING PHASE

The third phase was tough. River after river had to be crossed. In each instance dominating ground overlooked the rivers, and every one was a definite, separate, and difficult obstacle that was a severe test to an armored unit. At any moment an attempted river crossing could easily become an invitation to disaster. The physical aspects alone were difficult factors with which to contend; but add to them a determined, troublesome enemy, and a struggle of no mean proportions was sure to ensue. To the armored column pressing ever eastward, the stretch ahead looked formidable indeed.

Virtually every river had a canal paralleling it. Most often, the canal was a much more difficult and serious impediment than the river itself. The banks of the muddy canals were vertical and twelve or more feet high. More often than not, their composition was of concrete. Although the canal locks had generally been destroyed, a foot or two of water remained, and beneath there was a deep layer of soft, sticky, treacherous mud. This was a tank obstacle indeed!

The fast-flowing rivers were deep but often fordable by tanks in limited places. Here again banks were many times steep and high. It was a sure bet that bridges across both the canals and the rivers would be blown. To make matters worse, the dominating ground seemed always to favor the enemy. From the opposite side of the river, the high hills, like a sneering giant, loomed down upon the attacking elements.

The well-defended towns, situated at the crossings, were of necessity the initial objectives. In virtually all cases the defenders were in strong positions on the opposite side, but in some instances they defended on the near side of the river as well.

Two helpful factors gave the dark task ahead a touch of a silver lining. They were: (1) favorable terrain, and (2) land between water barriers. The high ground on the near side of the river overlooked the river, the town, and the shattered bridges, and gave observation on the dominating ground on the other side. Of material assistance, too, was the strip of ground that separated the canal and the river. Sometimes this strip was very wide, sometimes narrow; but in all cases it was big enough to divide the river-crossing job into two parts: the canal crossing and the river crossing. The strip enabled units to catch their breath after breaching the first obstacle and to get their second wind for the next crossing.

Canals and rivers were obstacles difficult to surmount, especially by tanks. Everyone knows that the initial crossing of a river and a canal and the securing of a strong bridgehead is primarily an infantry mission, and until such a task is completed, engineers cannot commence putting in their bridges. The tanks must wait until the two previous steps are successfully completed before they can even think about crossing. Once a bridgehead is established securely enough to permit engineers to work, the water obstacles will be quickly spanned and the tanks will be able to cross. Armored support is essential to ensure success, and tanks must get across as quickly as possible to support the infantry, to enlarge and strengthen the bridgehead, and to be ready to repulse the counterattack which is sure to come.

Realizing all this only too well, the combat command moved out on its unsavory mission. As it had in the latter part of the second phase, the combat command moved in two columns with the composition very much the same as before. Each column had its route to follow and river crossings to make. If both units were successful, two river crossings were made. On the other hand, if one had difficulty in securing a crossing while the other was successful, both columns crossed at one place and then moved off again in a double column.

As before, the column commanded by the tank battalion commander was led by a cavalry reconnaissance troop. It was followed closely by the light tank company of the tank battalion, and attached to the light tanks was a platoon of tank destroyers. Immediately behind the light tanks and tank destroyers came a platoon of medium tanks, the tank battalion assault-gun platoon, and an artillery battery. The remainder of the fighting elements of the tank battalion followed, and were in turn closely followed by an artillery battalion. Behind came more artillery, headquarters elements, and service units of all types. Attached to the tank battalion was a company of armored infantry, or when the going was expected to be especially arduous, a battalion of infantry from a nearby infantry division. The latter proved to be the wiser of the two arrangements, for a river crossing against stiff resistance for a single infantry company was to give a boy a man-sized job.

In any case, the attached infantry was carried on the back decks of the tanks. In the case of the armored infantry company, their empty half-tracks marched with the service elements of the tank battalion. The heavy weapons, however, were placed in the tank column where they were accessible, if needed, to the infantry commander. The infantry battalion's heavy weapons, too, were placed with the tanks.

The setup, as just described, was again able to make excellent progress. An artillery liaison pilot in a cub plane assisted immeasurably by staying always well in front of the column and reporting accurately on what lay ahead. Information from the plane was supplemented by pertinent observations by the cavalry.

The first evidence on the condition of a bridge came from the pilot. In addition, he divulged the presence of enemy and indicated what resistance could be expected. Like a batter getting stolen signals from a baseline coach, the cavalry was forewarned and proceeded cautiously, as close to the bridge site as possible. The reconnaissance element then was able to send back a more detailed report on the condition of the bridge, the status of the approaches to the bridge, and the strength, composition, and location of the enemy. An engineer reconnaissance officer was at once dispatched forward to the cavalry unit where he made his estimate as to what equipment he would need to construct a crossing, where he would build it, and how long it would take him.

In the meantime, the tank battalion with attached units moved forward, deployed, and took positions most protected from enemy fire. The artillery battalion followed suit and went into position ready to bring down all its fire immediately upon call. Light tanks and tank destroyers were sent out to protect the open flanks.

At this point all available information was discussed, since to be forewarned is to be forearmed. A plan was made as to how to reach the river and how to cross the river to establish a strong bridgehead. A thorough and detailed map study of the ground on the other side was then made, if it had not been made before, and what to expect and where it would be was considered. Supplementing the map reconnaissance was a personal and visual reconnaissance made from the best observation point available. After everything possible was completed in preparation for the task ahead, orders were issued for the capture of the bridgehead, order of march in which units would cross the completed bridge, actions to be followed, and objectives to be taken on the other side.

Before launching the attack, as many preliminary preparations as possible were made. All the tanks moved forward to the high ground overlooking the river and took defiladed positions in readiness to support, with direct fire, the infantry effort. The mortar and assault-gun platoons joined the tanks, as did the artillery forward observers. The field artillery battalion began to rain down heavy concentrations in swift swoops on all dangerous-looking areas, and was prepared to fire counterbattery fire once the attack was under way. The assault-gun platoon, together with the mortar platoon, and tanks joined hands with the artillery for the initial preparation on suspected danger areas.

After the infantry commander had gone forward to the cavalry position and had returned with all the information available, the infantry moved out to attack the river crossing and to win a secure bridgehead. Directly supporting the infantry was a platoon of tanks. This small unit virtually married itself to the doughboys and scurried around like a sheep dog tending to his flock. The tanks stayed with the infantry and covered them to the river. By this time, enemy small-arms fire and machine gun fire was sure to be heavy. The full weight of the fire from all the tank weapons was vital in disconcerting the enemy, and figuratively smoothed the road over which the footsloggers traveled.

On reaching the river or canal, the tanks moved along the banks to lend what support they could to doughboys as they made their valiant attempt to cross the water, as uninviting and costly an obstacle as an infantryman is called upon to hurdle. The tanks, on such a mission, are as vulnerable to antitank fire as a string of ducks at a Coney Island shooting gallery. They took what protection they could, however, from nearby buildings and stone walls. Their presence was a strong morale factor to the infantry. More important, tanks were immune to automatic fire, which was so painful and despairing to the infantry. A few well-placed tank shots could destroy a machine gun that would take the infantry much time and many lives to overcome. All the while, the artillery forward observer with the tanks was calling for fire as suitable targets presented themselves.

The infantry had the close support of the tank platoon, the artillery, and the remainder of the tank battalion, which fired direct from the high ground behind. The doughboys with such backing reconnoitered up and down the river until they found a suitable crossing. The securing of the bridgehead soon followed.

As soon as the bridgehead was strong enough to permit engineers to work in comparative safety, those rough-and-ready, daring jacks-of-all-trades immediately went into their specialty act and began constructing a bridge over the river or canal, whichever was first. Tanks now moved to the bridge site and covered the engineers as they worked. As soon as the span was in place, the platoon of tanks moved across and took positions between the river and the canal. The engineers then put on the finishing touches to the first bridge and moved forward, still covered by the tanks, to work on the next span. As soon as the last bridge was ready, the tanks moved across to the opposite shore and helped strengthen the bridgehead. The crossings were now ready for the passage of the entire column.

The pattern just described could not be followed in every instance. Each crossing presented many new and different problems. There were cases where infantry, with tanks supporting, as described, successfully crossed a canal only to be pinned down completely on the wide strip of land between the canal and the river by heavy enemy automatic fire. Because of terrain obstacles, the tanks could give the doughboys very little effective support from their positions along the canal bank; nor could the armor cross the canal, since a treadway bridge had not yet been placed across that obstacle. As no bridgehead had been established on the far shore, heavy enemy fire prevented the engineers from even commencing to work. A desperate situation had been born. As the river *had* to be crossed and since the tanks were without a bridge over the defiant canal, one course, and one alone, seemed open, and that was for the infantry to cross at any cost. "At any cost" meant very, very heavy losses.

Situations occurred where determination, courage, and initiative found other solutions. One historic crossing was made possible by a tank platoon leader who fired his tank guns at the banks of the canal to loosen them, only to have his tank get stuck in the canal mud once he got into it. Still not deterred, he had his tank towed back by another tank, and then set to work with fellow members of his platoon to build a ramp across the canal by using logs, rocks, concrete—in fact, anything and everything available. All this was being done under the same fire that prevented the infantry from advancing and the engineers from working. The canal bottom and the tanks offered protection that the other two units did not have. Eventually, one tank crossed the canal over the hand-laid ramp and towed successive tanks across. The platoon shouldered in at once to give the infantry the close support that it so critically needed. As far as the enemy was concerned, that canal-crossing achievement was the straw that broke the camel's back. The infantry soon crossed the river with the tanks covering, and although losses were sustained, the burden was lightened immeasurably by the steel friends. Alas, after crossing the river and with success in their grasp, the infantry once again were pinned down on the opposite shore by strong enemy fire. With the fragrance of one bold, successful accomplishment still in their nostrils, the tank platoon soon found, after a careful reconnaissance, a ford across the river. Once again, tanks and infantry were able to team up, and a firm bridgehead soon resulted.

Yet things did not always work that well. On other occasions the breaching of a deep canal without the help of a bridge, or the fording of a deep river, was impossible for tanks. Since the infantry had no close support except what the artillery and the tanks on the high bluff were able to give, the dogged doughboys took the only course open to them. They "grabbed the bull by the horns" and, in the face of withering and dismaying fire, finally made the bridgehead. In doing it that way, a great deal more time was consumed, but more important—much more—was the added cost in American lives.

Enemy antitank guns well placed close to the shore could and did limit the movement of tanks, and placed once again the burden on the perpetually weary shoulders of the selfsame individuals, the doughboys.

Before the attack to establish the bridgehead had been made, the tank battalion commander in his orders had divided his battalion and attachments into task forces. The units so organized were usually three in number, built around the medium tank companies and commanded by the medium tank company commanders. To alleviate the added burden upon the company commanders, it was more satisfactory when possible to put a responsible staff officer in charge of each force. Each company had a portion of the infantry attached to it. The battalion assault-gun platoon was assigned to one company, the battalion mortar platoon to a second, and the advance guard artillery battery to a third. The light tank company with attached tank destroyers and cavalry sometimes constituted a fourth task force. Often, however, they were divided up among the other three groups of forces to strengthen and balance them. The battalion reconnaissance platoon, together with the battalion command post, were usually near or at the most centrally located position.

When the time came to cross the bridges, the teams were formed and crossed the bridges one behind the other. Each group of elements had a specified locale to take on the opposite side of the river. Objectives were the dominating high ground, the locations most valuable to the enemy, and the ones, if they remained in enemy hands, that would cause our forces most trouble. All roads leading into the by now enlarged and strengthened bridgehead were covered by strong outposts, and small villages and towns within the bridgehead were taken by the task forces in their advance to complete their missions. In the process of reaching their goals, the groups usually met resistance consisting first of infantrymen with small arms and automatic weapons. Before reaching the designated spots, the task forces had to overcome antitank guns and tanks which fortunately were often well scattered. After all objectives had been taken, a large, strong, half-circle of steel extended from the bridge crossing at the focal point.

At virtually all river crossings, the speed of the column and the surprise it effected upon the enemy were apparently the vital factors in the subsequent rapid and successful crossings. Bridges were often blown by the enemy just before the advancing elements reached the crossings and just after fleeing Germans had made final use of the intact spans.

The terrain at virtually every river crossing was perfectly suited for strong, heavy, and prolonged defense. In fact, it was so outstanding that it was a defender's dream. If the Nazis had had time to prepare a planned defense consisting of well-placed artillery and cleverly positioned artillery observers ready to rain shells down upon the bridge crossing at the first signs of activity, they could have won for themselves a long delay. Similarly they could have placed their guns in strategic locations covering all approaches, established a tank unit for a mobile reserve, and dug in their infantry and machine guns. A combination like that would certainly have made a river crossing slow, painful, and terrifically costly. Much bloody fighting would have resulted. The losses, heavy as they were, in the actual crossing were insignificant when compared to what they could have been. Without a doubt, a crossing against an established defense would have called for a much more powerful and potent force.

Luckily, the advancing forces reached the bridges so quickly that the defenders, as has been mentioned, had time only to blow the bridges and to defend with what they could. Usually, after the friendly bridgehead was established, an enemy counterattack was launched. It appeared that while the river was being bridged, enemy forces were being gathered in an attempt to drive the attackers back and to destroy their bridge. By the time the Boche forces were formed, the bridgehead was usually too strong. The forces comprising it were sitting squarely astride all the key places which only a short time before could have proved disastrous to the advancing elements had the ground been held by the enemy. It was the same enemy who was trying desperately to win the very same ground, and who was being easily annihilated in the process. Enemy artillery, strangely enough, normally came down more heavily after the bridge was made than before. Once again such an unusual procedure seems to indicate that they arrived too late with too little. It must be emphasized that in some localities the enemy did have what they needed, and could not be dislodged until advancing forces which had crossed at other places routed them out.

After the bridgehead was secure and after the counterattack was quelled, action usually ceased. All elements of the column were then able to cross, the column was formed once again, and it moved off to the next river.

During this, the third phase of operations, the spotlight was held by the river crossings. The memory of them became ingrained in the minds of all members of the column because there were so many rivers, they were so close together, and they took such a tremendous effort and toll to cross. Soon after the last (for the time being) of the rivers had been successfully breached, the column slowed its already mincing steps to a virtual halt to gird itself for the next venture.

The days ahead will undoubtedly uncover much that is new in the ever-changing struggle of war. Already, different methods of employment and new kinds of strategy are being practiced to insure a steady and fruitful advance eastward to the ultimate objective for whose fall the world so restlessly and hopefully waits. Already, inklings of a new phase, a fourth phase, are discernible. But a discussion of it must wait for a later day, a day when history has already recorded the events. May that phase be the last phase.

CHAPTER THREE

8ᵀᴴ TANK BATALLION'S DARING MOSELLE CROSSING

Written by Brig. Gen. Albin F. Irzyk. Reprinted with permission from World War II Magazine, September, 1997.

The tanks of the 8th Tank Battalion, which I was a part of, rolled through Vaucouleurs, France, crossed the historic Meuse River and moved into a bivouac along its bank. It was early on September 1, 1944. The 8th was part of Combat Command "B" of the 4th Armored Division, the spearhead of Gen. George S. Patton's Third Army. Amazingly, those tanks had just advanced 328 miles in 12 days, moving forward as many as 51 miles in a single day. The 4th Armored Division's August sweep across the widest part of France was one of the most sensational operations in the annals of American military history and a triumph without parallel in the history of mobile warfare.

Pursuing the Germans relentlessly, the Americans reached the French border province of Lorraine. In 30 days they had covered a distance that Allied military planners had assumed would take nearly three times as long to travel. This astonishing advance was possible because conditions for armored operations were almost perfect. The days were long, the nights short. The terrain was dry, and the tanks could go cross-country almost unimpeded, often bypassing pockets of resistance. Opposition was scattered, and many enemy troops simply fled. Others had resisted fanatically, blowing up bridges or mining and defending roads with antitank guns. Many bridges had been destroyed, but the tanks were able to ford most of the creeks and streams, because the water in them was low.

No obstacles had deterred the aggressive tankers of the 4th Armored Division. Now we sat just 63 miles from the German border and no more than 140 miles from our objective, the Rhine River. That was less than half the distance we had come during the last 12 days, and at the rate we had been moving, the Rhine surely could not be more than a week or 10 days away. I was so optimistic about our prospects that I had already bet several of my associates that the war in Europe would be over by Thanksgiving. And it appeared that Patton would realize his hopes of a rapid dash into Germany and crossings over the Rhine at Mannheim and Mainz.

Much to our surprise, we did not move the next day or the day after. On the third day, we were informed that because of extended supply lines there was a shortage of gasoline, and we would be forced to remain in place. With that announcement, I knew the grand and glorious advance of the past month was over. The ideal conditions for armored operation would vanish, and the incessant rains would come. And even more disturbing, the enemy was being handed on a silver platter that most cherished of all commodities, time—time to reorganize, time to receive reinforcements from other parts of Europe.

Then came more demoralizing news. There was gasoline, but not enough for all the Allied forces. The Allied command gave logistical priority to British Field Marshal Bernard Montgomery and the armies in the north. This was difficult for us to accept. In the north were built-up areas and difficult cross-compartments, and Montgomery was a conservative and cautious commander. Patton was the one who had electrified the world with his August sweep, and he was closer to the German border and at least 100 miles closer to the Rhine than Montgomery. It is an established military principle that success should be reinforced. Since that principle was being violated, I could not believe that this had been a military decision.

At any rate, we sat. We read, swam, played touch football and basked in the sun. As we sat, we studied our maps and recognized that to the east we would soon be facing a formidable obstacle. The events occurring just to the north of us were not reassuring.

Maj. Gen. Manton S. Eddy, our XII Corps commander, had ordered a crossing of the Moselle River north of Nancy, France. The mission was given to the 317th Regiment of the 80th Infantry Division. When they launched an assault boat crossing on the morning of September 5, the attackers received enemy artillery and mortar fire from positions dug on forward slopes of the dominating terrain across the river. The intense, accurate fire paralyzed the attackers, broke the American ranks and destroyed most of the rubber boats intended for the river crossing.

Later, a night attack was launched. About four platoons were successful in reaching the east side, although casualties were heavy and more than half the assault boats were lost. Before the Americans could be reinforced, the Germans left their foxholes armed with bayonets, grenades and machine pistols and wiped out the American position by 11 AM on the 6th. For the time being, no further crossings would be attempted.

Sunday, September 10 began as just another sunny day. But on that glorious Sunday afternoon, the unsuspecting tankers were surprised by orders to move. The men wondered if this was for real, and, if so, why they were being told to move out so suddenly. They did not stop to ask questions; they hopped right to it, tore down their "homes" and got ready to move.

For the next few hours there was mild confusion because the orders kept being changed. Finally, after 10 days of marking time, the 8th began rolling again. Task Force Conley (named for the 8th's commanding officer) moved out at 7 PM, just as darkness was falling. In the days ahead, Col. Tom Conley would operate with my advance guard, out in front and leading, as he had prior to reaching the Meuse.

The tankers moved out smoothly, and after a few miles it was clear that the long rest period had not made any difference in the group's motivation. The men of the 8th had retained their aggressive combat edge. In no time, the eager troops reached and crossed the Madon River and continued east to a location south of Crantenoy, where they bivouacked for the night. A quick glance at the map located the command about 16 miles southeast of Nancy. During one day, the tankers had moved 31 miles.

Before retiring, I studied my map some more. I saw that we were now about 3 miles from the Moselle River, a major obstacle that had to be breached before the attack to the east could be continued. In the morning it would be our first objective, and there was bound to be trouble. Militarily, the spot was so advantageous for a defender that it cried out for a rugged, determined defense. The enemy had had ample time to round up the necessary forces and to reorganize and dig them in.

Early on September 11, lead elements of the 8th reached the Moselle and moved to a site overlooking the town of Bayou on the opposite side. We quickly sized up the situation facing us. Elements of the 35th Infantry Division had established a small bridgehead at that location.

A large, important river with its bridges down and defended by a dug-in, aggressive enemy is a major obstacle to an attacking force. Tanks can attack to the river's edge and fire on the opposite bank, but they do not assault the river. That is a job for infantry. They must either ford the river or, if it is too deep, cross over in assault boats. This is a difficult and dangerous operation because the infantry is exposed and vulnerable to enemy fire. Their mission is to cross any way they can, wrest a hunk of ground from the enemy and establish a bridgehead on the opposite side. During this complicated operation, the infantry is supported by artillery, so that the enemy will be pinned down while the infantry is exposed on the river. Once on the opposite bank, the infantry cannot hesitate, but must continue to fight and push back the enemy as succeeding waves of troops cross to help enlarge the bridgehead.

The goal of the assault is to push back enemy forces far enough so that they can no longer pour effective small-arms or artillery fire on the troops moving across the river. While the infantry and artillery engage the enemy, the engineers rush their bridging equipment to the riverbank, and when enemy fire lessens sufficiently, they work to quickly erect the appropriate bridge. The engineers also have an extremely dangerous mission, since they, too, are exposed and vulnerable as they work. The tanks are assembled nearby, and as soon as the bridge is completed, they begin crossing. Once on the other side, the tanks take over from the infantry and aggressively attack out of the bridgehead in typical armored style.

That is the way a river crossing is supposed to be made. However, as I had already learned many times, there are so many variables in combat that events rarely unfold as planned. The events that transpired at Bayon were an excellent example of plans gone wrong.

After the infantry had established its small bridgehead, aggressive enemy action kept them contained and prevented them from enlarging that bridgehead. The enemy was able to continue to bring effective fire on the damaged bridge site. The fire was heavy and accurate enough to deter the engineers from even beginning to construct a crossing for the tanks. The situation was getting no better, and the bridgehead was dangling by a thread. Someone in a position of authority must have recognized the danger and called for help from the tanks, which explained the abrupt departure of the 8ᵗʰ the evening before.

When their tanks reached the Moselle River and they found the bridge too badly damaged to cross, the men of the 8ᵗʰ Battalion should have backed off a bit—found cover and good firing positions and supported the infantry with direct covering fire concentrated on the opposite bank. But when they reached the river, the tankers quickly realized that the offensive had bogged down and sensed that not much was going right. They knew that something had to happen and that it was now up to them.

The first requirement was to get away from the bridge site quickly. The enemy had the location pinpointed and continued to pour fire onto it. So the lead elements of the 8th moved north and parallel to the river. Once out of enemy range, the tankers were able to pause and examine the problems and challenges that confronted them.

Commanding the advance guard, I stood with Lt. William ("Bill") J. Marshall, commander of the lead platoon of "C" Company. We stared at the mighty Moselle. Every man in the battalion knew that we were facing a formidable obstacle. To the north and south of our position, the Moselle was a wide, swiftly moving river that would certainly engulf tanks the moment they entered its waters. But there was something different about the part of the river at which we were now staring. We were fortunate to have reached the Moselle at this particular location.

At some point upstream, the river apparently had separated into three channels. So the part of the Moselle that we were analyzing appeared to have three fingers, and separating the fingers were sandy, gravelly spurs of land sprouting short, wild underbrush. Bill Marshall and I immediately recognized the exciting possibilities. Instead of one mighty river, we now faced three smaller, narrower rivers, which might be forded.

Fording the river now appeared to be at least an outside possibility. We were well aware, however, that there was another problem. The Canal de l'Est, which ran north to south and parallel to the Moselle, lay between us and the river. It had steep, soft, muddy sides and was wide and deep enough to permit the transit of large canal boats. This other formidable obstacle, like a massive tank trap, had to be overcome before we could even think of fording the Moselle.

Both Marshall and I knew that if ever there was a time to grab the bull by the horns, this was it. Although it seemed impossible, we knew that somehow we had to get ourselves across that canal and river.

I looked at Marshall and he looked at me. I asked, "Bill, can you do it?" Marshall, with his jaw set and determination in his eyes, nodded and declared, "We'll do our damnedest." Without another word, he spun on his heel and, having made a resolute decision, set in motion a series of remarkable events.

Marshall started the action by rapidly reconnoitering up the canal until he found the right spot for a crossing. If the depth of water in the canal had been normal, it would have been all over. But fortuitously, the locks somewhere had been opened or damaged, so the water in the bottom of the canal, though very muddy, was shallow. Marshall now pulled his platoon of tanks close to the canal and ordered the guns to open fire, pouring point-blank fire onto both sides of the canal. The high-explosive rounds, set on fuse delay, buried themselves in the muck and then exploded. The sides of the canal began to crumble. Large chunks of muck began to collect on the canal bottom, forming a rough bed. The continuous fire caused the banks to begin to collapse and increase the level of debris on the canal bed. Some abandoned railroad ties found nearby were dragged to the site and laid on top of the debris to give it some firmness and substance, hastily forming a rough ramp.

The moment of truth had now arrived. Marshall's lead tank, driven by Cpl. Ray Fisk, moved toward the broken bank and slowly, carefully slid down the steep slope, sending dirt and mud ahead of it onto the ramp. It then began to move slowly across the uneven ramp with its tracks churning and sliding through the low water as it inched along.

There was a loud roar as Fisk gunned his engine. The tank leaped off the ramp, its chevron tracks spinning wildly in the mud as it tried to get a grip on the steep, slippery bank. With the engine roaring in lowest gear and the tracks spinning, the tank gained only inches at a time, but it was moving. As the tank slowly climbed up the bank, its tracks began to bite into the higher, drier ground, and little by little it began to move more steadily. With a final roar, it leaped to the top of the bank. A tank had successfully forded the Canal de l'Est!

There was no time to celebrate. The hardest work was still ahead. Without hesitation, Fisk brought out the tow cable. Tankers grabbed it, dragged it across the canal ramp and hooked it to the front of the next tank. That tank, following the path of the first one, moved down the bank under its own power. Pulled by the first tank, it steadily negotiated the hazard and soon stood on the opposite bank. The process was repeated until the rest of the platoon was successfully across the canal. Each tank helped to progressively level the banks, making the journey easier for each succeeding tank, until they no longer needed to be towed.

For Marshall and his platoon this was a two-phase operation, and crossing the canal had been only the first phase. Now, what about the mighty Moselle? What good was crossing the canal if you were stranded between it and the river? Capt. Gene Bush, commanding officer of Company "C," let Marshall have his head. The rest of the company and battalion waited as he tackled the river.

As he had at the canal, Marshall again dismounted, reconnoitered the river in front of him, and tested the footing of the approaches. He waded into the river and determined the depth of the water. He quickly gathered the information that he needed and picked a crossing spot. Corporal Fisk's tank eased down the bank and gingerly entered the water. Slowly, steadily, it moved across the river bottom, and with each yard gained, the cold, swiftly moving water rose.

As the tank approached the midpoint, with Marshall (who, ironically, could not swim) hanging on to the gun tube, the water was dangerously high—already above the tracks and rising up the sides of the tank. They had reached the critical point. It was now or never. If the tank plunged forward into deeper water, its engine would surely be flooded and the tank would be stranded mid-river. Fisk, with one triumph behind him and knowing what to expect, gunned his engine. With a loud cough and roar, the tank leaped forward across the deep water and, without slackening its speed, moved into shallow water and up the bank. As it reached solid ground, water sprayed from its tracks. After letting the engine run to be sure that it had not absorbed too much water, Fisk eased the tank toward the next channel. He crossed the other two channels in the same manner.

As soon as Marshall had his platoon across, he established a small bridgehead on the east bank. Right behind his platoon came the rest of the company, then the rest of the battalion. Every tanker in the 8th knew that if one tank could do it, they could do it, too. The Moselle became a beehive of activity.

It was not necessary to follow the first tank's path across the river. There was ample room, so the tanks fanned out and picked their own crossing points. As was to be expected, some found water too deep or hesitated a bit too long in the deepest water before gunning the engine—and some tanks conked out. The tankers were prepared for this, and those already across had their tow cables ready. They quickly dragged their momentarily stranded brothers out of the river.

By the time darkness fell, all four tank companies of the 8th Tank Battalion not only had successfully crossed the canal and river but also had seized the dominating ground on the east side and thwarted a vicious counterattack. Astoundingly, a tank battalion had crossed a major river without a bridge. No military service school could have conceived an operation like it. This was truly an unprecedented river crossing by tanks.

A second task force of Combat Command "B," built around an armored infantry battalion, was assigned the mission of crossing the Moselle at Bainville-aux-Miroirs, about 2½ miles south of Bayon. The infantry was to establish a bridgehead there so that the engineers could repair a bridge that had been blown up.

After waiting for the engineers to bring boats, which did not arrive, one company found a ford and crossed the river. Other companies seeking to cross elsewhere were repulsed by strong enemy opposition. With such little progress, the force was ordered to withdraw and follow the tank crossing at Bayon.

Two days after the 8th's unprecedented crossing, Combat Command "A" of the 4th Armored Division crossed the Moselle at Dieulouard, north of Nancy. They made a traditional crossing, over a bridge that had been established by the 80th Infantry Division. It is the Moselle crossing at Dieulouard that is studied by students at Fort Leavenworth and Fort Knox.

The 8th's crossing may have had strategic implications that reached far beyond the bridge site at Bayon. There were rumors within the division that Montgomery wished to halt Patton's progress so that he could have the whole show to himself in the north. Patton, reportedly, was fighting hard to save a piece of the action for himself. Even though his logistical support had been cut to the bone, he still believed that he could do more than Montgomery if they gave him the chance, and he certainly wanted to keep trying.

Facing little support from his superiors, Patton reportedly had agreed to pull back if the Moselle could not be bridged by September 14. By crossing on the 11th and bridging on the 12th, the 8th Tank Battalion and Combat Command "B" more than met Patton's deadline. If there was any truth to the circulating reports, the 8th Battalion's action more than vindicated the Third Army commander.

CHAPTER FOUR

SINGLING

World War II in Europe ended in May, 1945. A year later, I was still in Germany involved in the occupation of that country. In late spring, an individual without comment handed me a rather thick booklet entitled, "Small Unit Actions." I asked, "What is this?" I quickly turned the cover to the title page, and much to my great surprise I saw the words, "France: 4th Armored Division at Singling." My first thought—4th Armored Division, but why Singling?

During the many weeks since the day the 4th Armored Division broke out of the Normandy stalemate in late July, until we reached Singling in early December, we had overrun, seized, or bypassed literally hundreds of villages and towns in a wide variety of actions. Consequently, I tried to recall what it was about Singling that was so different, so significant that the actions there would be highlighted in such a manner. As I studied the booklet more carefully, I found that Singling was one of four small unit actions that were covered in great detail. There were two in other theaters, and one other in France. The booklet was produced April 4, 1946 by the Historical Division War Department.

The publication recognized that most reports of battles were at the army, corps, or division level. On occasion such reports would dip down to the Battalion level, but only briefly, tersely, and superficially as, "The 3rd Battalion fought its way forward against heavy resistance." Hardly ever are the actions of the Company, Platoon, or Squad within the Battalion mentioned. So the fundamental purpose of "Small Unit Actions" is to zero in on the real, down to earth combat soldier, the grunt who daily and directly tangles with the enemy.

The four actions were chosen because the writers considered them average, and typical of scores of battles in their respective Theaters of Operations.

Singling was a small village with about 50 buildings scattered along a narrow, half mile, west to east road. Some of the farmhouses within the village had three-foot reinforced concrete walls. Garden walls were high and thick. Concrete pillboxes stood guard at the entrance to the village, east and west, on the hills and in the valley north, and on the ridge south, Singling, after all, was a part of the Maginot Line.

On December 6, the battle *within* Singling was, indeed, a small unit action, and, as intended by the publication, was covered in very great detail. The units within the village were a small tank/armored infantry team. Comprising this force was "B" Company of the 37th Tank Battalion, and "B" Company of the 51st Armored Infantry Battalion. Both units were under their authorized strength. B/37 had fourteen of its seventeen tanks. In far worse shape was B/51 which was radically under strength. Instead of the authorized strength of a rifle platoon of 56 men, the three platoons of B/51 numbered 19, 15, and 14 making it literally a platoon-sized company. That is the force that was sent in to capture Singling.

Opposing B/37 and B/51 were all four companies of the 111th Panzer Grenadier Regiment (armored infantry of the 11th Panzer Division). They were supported by two self-propelled guns, mortars, and light machine guns. The Germans inside the village received additional and formidable support from 105-mm howitzers close in and round the village, and from guns ranging from 75-mm to 210-mm from the 298th Volks Artillery Corps.

So, yes, the small unit action in the village of Singling on December 6, 1944 is described, as was the intent by the publication, in extreme detail. But that was anything but a limited, isolated, restricted battle. It was actually a very small part of something much, much bigger.

The fighting for the village of Singling actually began not on the 6th but on the 5th. There were more combat casualties on the 5th than there would be on the 6th. Amazingly, rarely mentioned or understood has been the recognition that the roots for the Battle of Singling extend back many weeks, and by the time the fight for that village had ended, nearly all the combat elements of the 4th Armored Division would be involved.

Historians who have written about this episode have found gaps in their research, which they filled with assumptions that were not entirely accurate. There are other inaccuracies and misconceptions. Also, there were factors that had a bearing on the situation which were not recognized, and, thus, have not been discussed.

The fundamental purpose of this narrative is to endeavor to paint a more complete and accurate picture of the Battle for Singling. This paper does not come from the pen of a historian. Rather, it is written by a participant.

I had a very prominent role in the Battle for Singling, and was deeply involved every step of the way. Although that series of events occurred sixty-five years ago, my memory remains vivid, and my recall is still excellent. Additionally, I possess some official documents that support certain of my statements. I clearly recognize that my recall may not be absolute, and others may differ with some of what I have to say. Nevertheless, I firmly believe that what I have to tell is much more valuable and accurate than that which has already been related by historians who have had, on occasion, to rely on uncertain sources.

BACKGROUND

During the last two weeks of August, 1944, tanks of my 4th Armored Division spearheaded General Patton's Third Army across the wide southern part of France. Using their mobility, firepower, and shock action, they operated like cavalry—slashing, sidestepping, bypassing, and using speed as surprise. This magnificent, heroic and unprecedented advance still has historians salivating, and is one of the main pillars upon which rests Patton's Military Immortality. Amazingly and incredibly, the tanks of my 8th Tank Battalion advanced 328 miles in 12 days, and on the evening of September 1 were sitting on the east bank of the Meuse River. We tankers were ecstatic. The German border was only 60 miles away with the Rhine River another 80 miles—140 miles altogether. That was less than half the distance we had advanced in 12 days. Patton had declared that we would be at the Rhine in 10 days, and I heartily agreed with him.

Suddenly we were stunned and shocked. Astonishingly and without any warning, our advance was abruptly halted. We were forced to sit and watch as day-by-day, virtually perfect tank operating conditions began to vanish. Simultaneously, we were providing the enemy with that most valuable battlefield commodity—time—time to regroup and to reorganize at which the Germans were masters.

We sat for ten days. We had learned that we were halted because of gasoline—rather the shortage of gasoline. We had moved so fast and so far that we had outrun the planners' logistical timetable. We were many, many miles and many days ahead of the planners' most optimistic estimates. There was gas at the port and on the beaches, but the great problem was getting it forward to the Canadian, British, American First, and American Third Army. It was obvious that General Eisenhower had to establish some sort of a priority, and he did. When we heard of his decision, we were rocked back on our heels. We found it astonishing, incredible, unbelievable. He had decided to give priority of gasoline and supplies to the conservative, cautious, plodding, unimaginative British Gen. Bernard Law Montgomery, who our tankers derided as the general who had pivoted around his D-Day objective—Caen—for two months. How could this be? In our society we go for the winner. In our service schools we were taught that you reinforce success, not failure. So this news for us was very difficult to accept.

On mid-afternoon, Sunday, September 10, ten days after we had reached the Meuse, we were suddenly ordered to move right out and to continue our attack to the east. We learned that although Montgomery had demanded everything of Eisenhower, Ike was concerned that if he stopped Patton cold after his sensational sweep in August, that there would be an outcry at home. So he allocated some gas to Patton. It was because of that we were able to move, and Patton resolved to go as far as he could before he ran out.

Not long after, we learned that on that day Eisenhower had approved a plan for an attack to the east that Montgomery had proposed to him which was surprisingly and extremely uncharacteristically bold for the cautious, conservative Montgomery. The plan was also glaringly risky—the operation would be called Market Garden.

With the passage of days, the nature of the war had changed dramatically. We had to fight to cross that major obstacle, the Moselle River, and continuously during the days that followed. Then astonishingly out of the fog early on the morning of the September 19, elements of the 4th Armored Division received a massive German tank counterattack. The enemy tanks were freshly minted Panthers just out of the factories. During the fighting that day, the 37th Tank Battalion with support from elements of the 704th Tank Destroyer Battalion knocked out 43 German tanks.

Two days before, on the 17th, Montgomery had launched his Market Garden operation. On this day, the 19th, that operation was fast failing, and would turn out to be a disaster.

The German counterattack (the Arracourt, Lorraine tank battles) would continue for ten days. The German Fifth Panzer Army which had been organized and equipped and had orders from Hitler to stop the Third Army, and to push it back across the Moselle, had fought until its combat resources were exhausted. When the battle was finally finished, there were 281 destroyed German tanks littering the hills and hollows of Lorraine. But, tragically, this was the end of the line for Patton's Third Army. He was stopped. Behind the disastrous defeat in Holland came a famine in supplies.

Now we of the Third Army moved back to a rest area mode. For the first time since Normandy, we were completely out of action. We watched as it began to rain in September, broke all records for rain in October. The fields became deep, muddy, sticky bogs. The mud was so deep that the tent pegs of our pup tents would not hold. The troops had to find shelter in sheds, barns, and rooms in farmhouses. And so we and the greatest offensive weapon that the Allies had, Gen. George S. Patton, Jr., SAT FOR OVER FOUR WEEKS.

With the approach of November, the weather became worse and then atrocious. The rain became sleet and snow, with constantly gray skies and a bitter cold winds. The mud was unbelievable. It was more like damp clay. It hung onto everything in huge clogs—on boots and tank tracks—and was almost impossible to dislodge.

While we sat, the Germans were extremely busy. Once again, we had provided them with that priceless battlefield commodity—time. They knew that we were coming, and precisely where we would be attacking. As defenders, they had a tremendous advantage.

They would move about and get to know the terrain in the area. That part of Lorraine consisted of many small towns with roads running through them. The enemy would be able to locate favorable ground from which their antitank guns would overlook and be able to zero in on advancing tanks, as they reached vulnerable points on the roads. Similarly, they had time to plot the most advantageous locations on the roads where they would install mines and blow craters, and cover them with fire that would cause our forces continued serious delays.

The ground was generally open, except for the scattered towns and the roads that went through them. So they would take great advantage of it by organizing their defenses in depth. That would force our attacking elements to fight yard by yard every step of the way.

So the big advantage went to the defender. But even he did not expect two tremendous bonuses that would aid him immensely, and add tremendously to our difficulties, when we began our attack. First, because of the unexpected ferocity of the weather—record rains, sleet, snow, bitter cold winds, ceiling zero—we could expect no critically needed air support. Conversely, for the enemy that was one element that they had greatly feared and now could completely ignore. Second, neither he nor we had expected the record-breaking rains that created mud so thick and sticky that it clung in globs to anything that touched it, even Sherman tank tracks. With the tanks unable to move freely across the ground, that now made roads critically important to the attackers, and to the defenders as well. Their plans for their antitank guns, mines, and craters now assumed greatly increased importance.

THE NEW (AND DIFFERENT) OFFENSIVE BEGINS

The sitting was finally over. We were ordered to continue our attack to the east on the morning of November 8, 1944. Shortly after first light, as always, our tanks moved out aggressively. Then almost immediately—disaster. Tanks had bogged down in the now very unforgiving mud, and were unable to advance. In that instant we all knew that we would be engaged in a far different war than we had experienced in late August and early September. No longer would our tanks be able to move over the open ground with impunity.

Tanks are tanks because of their mobility, shock action, and firepower. With their loss of mobility, they also lose their shock action. All that remains is firepower. That relegates the tank to nothing more than a roving pillbox. So in one fell swoop, our lethality, agility, and versatility were lost.

With the battlefield conditions, which we were now confronting, it should, initially, have been an infantry war. Up until now it was armor that had led, that did the attacking and advancing. The infantry divisions, which were far less mobile, kept up as best they could and cleaned up whatever the tanks had left behind. But now it was time for them to step up and lead the way. This would be a slow and plodding battle. This was not an armor situation. Yet, a decision must have been made that the infantry was not up to it, for armor was instantly and prematurely committed to action.

Historians and critics have faulted General Patton for the manner in which he conducted the Lorraine Campaign. They claim that he had lost his aggressiveness. Yes, they agreed, there was rain and mud, but sitting at their desks far removed from the action, they had absolutely no sense of what horrendous rain (sleet and snow) and mud we on the ground had to endure. Oh, yes, Patton should have more rapidly swept through Lorraine.

Since we had lost our invitation to freely use the fields, we were now forced to dramatically change our tactics. The only firm ground that we could expect were the roads, towns, and the areas around the towns. While in France, there were times when the two advancing combat commands were as much as 40 miles apart. That is a pretty wide front. Now for each attacking unit pretty much confined to the roads, the front would be one tank wide.

As we attacked, we would be subjected to the fire from well-placed antitank guns, mines and craters in the roads. Each of those would be covered by enemy fire, and each would cause us serious delay. With our tanks, artillery, and infantry, we would have to clear enemy fire up ahead, so that our engineers could repair the roads enabling us to advance. When we reached a town, it was sure to be defended. So we had to overcome them, as well. So it was plod, plod, plod—slow, dirty, dangerous, frustrating, time-consuming work.

And out there, as well, was the German's main battle and best tank—the Panther. It was that tank that we battled and defeated in September, until he had none left. The hills and hollows were filled with destroyed newly minted Panthers fresh out of the factories. How were we able to do this? We had mobility, and our tactics and gunnery were superior. He had a manual hydraulic system of gun laying, while we had power traverse. We were able to aim our gun more quickly, and to get two, three, or four shots off before he fired.

That was then. Now with our loss of mobility, and limited tactical capability, he had every advantage. His tracks had a flotation and cross-country terrain efficiency that was greater than ours. He had a high velocity 75-mm gun that easily penetrated from 2,000 yards the frontal armor of our tanks. Conversely, our low velocity 75-mm gun could not penetrate the 3⅛ inch frontal armor of the Panther. Thus, the Germans were able to occupy positions that provided them with extended fields of fire, and the ability to engage our forces at long range. Conversely, we were forced to engage at close range under cover of defilade, if we could find it, smoke, and artillery fire. It would be slow going—delay after delay. How more one-sided could a battle be?

The Germans were occupying the best defensive positions, and were widespread. To meet them, and to get through them now required us to attack on a broader front. It was normal for each Combat Command to operate with a tank battalion and an armored infantry battalion. Consequently, a decision was now made to cross reinforce each battalion and to operate them as task forces. The tank battalion would provide the infantry with tanks, and the armored infantry in turn would give infantrymen to the tankers. As required, these task forces would be subdivided into smaller task forces by operating with tank/armored infantry company teams—"B" Company, 8th Tank Battalion/"B" Company, 51st Armored Infantry Battalion. I was given command of a different task force called the "advance guard" composed of mostly light and some medium tanks.

For four days after our attack began, we slugged it out along roads, and through small-defended villages and towns. Our advances were being measured in increments of kilometers, not the many miles as in France in August.

By now we tankers were fighting, living, and eating our cold rations inside our tanks. The coldest place in the world, which I occupied, is a tank turret in winter-like weather.

As it had done each day before, at first light on November 13, my advance guard moved directly east. Our mission was to keep advancing to the east, and to seize a larger town called Morhange. Almost immediately, we entered the forbidding Bois de Serres, picked up speed, and much to our great relief, we were able to advance smartly through the width of the forest. As we emerged, we saw Oron, only a kilometer away, and we continued our aggressive and rapid advance. We surprised the defenders and overran the town with only slight resistance, and grabbed a big bag of prisoners in the process, which we sent to the rear.

Now the enemy would be concentrated, better organized, and fighting hard. For us it became slower going. My advance guard had to do considerable fighting along the four kilometers to Viller-sur-Nied, but we ultimately seized the town.

Now it was on to Marthille, which appeared to be between two and three kilometers away. I was just about to send my force aggressively forward along the road, but what I saw up ahead disturbed me. Just off to the right and paralleling the road was a narrow but swift moving creek. To the left was ground that rose rather sharply to a ridge topped by a forest that dominated the road below. My concern was that if my tanks were hit by enemy fire, they would be trapped. They could not readily deploy off the road either to the right or left.

The ridge dominated the road below all the way to Marthille. Because it was higher ground, I believed that it would be considerably drier than the flat, muddy fields, which had thus far been such a problem for us. Moving up to and driving along the ridge appeared to be the first opportunity since the attack started, to capitalize on the tank's mobility, to get off the road, and apply the tactics that in the past had been so successful for us.

So instead of moving east on the road to Marthille, I directed my tanks to move north and up the slope to the ridge, then to ride the ridge east, and to reconnoiter by fire as they moved. They had done this many times before with excellent results. This tactic was used when it was strongly suspected that concealed enemy might be waiting out there. The fire from the .30 caliber coaxial machine gun, which is mounted parallel to the tank cannon, was directed at suspected enemy locations. The purpose was to hit the enemy before they were aware of or ready for our advancing elements, thus revealing or flushing them out. If a target was uncovered, the tank cannon immediately went into action.

Now, the light tanks were put in the lead to feel out the enemy, followed closely by the Sherman medium tanks. We instantly knew that this maneuver would be working to perfection. The first light tank to reach the crest of the hill opened fire at the first suspected location.

Bingo! The .30 caliber tracers seemed to bounce off something, so the tank gun quickly shot the 37-mm round that it already had in the tube. The fire blew away brush concealing two antitank guns. Those weapons, of course, had rounds in their chambers, and were immediately fired by their crews. However, the guns had been aimed in a different direction, so landed harmlessly away, and the uncovered crews and guns were immediately destroyed by the follow-up fire from the Shermans.

It was late in the fall, but the Germans had cleverly used every bit of available cover to conceal their weapons and equipment. Reconnaissance by fire from the first tank had successfully laid bare the Germans' presence and vulnerability. Now like a bunch of hounds who had caught the scent of the fox, the tanks broadened their formation, and moved forward aggressively shooting at every suspicious location and object. Every suspicious object turned out to be an antitank gun. It was uncovered one moment, and destroyed the next. Almost immediately after the attack had started, hordes of Germans came streaking out of Marthille, breaking into small groups, running as fast as they could up the open slope—each group heading for a different spot. Apparently these were the relief crews, the ones off duty, who had been keeping warm in the cluster of nearby homes.

Each group headed for its own gun to help in the fight. Many were mowed down as they ran. Those who survived were totally winded by the time they reached their guns—and it proved to be too late, anyway, for their guns were gone. The tankers had advanced swiftly, fired furiously and super effectively, and in a period of thirty to forty-five minutes, incredibly, it was all over.

It would turn out to be the biggest catch in the shortest amount of time during the entire war in Europe. That hornet's nest would prove to have had one of the largest concentrations of antitank guns ever encountered in such a limited area.

The tally was staggering. There were twenty-one antitank guns destroyed. And what guns! Ten of them were the vaunted, vicious 88s, and the other eleven were the high velocity lethal 75s. Also destroyed were six mortars, seven half-tracks, and three trucks. More than a hundred of the enemy soldiers were killed, fifty were taken prisoner, and between two and three hundred went streaking back to the east as fast as their legs could carry them. They were accompanied by two Panther tanks, which had appeared out of nowhere, fired hastily and ineffectually at the Shermans, and then disappeared.

This was a triumph of absolutely staggering and tremendous proportions. The only casualty to our little force was one Sherman damaged when it rolled over a stray mine. How more one-sided could a victory be?

Conversely, it could easily have been a disaster of epic proportions. In the planning for their defense the Germans must have decided that this area was perfect for a super ambush. They appeared to be so confident of its potential lethality that they must have bled other defensive areas in order to be able to concentrate that mass of weapons. Then it required endless man-hours to roam the area to gather the scarce fall foliage in such abundance that they were able to skillfully and cleverly cover all the guns, so they could blend with the terrain. Before doing so, they had broadly deployed the guns so that they were aimed all along the road between Villers-sur-Nied and Marthille. They would probably have waited until the lead vehicle had reached Marthille with the others spaced behind it. Then with one thunderous volley they would have destroyed every vehicle in my advance guard, as well as the following vehicles from the battalion. Such an instant loss in men, vehicles, and equipment would have been a staggering, mortal blow—a disaster. Its repercussions and demoralizing effect would have immediately swept through the entire 4th Armored Division like wildfire.

What was sobering but frightening, as well, was the realization that it was just a simple battlefield decision that turned a catastrophe-in-waiting into an unprecedented triumph. Not continuing along the road, but choosing, instead, to ride the ridge above it was the difference between total disaster and an epic victory.

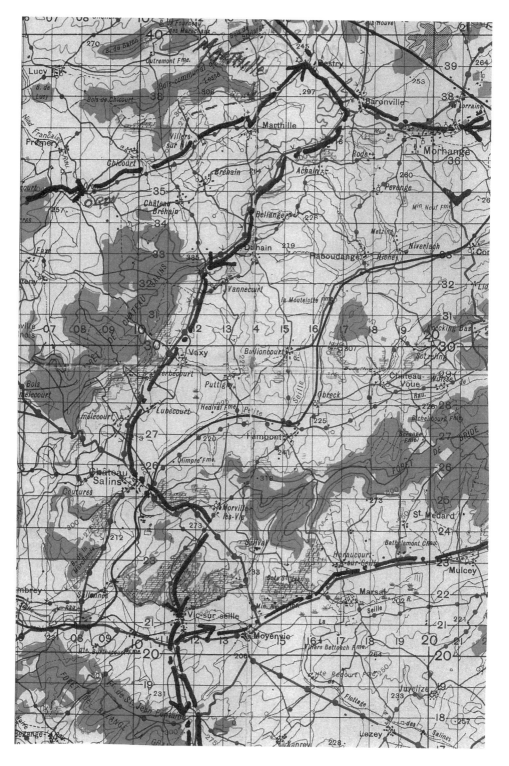

MARTHILLE (SINGLING)

As the days and weeks passed, the actions and results at Marthille would prove to be anything but normal or typical. It would turn out to be a one-of-a-kind aberration. From that time on, there would be no more triumphant moments.

After Marthille and reaching Destry, our forces made a radical turn and moved directly south all the way to the Dieuze/Sarre-Union road. There we turned to the east and were able to seize the important towns of Dieuze, Louderfing, Mittersheim, and then the very significant town of Fenetrange, over which we took control on November 23. Now that we had made a significant leap that brought us closer to the German border, German resistance intensified immensely. From then on it was again slug, slug under the most miserable battlefield conditions imaginable with both the enemy and weather extremely difficult adversaries. Yards, kilometers, miles were gained slowly with great difficulty, and were costly in lives, vehicles, and equipment. Each day was dangerous, dismal, dreary, and absolute drudgery.

The attacks would continue at first light each day. On the 24th another important milestone was reached. My battalion crossed the vaunted Sarre River, an objective to which we had for weeks looked forward to reaching. Now we were on its east side. We continued to advance, and by the end of the month, my battalion was located on the high ground near Rimsdorf, and plans were in place for a coordinated attack by elements of the division on the important city of Sarre-Union, and the high ground northeast of it.

The attack kicked off as planned, on the first day of December, and very soon there would be unpredictable and unexpected developments. Before the day was over, incidents that have not been recognized or reported upon by historians began to occur that would have a direct and indirect bearing on events during the next succeeding days.

During the morning, the 8th Tank Battalion working with the 51st Armored Infantry Battalion repulsed an enemy counterattack. Most unfortunately, during the engagement, Maj. Van Arnam, the Battalion Commander of the 51st, was wounded and evacuated. Ironically, he had

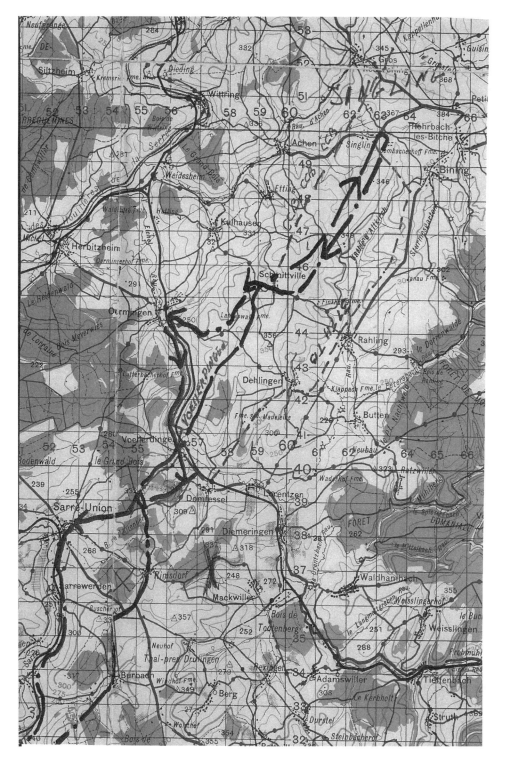

SINGLING

been in command for only two weeks, after succeeding the previous commander who was killed in action at the outset of the offensive.

As the battle continued undiminished, more bad and unbelievable news reached us. Now it came from Combat Command "A." We learned that Lt. Col. Arthur West, the Battalion Commander of the 10th Armored Infantry Battalion, while moving forward to reconnoiter the area over which they would be attacking, was also wounded and evacuated. Incredible! Two of the three divisions' Armored Infantry Battalion Commanders were lost within a couple of hours of one another. This is very tangible evidence of the ferocity of the action. Maj. Harold Cohen was soon placed in command of the 10th Armored Infantry Battalion.

Elements of both Combat Commands "A" and "B" continued to advance and, despite heavy fire and stiff resistance, were able to make modest gains.

The day's most significant news, of course, was the loss of the two Armored Infantry Battalion Commanders.

It was now December 2. More changes. One change occurred that would make this day one of the most memorable ones of my life. From the outset this day was characterized by enemy artillery, which was extremely active all day. Elements of both Combat Commands were constantly subjected to it.

The 8th and 51st repulsed an early morning counterattack, and they continued to advance north toward the Sarre-Union/Domfessel highway.

My tank had just pulled off the narrow road in the small town of Burbach. I was conversing on my radio, when a jeep stopped by my tank. I looked down and saw Maj. Dan Alanis looking up. After a quick exchange of greetings, he provided me with the surprising news that he was moving forward to assume command of the 51st Armored Infantry Battalion. Our conversation was brief, as he had to move on.

He had not been gone long when along came another surprise. Word came from my operations half-track that I was to report immediately to Brig. Gen. Holmes Dager, the commander of Combat Command "B," and my immediate superior. To be summoned so suddenly by him was a bit of a shock, but to be called while the battalion was heavily engaged was puzzling and unsettling. I would quickly receive the answer to my puzzle as I reported to General Dager. He immediately, bluntly, and with few words informed me that the commander of the 8th Tank Battalion had been relieved, and that I was to move right out to take command of the battalion during its ongoing battle.

In no time at all, I was in the turret of the battalion commander's Sherman tank. Without skipping a beat, the attack in progress continued, and elements of the 8th/51st Task Force crossed the Sarre-Union/Domfessel highway. By mid-afternoon, we had forced the enemy to withdraw from hill 332, just north of the highway, and consolidated our positions in the vicinity of Schlosshoff Farm. It had been a productive day, and we were now poised to continue the attack the next day. I reported to General Dager and provided him with an update on our day's actions, and was told that there would be no advance the next day, as the division would wait for the infantry to close up.

After nibbling on my cold rations, and before dozing off, I finally had time to think back upon the day's significant events. The day just ending saw the division acquire two new battalion commanders, Dan Alanis of the 51st Armored Infantry, and me of the 8th Tank Battalion. By taking command of the 51st, Alanis had vacated command of the 704th Tank Destroyer Battalion. The 704th was an attached battalion, but operated throughout the war as an integral part of the division. To fill its vacancy, Maj. Charles Kimsey was placed in command of the Battalion. That meant that on this day, the division acquired three new battalion commanders. Adding to it the change made the previous day in the 10th Armored Infantry, that added up to four new battalion commanders in two days. That just had to be an unprecedented transformation.

Amazingly, it was not yet over, and there had been no way of suspecting the radical changes and explosion that would occur the next day.

After an understandably restless night, I awoke early on the morning of December 3. I quickly learned that the enemy was not aware that this had been expected to be a quieter day. Early in the morning as the infantry on our flank was endeavoring to close up, they received a German counterattack at Sarre-Union. As part of the attack, enemy tanks pushed out from the woods north of the highway. These were quickly observed and taken under fire by my tankers, who quickly knocked out four of them.

Just as the situation appeared to be settling down somewhat, I was told that I was to report at once to General Dager at CCB. Dan Alanis, who was also well forward with his units, had received the same instructions, so we made the trip back together. For two battalion commanders to be pulled out suddenly while involved in an operation with the enemy, we concluded that there had to be something extremely important happening.

As soon as we had reported to him, a very shaken General Dager surprised and stunned us with the incomprehensible news that our greatly admired and deeply respected division commander, Maj. Gen. John S. Wood, had been relieved of command of the division. He was being replaced by General Patton's Chief of Staff, Maj. Gen. Hugh Gaffey. Dan Alanis and I sat there absolutely transfixed. How could this have happened?

General Dager was not yet finished. More surprising information. He next announced that a Brig. Gen. Herbert Earnest, an infantryman, had assumed command of Combat Command "A." That would give the division two Brigadier Generals, although it was authorized but one.

Amazingly, in addition to the four battalion command changes that had just been made, there were changes, as well, in the two most senior positions in the division. Incredible! The division during the first three days in December had suffered a staggering, totally unprecedented command face-lifting. These changes immediately raised the question, how much would they affect the operations of the division during the immediate days ahead?

I was awakened at 2 AM on December 4 with my next day's orders from CCB. The 8th with its supporting armored infantry, now the 10th, was to attack early in the morning with the mission of capturing the large town of Vœllerdingen, seizing the bridge in that town over the Eichel River, and establishing a bridgehead on the east side.

Division had just shuffled its combat battalions. The 10th Armored Infantry had been assigned to CCB. The 37th Tank Battalion had been moved from Reserve Command to CCA. Thus, CCA would become unusually heavy. It would have within its command the 35th and 37th Tank Battalions and the 51st and 53rd Armored Infantry Battalions. CCA would have within its folds two-thirds of the fighting elements of the division, and would make it twice as strong as CCB.

After an artillery preparation over ground that they would be attacking, the 8th/10th Task Force moved out early, advanced through light resistance to the high ground north of the Sarre-Union/Domfessel road. Since the task force had to move northeast toward Vœllerdingen, it was necessary to clear the woods of enemy holding the exposed flank, which was accomplished. The task force successfully negotiated le Grand Bois, and advanced to Hill 280, almost directly west and only about a kilometer and a half from Vœllerdingen. Although the town was that close, it was virtually out of sight. It sat down at the bottom along the river. It would be a downhill attack. Once deep inside the town, the attacking elements could easily be trapped within the town's narrow confines.

As I was considering plans for the attack on the town, ten enemy tanks left the cover of the woods on our left flank, and began heading our way. My very alert gunners spotted them immediately, and poured out a volume of fire. The two lead tanks were instantly hit and set on fire. With that, the remaining tanks quickly retreated into the cover of the woods.

Even though nightfall was approaching, I delayed our attack so that I could get a multi-artillery battalion TOT (Time on Target). When it was delivered, it was thunderous, earthshaking, awesome. It did the trick, for as soon as the fire lifted, the tanks charged safely into town.

However, once in town they quickly discovered that before they could reach the Eichel River Bridge, they faced a most formidable obstacle—a high embankment topped with rails upon which the railroad train rode. The tankers continued moving within the town and fortuitously found at the bottom of one of the streets an underpass through the embankment.

As they prepared to rush through it, they received heavy direct fire from what appeared to be self-propelled carriers that had moved in close. The tankers instantly retaliated, and began pouring AP (armor piercing) and HE (high explosive) fire through the small, square aperture. Momentarily it was a duel. This was ticklish business because if any of the fire hit the sides of the opening, loosened rubble could easily block the passage. After a heavy exchange of fire, the tanks in close column rushed the opening, and charged to and across the bridge, and were on the other side of the Eichel, before the bridge could be defended or blown. The tanks fanned out, more tanks followed, and then the Armored Infantry. Together they formed a firm and secure bridgehead over the Eichel River, as day was ending and night falling.

The river was swollen and overflowing its banks. Once across the bridge the road to the east petered out. It intersected with a small road running parallel to the river from Oermingen in the north to Domfessel to the south. *From the bridge at Vœllerdingen all the way to Singling there was no road, only muddy, open fields with patches of higher ground.* This was in marked and sharp contrast to the high-speed road from Domfessel to Bining assigned to CCA.

Yet another irony. A book published many years later would state, "When a bridge was seized at Vœllerdingen, the 37th Tank Battalion dashed across, headed for the Maginot Line." A similar statement would appear in the *New York Times*. Reminder: At the time of that river crossing, the 37th had just moved from Reserve Command to CCA, and was located miles from the bridge.

The mission for CCA was similar to the one that had been assigned to CCB. A task force led by Maj. Henry A. Crosby, executive officer of the 53rd Armored Infantry Battalion, and composed of elements of his battalion and that of the 35th Tank Battalion, had been directed to attack early on the morning of the 4th to capture the large town of Domfessel, seize two bridges, move across the Eichel River, and establish a strong and secure bridgehead on the east side of the river.

After a thirty-minute artillery preparation, the task force moved into the attack at 0930 hours. By 1010 hours, the attacking elements had reached the town, and were immediately hit by heavy sniper fire. This would require time clearing the snipers, of which there were many, from their hiding places. Delaying the force also was the requirement for a great deal of engineering to be done, because the streets in the town were covered with debris. Also troubling were the large craters that had been blown in the streets. It was soon learned that the bridge in town had been blown, as well as the railroad overpass similar to the one in Vœllerdingen.

While the troops were engaged in clearing up the very many impediments, artillery fire fell upon them from the northeast. The task force commander quickly realized that it would take at least the balance of the day to complete the clearance and repair work required to enable the troops and their vehicles to continue their advance through Domfessel. More bad news reached them. A patrol reported that the bridge over the Eichel north of the town had also been destroyed, and artillery shells continued to be dropped on the town.

The division's 24th Armored Engineer Battalion had the daunting task of installing two 36-foot treadway bridges at the site of the blown bridge in town, and an 80-foot floating bridge over the Eichel north of the town. These challenging jobs would be particularly difficult, as incoming artillery would still be active as they worked.

Because of the delays encountered, the task force suffered casualties. Five tanks of the 35th were lost from artillery fire, and two

more would be disabled by mines. Night fell before the task force could make any more progress.

Thus, after nightfall, there was a considerable difference in the situations for the division's two combat commands. CCB had seized intact a bridge over the Eichel River and had established a bridgehead east of the river, which was securely held during the night despite probing and patrol activity. At daylight on the 5th, *the elements of CCB were ready to roll.*

Conversely, CCA's forces were *not able to move right out* because more work needed to be done to be able to move tanks and armored infantry east of the Eichel River over installed engineer bridges.

As soon as my situation had stabilized, I reported it to CCB. That headquarters, as might be expected, was greatly elated. Gen. Dager immediately informed me that my mission the next day was to enlarge the bridgehead, clear the Nichelbusch Woods northeast of Vœllerdingen, and then to advance to the high ground southwest of the little settlement of Schmittville. He cautioned me to stay put, not to advance any further, once we had reached that high ground. He was concerned that CCA was not yet across the Eichel. He did not know how much longer they would be delayed, and he did not want me to get too far out in front with the river between two combat commands.

However, he told me to be prepared to move out *once the other combat command had caught up.*

It was now early on the morning of the 5th. We were ready to go. I quickly had my elements moving out, and enlarging the bridgehead. I instructed Captain McGlamery's "B" Company with members of the 10th Armored Infantry mounted on each tank to push out and take the lead. Their mission was to advance, seize, and occupy the high ground southwest of Schmittville. I moved out behind the little task force. They had not moved very far before they began to receive machine gun and small-arms fire from the woods. Because of the density of the woods, the enemy could only take up positions and fire from the edges of the woods. My tankers rode the ridge west of the woods, immediately poured fire at them with their coaxial machine guns and, when necessary, a shot from the tank cannon. The infantry jumped off the tanks, followed the fire, and quickly moved to and swept the woods. Recognizing that the woods were no longer a threat, the tanks continued to ride the ridge. Although the mud was deep in the fields all around them, by staying on the drier spur they had no difficulty reaching their objective, the high ground in the vicinity of Langenwald Farms. This early jaunt of "B" Company *was completed before noon.* It positioned them about 2 kilometers southwest of Schmittville, a little more than 4 kilometers northwest of Rahling, and 4½ kilometers southwest of the small village of Singling.

The moment that I knew that Captain McGlamery was on his objective, I moved forward to join him. When I arrived, things were quiet and peaceful. We both sat on the ground and had a lengthy, pleasant chat. As I rose to leave, I reminded him once again that he should be ready to move out at a moment's notice, and that the rest of the task force was in position to quickly close up on him.

I hastened back to my command post, expecting to learn that movement orders had arrived for me, but, surprisingly, the afternoon had remained uncharacteristically quiet. It was very late in the afternoon when I was summoned back to CCB. The first thing that I had expected from General Dager was a situation report on CCA's activities. There was none. General Dager immediately got down to business. He informed me that Division had assigned to CCB the mission of seizing Rimling. He had been told that CCA would operate on CCB's right with the mission of attacking Bining, then Rohrbach-lès-Bitche, virtually connected to it, and the high ground to its north.

It is necessary to note that the two combat command's assigned missions from Division were important, well-established towns of military significance. There was absolutely no mention of a place called Singling as a prime objective. Why should there have been? Singling was a village with only about 50 buildings scattered along a west-east road. There was absolutely no road that went north from Vœllerdingen to and through the village and beyond. Access to the village was limited. The village was not much different than the hundreds of tiny villages and small towns that we had bypassed all the way from Normandy. It was of little tactical value in its own right. If anything, it was not important as a town but as a terrain feature, merely a way station sitting just east of CCB's axis of advance.

General Dager's specific instructions to me were quite simple. He directed me to attack early in the morning with the town of Singling as my objective, and to continue on to the town of Rimling. I knew from many weeks of association that Singling to General Dager was a directional objective (via Singling) not one to be fought for. When I returned to my CP, I studied my map and noted that my axis of advance would be Schmittville, Singling, Gros Rederching, and northeast to Rimling. CCA's axis would be from Domfessel to Dehlingen, Rahling, Bining-Rohrbach. Operating along their axes, the two combat commands would be separated by 3 to 4 kilometers.

For my force it would be a direct shoot of 6 kilometers to Gros Rederching with a slight turn to the northeast to Rimling, another 3 kilometers. My axis would cross the Achen-Singling, east-west road about 2 kilometers west of Singling. My route would take me cross-country all the way to Gros Rederching, except for perhaps the last couple of kilometers.

December 6 started very early. While still dark, I had a meeting with my commanders, and issued the necessary orders for the move to Rimling via Singling. Elements of the task force moved out quickly at first light. As soon as they were closing in, "B" Company shoved off. They rode the higher, drier, open ground, and rapidly covered the 2 kilometers to Schmittville, and then it would soon be down the slope toward Singling. In keeping with my resolve upon assuming command to actively fight the battalion, I was with the lead elements as they advanced.

Although it was not raining, it was a gray, cold, dreary, very unpleasant day with a dark, heavy overcast. As we began our descent to lower ground, I received a staggering blow, the shock of my young life. What I looked at out in front of me was unbelievable, incredible, incomprehensible. It was not the expected open terrain, but a large number of widely deployed military vehicles. They were not enemy vehicles but American vehicles facing Singling. There is no way that I could ever have been prepared for the scene unfolding before me. As we were advancing, I had expected at any moment to engage or be engaged by an enemy force, but it was beyond comprehension to find, instead, an American unit. Who are they? How did they get here? I strained to read the markings on the first vehicle—more astonishment, more disbelief. The vehicle unbelievably belonged to *the 37ᵗʰ Tank Battalion*! NOT THE 37ᵗʰ—that just could not be!

At last word on the 4ᵗʰ as light had fallen, the 35ᵗʰ and 53ʳᵈ were still west of the Eichel. A mammoth challenge still awaited them and the 24ᵗʰ Engineers. Bridges had to be installed at Domfessel and north of it. Once the bridges were in came the tedious, laborious task of tanks and infantry half-tracks individually negotiating the bridges. The task force could not move out into the attack until its forces were assembled. All of this was difficult, and, particularly, would take time.

At last word on the 4ᵗʰ, the 37ᵗʰ had been assigned to the Reserve Command positioned to the rear of CCA. The new Division Troop List had moved the battalion to CCA, but this initially was only a paper move, not a physical one. The 37ᵗʰ still occupied their position in the rear. Knowing all of this, it is no wonder that I was absolutely astonished, dumbfounded to suddenly find them broadly positioned in front of my most forward element. It almost seemed as though they had just dropped down from the sky.

Enough conjecture. It was necessary to solve the riddle. I had to find without delay its commander, Abe Abrams. I quickly determined his whereabouts, and moved my tank forward to his command tank. I pulled up close to it, dismounted, and jogged briskly to it. When I reached the tank, I found Dan Alanis, CO of the 51ˢᵗ Armored Infantry Battalion, standing beside it. I knew instantly that Dan's battalion was now working with the 37th. Dan and I quickly exchanged greetings. Then without hesitation, I climbed up onto the deck of the tank to talk to Abe, who was standing in his turret talking into his radio mike. As I had climbed up, Dan followed. We had no sooner reached Abe when he pushed away his mike and erupted. His outburst—a loud, shouted torrent of words—almost tore my head off. There were no preliminaries, no questions, no discussion. It was so totally and completely unexpected that I virtually recoiled as from a blow. The torrent of words continued undiminished.

"Where have you been? What took you so long?" Abe shouted. "You're too slow. I'm occupying *your* axis of advance. I've attacked *your* town. I can't stay here any longer. I've got to get right out. I've got to get back on my own route, on my own mission. It's about time that you took over the town. I've got a tank/infantry team in it. I want your tanks and infantry to relieve them in place. Do it right now. I can't spend any more time here. The town is clear, so you can move right in—you won't have to fight."

The meeting was finished. I blinked my eyes, and knew this was it. There was no room for questions or discussion. So I in deference to the senior officer simply nodded and said, "Yes, Sir," saluted and clambered down to the ground. I rushed back to my tank to issue the instructions necessary to effect the relief. As I moved, I was in a daze, as a multitude of thoughts swirled through my head. I was trying with great difficulty to compose myself, as I felt devastated. In my long years in the military I would never be talked down to, and so unfairly, as I had just moments ago.

I had been orally lashed by an individual who, at that moment, had been overbearing, imperious. I had no opportunity for discussion, explanation, clarification. No, this was it. On the face of it, Abe handled me disdainfully, and had in a sense belittled me. But why not: this was a mere Major, and a brand new rookie battalion commander at that. Abe was a ranking lieutenant colonel, a West Pointer, the most experienced tank battalion commander in the division, a hero and an architect of the tank victories at Arracourt.

While all of that is very impressive and true, something significantly important must definitely not be overlooked.

At that very moment when I stood head to head with Abe on his tank, I commanded one-third of the division's tanks, as did Abe. At that moment I had the same number of tanks, the same number of men, the same organization, the same responsibilities, the same authority as Abe. On that tank, we were organizational equals.

Although Abrams was the senior officer in the area, he had no direct command authority over me. My immediate superior who gave me my orders was General Dager.

Yes, Abe was by far the more experienced tank battalion commander, but I, as the 8th Tank Battalion's advance guard commander until I assumed command of the battalion, had on a daily basis been on much more intimate terms with the enemy.

It was understandable that Abe was overwrought, exasperated, frustrated, and edgy. The day before was a most difficult one for him. He had been sidetracked in his efforts to reach Bining, and late in the day he lost a whole company of medium tanks. When I reached him on his tank, he was on the radio talking to his combat commander, who had ordered him to move away from the CCB axis, and reminded him that his objective was Bining, not Singling. Abe had grabbed a tiger by the tail, and was now most anxious to let it go.

I soon learned that Singling had not been taken (parts had been), and was not clear. Apparently Abe had misinterpreted a report, was unaware of the true situation, was in great haste to leave, and passed on to me information that was not entirely accurate.

When I got back into my tank, there still appeared to be fire from the direction of Singling, but I relied on the information that I had received, and assumed that we would receive no enemy resistance as we entered the town.

I ordered Company "C," commanded by Bill Marshall, to pick up the infantry of Company "B" of the 10th, go into Singling, contact Capt. Jimmie Leach, the CO of the 37th's "B" Company in town, take over their positions by relieving them in place, outpost the town, and send out patrols north of the town.

I told Bill that there was no need for caution, and to proceed rapidly and enter the town as the others had done.

I moved my tank to get closer to Singling, and punched the radio button to get on the "C" Company channel, so that I could follow the action. I learned from listening to the transmissions that at the south edge of town, "C" Company's First Platoon commanded by Second Lt. George Gray, noticed tank tracks. They turned northwest to follow these tracks. Up ahead were two American tanks, which Gray assumed were the ones he would relieve. As he approached them, he noticed that the hatches were open, but there was no sign of any crew members. Then Gray saw near a road up ahead another tank, which he assumed was also American, since he believed that the enemy was no longer in town.

He continued to advance, and as he moved around the corner of a wall, he was hit by two armor-piercing rounds. His gunner, Corporal Aro, was killed, and Gray was seriously wounded.

I, listening on the radio, was thunderstruck by this staggering development. The day had not yet run out of shockers. The balloon had again burst. My units were barely at the edge of town, and had already suffered a kill. It did not take a seer to recognize that the town *was not* clear. This development was confusing and most disheartening. It was now obvious that the two American tanks had been knocked out much earlier, and that the area was not any safer.

Lt. Bill Marshall immediately ordered the Second Platoon, commanded by Staff Sergeant DeRosia to move east and try to get behind the enemy tank that had apparently knocked out Gray. DeRosia had not moved far when he received direct fire from the north and east, which was so heavy that he had to move at once without being able to locate the fire.

The situation was now so confused and unclear that Marshall ordered all his tanks to withdraw to the reverse slope of the ridge south of town. Having done that, Marshall moved back to talk to me. His tank soon appeared. I dismounted from mine and met him on the ground. He was very upset, probably from the double blow that he just received, having an expected safe approach into town hit him in the face, and seeing his extremely close friend, Lieutenant Gray, a battlefield commissioned officer, wind up a severe casualty. Bill seemed to be blaming himself for barging forward and getting Gray hurt. I tried to reassure him that his actions could not be faulted, and suggested that he go back to the rear for a breather.

I was now presented with an immediate and serious problem. As result of attrition during the preceding weeks, and now with Marshall and Gray gone, "C" was left without a single officer. Without hesitation, I placed S.Sgt. Edwin DeRosia in immediate but temporary command of the company.

Apparently no one in the 37th Tank Battalion, until the team in town commanded by Capt. Jimmie Leach was later being relieved, had a really accurate picture of just what the situation was in that part of town. The two American tanks, which Gray had moved up to relieve, belonged to Lieutenant Farese's platoon of the 37th, and had been knocked out earlier in the day.

Lieutenant Farese had run into a nest of armor and defensive emplacements—a perfect defensive position that the enemy used cleverly. This nest consisted of at least three Mark V tanks, two SP guns, and one towed gun, which had successfully blocked every attempt at direct assault or envelopment. They were so well placed and so well located that if one of our tanks moved against them and merely bared their radio antenna, as Staff Sergeant DeRosia well knew, it immediately received armor piercing fire. The enemy owned this part of town. Yet this is the area that "C" Company was encouraged to approach confidently—without a word of caution or warning. No wonder that there would be some acrimony.

The armored infantry of Company "B" of the 10th AJB commanded by First Lieutenant Lange had remained on top of the "C" Company tanks, excluding Gray's; as they withdrew to the ridge, Lieutenant Lange then dismounted his doughs and moved them into town to relieve the infantry, as he had been instructed to do.

After Bill Marshall had departed, and with the "C" Company situation somewhat stabilized, I was concerned about the armored infantry who were without tank support. The best way for me to determine this was to move down to the edge of town to see for myself. When I reached Lange's company, I found that after deploying his troops, he had moved back trying to locate Marshall and the tanks that were to support him. He found Staff Sergeant DeRosia instead. My arrival was most timely, for some immediate decisions had to be made. Abe Baum, S3 Operations Officer of the 10th, soon joined me.

After a brief discussion with Lange, I was able to make an assessment of the situation. It appeared that the 37th's team had never totally controlled the part of town that they were now in. At best, they had occupied the center of town, a substantial number of the fifty or so buildings. But they had been inside the buildings because they were periodically under fire along the main street, and movement outside of and between buildings was hazardous. Even the infantry CP had been harassed by direct fire much of the day.

The enemy had tight control of the west, and they dominated from the north and northeast, as they occupied that ground.

When Lange moved into town, his company was a shadow of its former self. The fighting strength was that of a platoon, not a company. His fewer than fifty men were strung out thinly, and were vulnerable to enemy probing, and worst of all—infiltration. They were anything but a concentrated fighting force. During their brief time in town, they had already suffered casualties from mortar fire.

As I was about to make my decision, night had already fallen. Although Lange occupied the center of the tiny village, he was outnumbered, and the enemy still held the outskirts and areas in the west and north. Lange with his limited resources just could not hang in there alone. Yet, I could see absolutely no reason to push in my tanks to provide him with the needed muscle. All across Europe, thus far, we tried to avoid getting involved in towns and villages with our tanks. At times we had to, if for example, it was necessary to clear the road through the town. Most of the time, if the terrain permitted it, we bypassed those settlements.

Once inside a town, the tank loses its mobility and with it its shock action. It is left only with its firepower. Accordingly, it stops being a tank, and becomes merely a roving pillbox. Even here it is limited because it cannot fire from behind buildings, walled yards or around corners. So I just could not see one good reason for pushing in my tanks. It was dark, vision from the tanks was extremely limited, they would have to feel their way along the narrow streets, and it would be extremely easy for a single German soldier to destroy or damage a tank with a handheld Panzerfaust or a tossed grenade.

So I ordered Lange to withdraw his troops immediately from the village. I instructed Staff Sergeant DeRosia to jockey his tanks back and forth on the reverse slope of the ridge to make the enemy believe that more tanks were advancing into the town. As the infantry withdrew, they positioned themselves with the tanks. The two elements now had excellent defensive positions south of the village.

With Singling now clear of U.S. troops, I decided that now was the perfect time to hit the village with artillery. Just two days before, I called for and received a TOT (Time on Target) on the city of Vœllerdingen. I firmly believed that it was an important reason why I was able to get through it and to seize intact the bridge across the Eichel. I was convinced that now was the time for another, so I made my request for a TOT on Singling. A TOT is the concentration of several battalions of artillery coordinated by corps that destroys men and equipment, and has a powerful demoralizing effect.

My request was soon answered, and down it came! Screaming, squealing, screeching sounds of artillery shells exploding overhead abruptly shattered the silence of the dark, still night. Instantly there was pounding, blasting explosions, flashes all over and inside Singling. The action was so close in front that the ground shook where I stood. Once again I had received more than I had expected.

As I stood back and watched the rounds hit and explode, I knew with a certainty that I had made the correct decision. Breaking developments would soon emphasize how right I was. After the TOT, there would not be a single sound or action—not a peep—from the enemy that night or the next morning. Before retiring, I was informed by CCB that I was to hold my present positions, and not to move in the morning.

Very early the next day, I learned that as probably the last action on the 6th, the 37th finally captured their objective, Bining. Some ironies abound. Not a single medium tank was involved. Those not knocked out of action had been fully engaged. It was the 37th's light tanks reinforced by a "borrowed" infantry battalion that seized the town. The town in comparison to Singling was extremely lightly defended. Had the 37th been able to hit it directly, as planned, seizing it would have been a cakewalk.

The morning was not too advanced when word was received that the 4th would immediately be relieved in place by the brand new 12th Armored Division. That was most welcomed news, for the 4th had gone for more that four weeks without a hot meal for its troops, and hardly a minute for the maintenance of its vehicles. A period devoted to rehabilitation had been desperately needed, and now it was at hand. This also meant that for the 4th Armored the Battle for Singling was over, and its advance to the east was momentarily halted.

Singling had never been designated as a prime objective for the 4th Armored Division, as it had no tactical or strategic value. It did not even have a road going north and south through it. It became a major player by accident.

The day's skirmishes by the small tank/infantry team explored in detail by the "Small Unit Actions" booklet had several highlights and accomplishments. The initial attack featured a most impressive charge of tanks into the village. From then on, as in most congested areas, it was an infantry battle. B/51 was outnumbered by its enemy counterparts at least 3 to 4 to 1. Yet, it was able to take control of and to hold on to a considerable portion of the village. During the day's seesaw engagements, the courageous troops of the 51st were able to capture a surprisingly large number of the enemy. All of this was made possible by the presence of the tanks that were backing them up. Although restricted from offensive action, the tanks were able to make quick moves, and to pop out quick shots. Importantly, the enemy knew that they were there.

What were the results of the "Small Unit Battle?" At day's end the "B" Team had still controlled a portion of the village, and they had been successful in holding off all day a much larger force, and preventing them from advancing through and out of the village.

For the enemy, it was probably a more successful day. They had stopped the advance of the 4th Armored Division. Additionally, they had tied up completely an entire tank battalion, and much of the rest of the division behind it. As night descended upon them, they had, however, become ineffective inside the village.

And that is how the Battle for Singling ended on the night of the December 6.

POST BATTLE ANALYSIS AND COMMENTARY

How did the 37th Tank Battalion get from the rear of CCA to Singling? Did they just drop down out of the sky?

The writers of "Small Unit Actions" seem to accept that they did. On page 180, they include a map that shows a broad arrow with the words, "TF ABRAMS," going directly from Schmittville to Singling.

However, there is no arrow showing how Abrams arrived in the area. The accompanying narrative states for December 5, "37th Tank Battalion attacked from Schmittville under orders to advance as far as possible with Rimling as a limiting objective." That short statement contains errors and is confusing. The 37th was never in Schmittville. Rimling was not CCA's objective—Bining was. Rimling would be CCB's ultimate objective. YES, THERE WAS CONFUSION EVEN IN THE RANKS OF THE BOOKLET'S AUTHORS.

So how did the 37th emerge seemingly out of nowhere from the rear of CCA, suddenly appear in front on center stage, and become the division's most prominent and virtually sole performer in a puzzling, confusing operation? There are very many unanswered questions.

At some point, the 35th, 53rd, and 24th were successful at installing the bridges and getting the fighting elements of the task force across the river. The difficult and demanding actions all day in Domfessel on the 4th and into the early hours of the 5th must have taken their toll. Consequently, were their actions now slow and sluggish? The day was already well advanced, and since this was December, darkness would settle in early. Someone must have decided that there was a faster way for CCA to reach its objective—Bining. Was it Brigadier General Earnest, the new, two-day CCA Commander, the infantryman with his first armor experience? Undoubtedly not. Was it the new, two-day Commanding General of the 4th Armored Division, Maj. Gen. Hugh Gaffey? He had been an Armor Commander, but prior to this assignment he had been General Patton's chief of staff. It could have been, although in two days he had barely gotten the "feel" of the division. Or was it Lieutenant Colonel Abrams? He had been chomping on the bit, very anxious to get back into action. Now that the division had a brand-new combat and division commander was it not time to make his move? Did he propose to and convince General Gaffey that with his fresher battalion and a bold move he could quickly advance the relatively short distance to Bining?

It is more than probable that he may have. As Patton's chief of staff, Gaffey was well aware of the high regard in which Patton himself held Abrams. Both knew that Abrams was an aggressive tanker, the senior one in the division, a West Pointer, and a hero of the September Arracourt tank battles.

Abrams was an extremely self-confident, even a bit cocky individual. For his temperament and background this could not have been a more ideal situation. All he needed was the green light and a wide-open battlefield, and he got just that. General Gaffey must have decided or been convinced that the situation now required a bold, aggressive move, and he had a bold aggressive commander to execute it.

Consequently, the 37th Tank Battalion bolted forward, and passed through the 35th and 53rd Task Force in the vicinity of Dehlingen. Once clear of it, the battalion quickly covered the three kilometers to Rahling and moved onto the main, hard-topped road with a direct, unimpeded shot to Bining only five kilometers away. Now was the time for the 37th to make its bold, aggressive charge to the division's objective. The road was on a prominent ridge all the way. Since the ground on both sides of the road was too soft for cross-country movement, the vehicles were required to advance on the road.

From the very beginning of the drive there was on the 37th's right and parallel to it the massive Forêt-de-Montbronn. As the force got closer to Bining, it would pass a series of prominent knobs, to which the 37th was very vulnerable.

The bold, aggressive move appeared to be working, for the force was soon closing in on Bining. Suddenly, seemingly out of nowhere, descending upon them was an extremely heavy volume of fire. The battalion was forced to jam on its brakes, and to quickly evacuate to the muddy ground to the left of the road. In just a moment, the prospect of a quick, direct seizure of Bining completely vanished. The immediate important challenge was to negotiate the muddy terrain so as to get out of range of the enemy weapons.

Once Abrams had reorganized his battalion, he recognized that to capture Bining he would now be forced to do it from the west. To the west of his position, and parallel to the Bining ridge, was another prominent ridge that ran from a settlement called Schmittville to a small village named Singling. That ridge had no road. However, since the ground on the ridge was higher, it was also drier and tanks could negotiate it. In order to get his force to the ridge, he would have to overcome another challenge. His tanks would somehow have to find their way across the treacherous and very muddy Vallee d'Altkirch.

His tanks were eventually successful in reaching the ridge in an area south of the village of Singling, which was about 2½ kilometers northwest of Bining.

To get abreast of Bining and in position to attack that town directly from the west, Abrams had to move closer to Singling. Once abreast of Bining, the tanks were forced to make a right angle turn. As they were moving, they exposed their left flank. Once again, seemingly out of nowhere, down came another torrent of fire. It came from direct fire weapons, as well as from artillery. In a matter of seconds, five closely deployed tanks were knocked out by high velocity, direct fire weapons. Nine others, which had been slowed and bogged down by the sticky mud, were quickly destroyed or disabled. This was a real shocker, absolutely devastating, demoralizing, so sudden, so powerful. All fourteen tanks of "C" Company gone, completely out of action, a wipeout. Gone in almost an instant one-third of the tanks of a tank battalion.

Normally at this point it would have been wise to push the infantry out toward the village to secure its forward edge. But not this time, for there was no infantry. In this situation that was not critical, for the devastating fire had not come from within the village, but from the dominating ground around it.

The only thing left to do for the remainder of the battalion was to pull back to a safe and secure location.

What had started out with high hopes for a speedy and successful operation turned absolutely sour, and ended tragically and most dismally. It would prove to be a long, painful, miserable, cold night for the 37th Tank Battalion.

And that is how the 37th had moved from the rear of CCA to Singling in the Maginot Line.

This operation has generated questions that still remain unanswered.

When Abrams landed squarely on the Schmittville/Singling ridge, did he know that he was sitting right on the CCB axis of advance?

Did he request approval from CCA or division headquarters to leave his axis and move the 3 to 4 kilometers west to CCB's axis?

Did he notify higher headquarters that he was doing it or had done it?

After he had passed through the 35th/53rd Task Force, did CCA or division request situation reports from him?

When did CCA and division know that he had reached Singling?

When General Gaffey did learn about it, did he ask, "What are you doing in Singling when your assigned objective is Bining?"

If division was aware of CCA's location, why was the information not passed on to CCB that Abrams had put Singling into play?

(When CCB's forces moved out the morning of the 6th, nothing had been mentioned to them that morning or the evening before about the location of the 37th.)

WHAT HAPPENED TO CCB?

As historians have probed the Singling affair, they apparently have been unable to explain why CCB was not on hand when CCA's 37th Tank Battalion became heavily involved with that village. So, they have resorted to suppositions. Some of those are listed below.

- "It was necessary to clear away rear guards from the Nichelbusch Woods northeast of Vœllerdingen, as fire from that direction had harassed the column. This action coupled with the slow cross-country travel forced

81

the column to halt for the night at Langenwald Farms southwest of Schmittville."

- "CCB was still some distance from the battlefield."
- "Singling was one of CCB's objectives, but CCB had not advanced rapidly enough to be in position to deal with the town."
- "The cross-country march (by the 8th) was slow because of fog and soft terrain conditions."
- "Going was slow because of mud and harassing fire. B/8th had moved to high ground south of Schmittville, where AF Irzyk was ordered to halt for the night."
- "After Abrams, Singling was one of CCB's objectives, but CCB had not advanced rapidly enough to be in position to deal with that town, and then to move aggressively to the high ground southwest of the tiny settlement of Schmittville."
- "Singling was one of CCB's objectives, but CCB had not advanced rapidly enough to be in position to deal with the town. In order to relieve the situation and to per-mit his forces to continue to attack, Lieutenant Colonel Abrams ordered B/51 to attack Singling."
- "As the attack on Bining progressed, Combat Command 'B' passed Combat Command 'A' and attacked Singling."

All of the above are manifestly incorrect, confusing and dead wrong assumptions, suppositions, and theories. That they have been written is a clear indication that their writers were totally unaware that CCB was the first element out of the blocks on the 5th, easily reached the high ground southeast of Schmittville before noon, and sat and sat for the rest of that day with absolutely no instructions to move.

Those writers seem to accept that it was a breeze for the 37th to move from the rear of CCA west of Domfessel and the Eichel River all the way to Singling, but for some reason they simply conjecture that the 8th Tank Battalion had great difficulty negotiating the short distance from their bridgehead east of Vœllerdingen to nearby Schmittville.

What Should Have Happened

If the 4th Armored Division's high command had made a simple, timely, proper decision on December 5, *there might never have been a Battle for Singling*. CCB had been successful on the 4th in seizing intact a bridge over the Eichel River, crossing it, and establishing a bridgehead on the east side, a feat which CCA was unable to accomplish at Dom-fessel.

Early on the morning of the 5th, the 8th Tank Battalion, the first unit out of the blocks, eliminated all resistance from the Nichelbusch Woods, avoided the muddy terrain by picking higher and drier ground, and reached their objective, the high ground southeast of Schmittville, *before noon*. They were told not to advance further until CCA on the right had caught up to it.

If CCB had been ordered to move soon after, perhaps early afternoon when the 37th had passed through the 35th/53rd Task Force, as should have happened, CCB and CCA would have been advancing on parallel axes, as they had done all the way across France, and until now had been doing. If that had occurred, CCB would have immediately thrust *toward* Singling along the ridge from Schmittville. The west-east road from Achen through Singling was less than 6 kilometers away. As we moved on our direct axis to the north and neared Singling, we would have left the ridge to the left, so as to be able to bypass the village. The uncertain terrain may have forced us closer to Singling. If that happened, my lead elements would surely have received long-range fire from the hornet's nest so well emplaced just west of the village. In that event we would immediately have returned fire, and I would instantly have called for artillery support from my closely supporting artillery battalion, which always was deployed close behind. As that fire began falling on the suspected enemy targets, it would have joined the direct fire already spewing forth from my deployed tanks. This combination would surely have been effective in pinning down the enemy tanks and SP's, as well as artillery pieces, which were out in the open and extremely vulnerable. As we had done so many times during the previous weeks, we would have dueled it out with the enemy. However, with the tanks of my battalion we were at greater strength, and would soon have prevailed and eliminated the initial enemy resistance. With that we would have been past the main part of Singling, for which there was no reason to clear. As we continued our advance to the north, our next concern would have been the dominating ridge north of Singling. We would have continued to pound it as well as other critical defense features with more and heavier supporting artillery battalions (the ones that had provided me with the TOT at Vœllerdingen). By the latter part of the afternoon we would have left Singling behind, and would have been well on our way to our division objective—Rimling.

During those past hours, the enemy would have been so heavily involved with us that they would have been forced to lessen their attention to their east. While all this was happening, the 37th's charge to Bining was stopped in its tracks by heavy fire from their right, and they instantly had to evacuate the road to their left.

Abrams would have had to reorganize his battalion on the left side of the Bining road. While doing so, he would have realized that he could not now seize that town as he had planned. He would have to operate on the left side of the main road. That would require him to attack Bining not from the north, but from the west.

If the division's command structure was operating as it had done for the many previous weeks, CCB would be abreast of the activities and current status of my 8th Tank Battalion and my supporting 10th Armored Infantry Battalion. Similarly, CCA would have been well aware of the 37th's operations.

Now that Abrams had to abandon his previous plan and had to improvise a new one, he would quickly have realized that to attack Bining from the west, he would have to do so from the next ridge to his left. If things were properly working, he would by now know from

CCA that forces from CCB had moved out and were operating on their assigned axis, which he recognized as the ridge to which he had to move. So, unquestionably, he would have asked CCA to get from CCB the location of the 8th, and if they had left the area that he needed to occupy, he would have asked for clearance to move to that area on the ridge.

After his tanks had successfully negotiated the treacherous and muddy terrain and reached the ridge, he would have had them quickly ready for their move on Bining. Since he was south of Singling, he would, initially, have moved them closer to that village. That would have put him directly west of Bining. An added bonus was the knowledge that by attacking from that direction, he would be on favorable terrain, and he would not have to contend again with the Vallee d'Altkirch because he would be moving just north of its reaches.

However, he had to make a sharp turn to the right, exposing his left flank. He had every right to believe that based on the report that he received about CCB's actions in the vicinity of Singling that there would not be much of the enemy waiting for him. He could now make his dash to Bining before darkness fell, and to his great and most pleasant surprise would have found it lightly held, and it was not long before the town was his.

Once past Singling and environs CCB's forces still had considerable daylight remaining, and the farther beyond Singling they moved the lighter was the enemy resistance.

By the time night fell, it was conceivable that both of the division's objectives had been seized—Bining by CCA and Rimling by CCB. This would have been the night of December 5.

Of course, we will never know what the outcome would have been, if division had chosen to have both Combat Commands operating simultaneously on parallel axes. There are many questions about that operation that will never be answered. Admittedly, this is merely a scenario of what might have happened. However, it is a plausible, believable scenario, for it is typical of the actual operation of the division over a period of many weeks under a great variety of situations. The operation of the division on the 5th and 6th, one must conclude, was an aberration.

Questions Abound

Why was the 37th Tank Battalion, by itself, turned loose like a lone eagle to roam the battlefield, while all other forces stayed relatively "put?" Did General Gaffey believe that a bold, sudden, quick thrust to Bining would do the trick?

It had been habitual during previous actions that when a combat command sent out a tank battalion into the attack, it would have along with it armored infantry and armored artillery, as well as such detachments as engineers, tank destroyers, and reconnaissance elements. But not in this case. It was time-consuming for the vehicles of supporting elements to negotiate in single file the engineer installed bridges. Was it decided not to wait for that to happen, but, instead, to make a quick, hasty charge to Bining without them?

There are questions about the 37th's Singling attack on the morning of December 6. Just late in the afternoon of the day before, they had been bloodied by fire from Singling and environs.

Now it had its armored infantry and its direct support armored artillery, the 94th, on hand. At this point, the 37th was not receiving any enemy fire, and the situation did not seem to require quick action. Nevertheless, there was an immediate attack by a small company team composed of tanks and armored infantry. Both elements, particularly the armored infantry, were under strength. As it turned out, the B/37 and B/51 team never had a chance. They would operate against heavy odds, and were involved in a confused, hastily improvised maneuver. Their force was greatly outnumbered. The enemy was not only at greater strength, but possessed every terrain advantage. They controlled the main street, the nose of the ridge, west of town, and all of the surrounding terrain.

In order to help level the playing field, why did the 37th not accept a forty-five minute or so delay, and request an artillery TOT of five or six battalions of heavy artillery? Such a massive amount of instant, concentrated fire on the tiny village, and the surrounding, dominant terrain would certainly have caused considerable havoc and suppressed enemy activity. I had requested a TOT just two days before at Vœllerdingen, and for me that proved decisive.

A clear indicator that the attack had been hasty became evident at day's end. Because they pushed quickly into the attack, coordination by radio had not been completed. Accordingly, that night after the day's action, some tank and infantry platoon leaders believed that they had been in Bining, as, among other things, they mistook the Welschoff Farms north of Singling for the barracks they had expected to find at Bining.

It was a MISNOMER to call the Battle of Singling a "Small Unit Action." It actually involved much of the division.

That the operation called the BATTLE FOR SINGLING unfolded as it did was a clear indicator that something had been very wrong at the top. Was it a failure of leadership, lack of awareness, confusion, momentary ineptness? As that battle developed on December 5 and 6, such would never have happened if General Wood had still been in command! So, yes, the radical command changes DID have an immediate effect on the operations of the division. How else can it be explained why a highly successful, battle-tested division like the 4th would have been stopped, while a lone battalion without support would have operated so freely on the battlefield?

What happened to the 35th/53rd after the 37th passed through them? They were never heard from again.

Despite the attention paid to it, Singling was anything but a big or important action. The insignificance of the battle is emphasized by the lack of awareness and knowledge by Corps Headquarters of what actually transpired there. Like so very many towns before it, Singling was easily and quickly forgotten, particularly since the division had not particularly distinguished itself. It would move on to many momentous, memorable achievements. It was not until months after the war that Singling was most surprisingly somehow resurrected by young War Department historians.

Singling was certainly not one of Lieutenant Colonel Abrams' finest moments. It was unheard of for him to be stopped dead in his tracks. That battle may well have been the low point, the nadir of what would turn out to be a brilliant career. In the years ahead he would have many triumphant moments, and Singling would be an unmentioned flyspeck on that long, illustrious career.

During the advance to Singling, the division had rolled up the German defense line in the Sarre for a distance of thirty miles across the XII Corps front.

The drive to Singling was the farthest northeast advance of the division in its push to the Rhine. That engagement was the final action on French soil.

By its actions at Singling and environs, where the Germans had strong prepared defenses, the division opened the way for later advances by the 12th Armored Division.

CHAPTER FIVE

THE MYSTERY OF "TIGER JACK"

Written by Brig. Gen. Albin F. Irzyk. Reprinted with permission from ARMOR *Magazine, Jan-Feb 1990.*

This is the extraordinary story of a remarkable general who figuratively commanded his division in combat while sitting at a desk at Fort Knox, Kentucky, nearly 3,000 miles away from the action. His division was the 4th Armored Division.

He was Maj. Gen. John Shirley Wood, nicknamed "Tiger Jack" and "P" Wood. He picked up the "P" at West Point, where he had spent endless hours tutoring fellow cadets. His habit of nervously pacing was reflected in his other nickname, one the Germans found accurate enough to use routinely.

Of his division, General Patton declared, "The accomplishments of this division have never been equaled. And by that statement I do not mean in this war, I mean in the history of warfare. There has never been such a superb fighting organization as the 4th Armored Division."

Freed American PWs reported, "The 4th Armored Division is both feared and hated by German front line troops because of its high combat efficiency." GIs themselves said, "It is the best damned armored division in the European Theater of War."

Liddell Hart, eminent British historian, military writer, and critic, said Wood was, "The Rommel of the American armored forces . . . one of the most dynamic commanders of armor in World War II and the first in the Allied Armies to demonstrate in Europe the essence of the art and tempo of handling a mobile force."

Lt. Gen. Willis D. Crittenberger said, "He far exceeded in his leadership capabilities any man I have ever known."

And Gen. Jacob L. Devers simply stated, "They would follow him to hell today."

Yet, this man, commander of that division, who had achieved outstanding and unprecedented success in the employment of armor, who was at the height of his success, at the very apex of his fame in Europe, was relieved of his command and sent home, after little more than four months in combat.

"Impossible," you say, "This could not happen!" Why, this would be heresy—almost like trading off a star NFL quarterback at the height of an undefeated season.

After all, division commanders are relieved because their troops will not move, will not fight, are not aggressive; their tactics are poor, and they suffer unnecessary and heavy losses, or they don't seize objectives or accomplish assigned missions. But highly successful division commanders relieved—never!

Never say never, for it happened to Maj. Gen. John S. Wood.

Air Force Gen. O. P. Weyland had admiringly stated, "Whereas more cautious division commanders occasionally warranted some prodding, 'P' just as often had to be restrained." Yet, this man was gone from the combat arena before word of his great accomplishments ever filtered back to the American public. Today, one will not find him listed among Eisenhower's lieutenants. Moreover, historians, military buffs, even the keenest students of World War II hardly know of him. Tragically, he was a great man, but virtually unknown.

I began my connection with the man and his division in August of 1942. As a cavalry officer in probably the last horse regiment, I had recently had to give up my mounts. The powers that be found me a new home and mounts of a different type at Pine Camp, New York.

Shortly after my arrival there, one of the first questions I asked was, "How is our division commander?" The answer: "He's kind of weak."

"Why do you say that?" I asked.

"Well," came the reply, "we recently had a division review and after it, he made a speech and ended it by saying 'God bless you men.'"

Weakness? That man was to utter those words in his remarks to his troops endless times, so fervently, so emotionally that he sometimes brought tears to the eyes of his listeners.

Initially, he was not liked or admired. There was plenty of bitching and griping at Pine Camp. The men referred to him as "Paper and Butts," because he insisted on immaculate unit areas.

His troops trained hard all day and had to attend schools at night. All were restricted to camp, except for Wednesday evenings and brief weekends. Such actions did not stimulate popularity.

When he had his commanders and staff together, he announced, "I don't expect much—all I expect is perfection." As his listeners recoiled, he continued, "Of course we'll not achieve perfection, but that's what we'll always be striving for."

He was recognized early as warm and caring. He stopped wherever he observed groups of his troops. He talked to them and showed concern. "When have you last written home?" If the answer was not satisfactory, he would tell them, "Do something for me when you're in the barracks tonight. Please write home—tell them you're alright, tell them what you're doing."

In the early fall, we cut our ties to Pine Camp and headed for maneuvers in Tennessee. While there, General Wood was reprimanded, ridiculed, and rebuked by more senior officers during weekend maneuver critiques. They chastised him for being too bold, too unorthodox, for moving too fast, too far, covering too much ground, and forcing problems to end prematurely. They informed him that he just could not do it in combat with the enemy shooting, fighting, attacking, so why was he doing it in Tennessee? General Wood stood his ground, and quietly told them, "We can do it, and we will do it." (What a prophet he was.)

It was during these maneuver critiques that General Wood, on two separate occasions, challenged—actually called the hand of—Lt.

Gen. Ben Lear, Second Army and maneuver commander, who reputedly ruled by fear and commanded "by the book." Wood objected to certain criticism of his actions, and passionately and emotionally defended his troops, who had been the targets of critical remarks he considered totally unfair.

A witness later stated, "This was the greatest act of cold courage I have ever observed or have known of, and also the finest act of loyalty from the top down imaginable . . . . This man . . . had actually put his career in the United States Army on the line. . . ." (A harbinger?)

Word of this exchange spread quickly throughout the division, and General Wood instantly became a great hero to his men, for they now knew he would always stand up for them, and between them and difficulty. It was during these maneuvers that a bonding took place that has lasted to this day. General Wood and the 4th Armored Division became inextricably entwined, a marriage forever. The man and the division became one. It has been said that the great divisions of history have been known by the names of its commanders. One of the best examples is the 4th Armored Division, with which "P" Wood's name will be permanently and forever linked.

The Mojave Desert was the next stop for the division. Despite the intense heat of the desert, he required his men to wear their fatigues with sleeves rolled down and collars buttoned—certainly far from a popular requirement, but one he deemed necessary in the development of his division his way.

As we expected, his training was innovative and realistic. Two of his tank companies, buttoned up with live .30 caliber rounds in the coaxial machine guns, would start at opposite ends of a wadi and soon have a meeting engagement. In one of these problems I rode in one of the tanks, commanded one of the tank companies. I can assure you there was plenty of activity and excitement when we spotted an "enemy" tank moving from cover, fired live bursts at him, saw our rounds "splash" against his sides or turret, knowing instantly we had scored a "kill." How more realistic can you get, what better preparation for combat than that?

Then it was on to Camp Bowie, Texas, and more insights into this fellow, Wood. Not long after his division had settled in, a great hue and cry arose from the nearby civilian community. We were in the dry belt of Texas, and Wood had authorized the sale of beer in the post exchanges. Community leaders screamed in anguish, preachers pounded their fists in their pulpits, and letters of protest flooded congressmen and other influential officials. Wood held fast, declared his soldiers would have beer if they wanted it, and beer remained at Camp Bowie as long as the 4th was there.

By this time, every man in the division was beginning to feel that General Wood was a personal friend. The men knew that their commander was genuinely, sincerely interested in them, that he identified with them, and had an emotional involvement in their lives. They knew he referred to them as "my people." Whenever he traveled by jeep in the presence of his troops, he stood in the jeep constantly saluting. The troopers marveled, "He saluted me before I saluted him." Soon the men were trying to salute their division commander as far as they could see him, to beat him to the draw.

He trusted his men. They treasured this trust. He obviously believed in the credo of Ralph Waldo Emerson; "Trust men and they will be true to you; treat them greatly and they will show greatness themselves."

Before the division embarked for England, Wood informed his troops, "This division will attack and attack, and if an order is given to fall back, that order will not come from me."

By this time, other divisions were acquiring nicknames. When pressed to come up with one for his, General Wood declared, "The 4th Armored Division will have no nickname—they shall be known by their deeds alone." Those words from that day forward became the division's motto. Although never with a formal nickname, the division in the months ahead was often known as the "Name Enough Division" and "Patton's Best," and was variously labeled, "Breakthrough," "Whirlwind," "Glorious," "Irrepressible," "Immortal."

The division did win its military immortality in the Normandy breakout, when it slashed rapidly and aggressively out of a depressingly stalemated situation to seize the tactically and strategically important city of Avranches, a decisive objective that gave access to Brittany on the south and west, and to Le Mans, Chartres, and Paris on the east.

For us, the action in Normandy was strongly reminiscent of Tennessee. We shouted excitedly at one another, "Just like maneuvers!" (Except that our ammunition was live, the incoming fire was real, and the prisoners did not have "aggressor" armbands, but strange uniforms.) Wood's troops were obviously seasoned from the outset.

General Wood quickly established his leadership literally, figuratively, and every other way. Near Coutances on the way to Avranches, Wood marched into town under fire, captured a German soldier, found a path through a mined area, picked his way through on foot, and sent back a cryptic, classic message. It was scrawled in pencil on a message blank and ordered, "General Dager [his combat commander] send the infantry through after me."

Later, he was to say, "If you can't see it happen, it is too late to hear about it back in a rear area and meet it with proper force."

From Avranches, his division was ordered southwest to seize the Atlantic ports of Lorient, Vannes, and St. Nazaire. While his units were moving in that direction, he protested such employment to his senior commanders long, loud, and vehemently. He reminded them, in no uncertain terms, that the enemy was to the east, that the war was not going to be won by going west. But the plans had been conceived before the invasion and, because of strategic inflexibility, were being doggedly carried out. The high command did not like Wood's reminding them that they were winning the war the wrong way. By the time they reoriented their thinking, Wood had already reached the outskirts of the Atlantic ports and had lost much valuable time. In the process, he won few friends and undoubtedly picked up resentment, for it must have been galling for his superiors to know that he was right.

Once the division was finally turned around, we began what was to be an epochal sweep through France. General Patton plotted the strategy, and General Wood executed it. He was a bold and daring commander who was willing to take risks and was really the architect of the rampage through France. For weeks, as the 4th Armored Division went, so went Third Army. Wood's vision set the pattern for armor operations in Europe. Accomplishing the impossible prescribed by Patton became routine.

We moved too rapidly, were too widely scattered for the conventional gathering of commanders for the typically detailed, specific orders. Wood resorted to "mission type" orders. These consisted of a line of departure, a broad, directional arrow (axis of advance), a goose egg (objective), and the, terse order to "get going at first light." That's all we had; that's all we needed.

The hallmarks of his division were rapid flanking movements, deep penetration, constant momentum and violent execution of fire and maneuver. Like cavalry, Wood slashed and sidestepped with speed and surprise. He echeloned in depth and did not worry about his flanks.

After two and a half months of intense and constant action and, by now, deep in France, the division halted in the October mud and rain for its first "break." On the second day, word came that General Wood would visit our battalion early the next morning. We arose at dawn and assembled quickly. As the battalion S3 Operations Officer, I spent many minutes getting the overshoes off and hidden and endeavoring to line up the men without getting their boots muddy. Shortly after I had made a final check of their appearance, and had them dressed in straight lines, we looked up and there, suddenly, was our commanding general. We watched fascinated as his large, bulky, tank-like form bounded lightly upon the temporary platform we had built for him. With legs spread, he glanced momentarily at his smartly assembled troops, and then called out, "Gather 'round, men." (Find

that command in any drill manual.) In an instant, the carefully formed ranks were broken as the men rushed to get as close to their commander as they could. They jammed in a tight circle around him, eager to be near him, to hear his words. He related all that they had done. He told his men how very proud he was of them and how very humble he felt to be in the presence of those who had accomplished so much. His voice broke, and tears rolled. He was obviously very moved, and so were his troops. He concluded with, "God bless you, men."

About this time he began to receive recommendations for the Presidential Unit Citation for platoons, companies, and battalions which had distinguished themselves during the weeks of combat. He refused to approve any, and declared that he would not single out any unit within his division. He said that if such an award were granted, he would wait until the entire division received it as a unit. Again, he showed great prescience and faith in his division because later, the 4th Armored Division became the only tank division and the second entire division to be so decorated by order of the president. There was an added and unexpected bonus. The French government twice cited the whole division with the Fourragère.

October soon became early December, with the rain heavier and the mud deeper and stickier. The attacks continued down narrow roads in atrocious weather. The war became a slugfest. "Penny-packet" tactics had replaced massed armor employment. And then, without warning, the 4th Armored Division received an almost mortal blow. For the first time since entering combat it was stunned, reeling, demoralized; it recoiled, was severely wounded. Word, like winds before a tornado, instantly reached every last man in the division that their beloved commanding general had been relieved of his command and sent home. All were shocked, disbelieving. This just could not happen, was not true, was not possible.

When the news had finally sunk in, and some semblance of composure returned, the first word universally uttered was the question, "Why?" the same question that persists to this day. Almost immediately, answers in the form of rumors and speculation swept the division like a prairie fire. The "real reason" soon reached us. General Wood, we were told, was relieved because he was tired and sick, and was being sent home for a rest.

BUNK! We all agreed. We knew that he was every bit as tired as we were, but not more so. If he was sick, so were we.

So speculation about "the true story" intensified and in some sources continues to this day. Wood himself, speculating in later years, rejected the medical verdict and declared, "I suppose I will never know the entire story . . . ."

Within the division, we also universally rejected the medical version, and continued to speculate.

Was he relieved because:

- in his desire to press the attack, he had crossed the boundary between Third and Seventh Armies, and had, for a period, operated in the Seventh Army sector?
- he was openly critical of the misuse of armor and of his division, particularly?
- he pleaded with General Eddy, his corps commander, for a little rest for his exhausted men and vehicles, and for time to reorganize?
- there was a severe personality clash between Wood and Eddy, two very strong and dominant commanders, undoubtedly exacerbated by the three reasons above?

Comment upon each of these items of speculation is necessary to flesh out this most fascinating combat episode.

General Wood, in typical fashion, most certainly crossed the army boundary. He later wrote, ". . . such lines meant little to me, and I went where the going was good." However, in this case, he received permission to cross the boundary with XV Corps of Seventh Army to turn the enemy's positions facing the XII Corps. He not only helped his own situation, but did the XV Corps a great big favor by destroying the salient that a German counterattack by the Panzer Lehr Division had sliced into the XV Corps flank. So, this excursion surely did not cost him his command.

Most assuredly he complained of the misuse of his armor. Initially and briefly, the division had been held back pending an exploitation situation, but the corps infantry divisions were bogged down, and the armor was soon committed to "retrieve the setback."

Thereafter, because of rain, mud, and terrain, the division had to operate almost on a one-tank front. Some of the tanks were badly shot up by 88s, causing numerous casualties. Although the division ground ahead slowly, it took its lumps. The armored divisions were not concentrated. The only armor breakthrough at that time occurred at the Saverne Gap by the 2nd French Armored Division, and that success was not exploited. A corroborating voice came later from German General von Mellenthin: " . . . the armored divisions were committed too early and . . . [Lt. Gen.] Eddy [commanding XII Corps] would have done better to wait until his infantry had eaten away more of our main defense zone."

All of this certainly aggravated General Wood, who saw his division being whittled away because of poor tactics. Certainly, Wood's criticism didn't set well with his superiors, some of whom undoubtedly still smarted from being embarrassed by Wood, who had been so very correct about Brittany.

General Wood deeply believed in the unceasing endeavor to spare the men he had the honor to lead unnecessary hardships and useless losses, and possessed the willingness and desire to share their hardships and face the same dangers. He tried to do the most with the least possible cost in the blood of his men. Stupidities and mistakes that caused needless casualties infuriated him. His division had pressed the attack, day after day, for many weeks, from first light until darkness, taking on fuel and ammunition during the night. The vehicles, which received maintenance every day during training, had not been touched for weeks.

The continuous fighting under almost impossible conditions for armor had seriously reduced its tank complement and caused heavy losses among experienced personnel, particularly officers. The men were exhausted. Both men and vehicles had been pushed virtually beyond endurance. Certainly, General Wood interceded for his men. He wanted a period of rest for his troops and vehicles and a chance to reorganize. Herein rests a tremendous irony. The "break" which General Wood must have fought so hard for, at great personal sacrifice, was granted just five days after he was relieved of his command. His division, whose forward elements were in the Maginot Line, was relieved by the new and fresh 12th Armored Division.

And there is yet another great irony that apparently has eluded historians and gone unrecognized and unappreciated. If it had not been for the "break" that permitted the 4th Armored Division to rest, refit, and reorganize, it would have been impossible for it to make the historic forced march of 151 miles to the environs of Bastogne, and then, in five days of bitter fighting, succeed in breaking through to the 101st Airborne in that beleaguered city.

It was inevitable that Wood and Eddy would lock horns. Unquestionably, Eddy wanted to keep pushing (undoubtedly pressed by Patton) and could not help but be irritated and annoyed at Wood's pleas on behalf of his troops. He probably interpreted this as a sign of Wood's developing softness because of the pressures of the campaign. To Eddy, Wood's insistence may also have spelled taut nerves.

It did not help that Wood was not an easy subordinate. He was a highly intelligent and perceptive man who did not "suffer fools gladly, no matter what their station." He had little toleration or respect for men of lesser minds, lesser competence. He had difficulty practicing allegiance to those above him whose capabilities he believed were inferior to his own. He was never a "yes" man, and sometimes expressed dissent so vigorously he may have appeared insubordinate. So, the sparks that flew must have caused an explosion, for when the dust settled, Wood was on his way home. Patton must have decided that one or the other had to go, and the decision was—Wood.

Wood said of his relief, "I will never know the entire story . . . ." Over the years, those who have known and speculated about this World War II episode generally conclude that the full story of Wood's relief has never been told.

I, too, have speculated, pondered, and reflected on the reason for his relief. But suddenly for me there is no longer a mystery. I have deciphered the reason, and the solution is quite simple and basic. General Wood was relieved because he was just being General Wood.

Now, in an eerie resemblance of his actions during Tennessee maneuvers, he once again "stood up" to his superiors, was critical of their tactics, pleaded for a respite for his exhausted men and vehicles, and finally did in late 1944 what he came within a hair of doing in 1942—he committed career suicide.

This need not have happened. General Wood could have been unfeeling, less humane about the condition of his men and vehicles; he could have diluted the fierce, almost obsessive loyalty to those he led. He could have ignored what he saw as the misuse of his forces and the improper tactics employed. His demeanor and remarks could have been more tactful, diplomatic, respectful.

Had he done all of this, he undoubtedly would have continued in command of his division and could possibly have finished the war as a corps commander with a third star (if he could have torn himself away from his division).

But if he had done all of that, he just would not have been "P" Wood.

Yet, because he was so good and so successful, there has to remain some suspicion about the motives of his superiors and the so-called "system." On the date of his relief, there must have been broad knowledge that merely five days later the division was to get its well-deserved "break." If Wood needed rest, as they claimed, why didn't "they" wait five days so that he could get his rest along with his troops?

Of an action only nine days before his relief, German General von Mellenthin related, " . . . Bayerlein might well have broken through to the Sarrebourg-Saverna road, but unfortunately was taken in the flank by the 4th Armored Division, which had forced its way across the Saar at Fenetrange."

At the end of November, three days before his relief, the 4th Armored was east of Sarre-Union and "pushing forward with violent fire." Could those have been the actions of a division led by a tired, sick commander?

In Europe, there was a paucity of good division commanders. Consequently, division commanders who were timid, mediocre, colorless, and, at best marginally successful, were retained. Realizing this, it certainly flies in the face of logic that Wood, a proven, successful division commander, would sit out the bulk of the war at Fort Knox.

Maj. Gen. Hugh J. Gaffey, Patton's chief of staff, succeeded Major General Wood. Here was a safe, don't-rock-the-boat choice with whom Eddy, Patton, and others would be comfortable and certainly have no problem. Gaffey commanded for 3½ months and was followed by Maj. Gen. William M. Hoge, who commanded for a brief period until the end of the war. They hardly counted. In the eyes of the men in the 4th, they were still led by Wood; the other two went along for the ride. There was no perceptible change in its method of operating or its indomitable spirit.

For the rest of the war, the division bore the distinctive mark of Wood's training, tactical ingenuity, and military genius. Not long after Gaffey assumed command, the division made its historic link-up with the 101st Airborne at Bastogne.

In the fall of 1945, at a gathering at Fort Knox at the quarters of Lt. Col. (later Maj. Gen.) Arthur L. West, 4th Armored veterans were rehashing the war and discussing the division's exploits. General Gaffey was present and himself admitted, "I had little influence on the division and its actions because you carried on under the influence and momentum of General Wood."

At another time, General Hoge said, "Wood was much revered and loved by both officers and men of his division . . . I still marvel at the depth of leadership when I took command."

The 4th Armored Division, until the end of combat, and for 40 years after as the 4th Armored Division Association, has been General Wood's division.

For many years, the New York chapter of the association celebrated Activation Day with a pilgrimage to West Point. The highlight of that weekend each year was the solemn, touching memorial service conducted at the gravesite of General Wood.

The division association has met in convention for 40 successive years. General Wood remains the favorite and most frequent topic of conversation.

His was leadership at its absolute best. Volumes that endeavor to answer the question, "What is leadership?" crowd library bookshelves. One could obtain the answer by discarding many of the texts and theories and merely studying Wood. It is too bad that we cannot break down into component parts the Wood charisma and "magic."

He knew that the division he trained and led in combat was one of the most outstanding in World War II. He lived to realize that he was worshipped by his men, and recognized that their deep affection would last to the end of his days and long after he was gone.

Years later, Gen. Bruce C. Clarke remarked, "The 'Gods of War' did not smile on 'P' Wood . . . . Under different circumstances 'P' had the brains, the knowledge, the drive, the magnetic hold on his men to have been listed on the rolls of the Great Captains of history."

This story of General Wood has not been written by an impressionable, starry-eyed, hero-worshipping second lieutenant. Hardly. I have commanded a company, tank battalion in combat, an armored cavalry regiment in Germany, and for brief periods a division in Vietnam. I have served on joint and NATO staffs. During a full military career, I have watched from a very close vantage point many senior officers of all our services and of many allied nations. I have studied, taught, and endeavored to apply leadership. In my lifetime, I have looked up to few heroes.

It is now more than 40 years since WWII. Yet, in my eyes, Maj. Gen. John S. Wood remains a genuine, authentic hero. I have long admired him, always looked up to him. I consider him the finest soldier, the greatest leader I have ever known. I shall never forget him for what he was and what he stood for. For me, his greatness grows, as my years recede.

CHAPTER SIX

4ᵀᴴ ARMORED DIVISION'S SPEARHEAD AT BASTOGNE

Written by Brig. Gen. Albin F. Irzyk. Reprinted with permission from World War II Magazine, *November 1999.*

J ust before dark on the day after Christmas 1944, elements of Lt. Gen. George S. Patton, Jr.'s 4ᵗʰ Armored Division, attacking from the south, succeeded in making contact with the beleaguered Americans at Bastogne. The encircled 101ˢᵗ Airborne Division had occupied that critically vital Belgian town for several days, categorically refusing German demands for surrender.

The dramatic linkup of the two forces broke the siege of Bastogne and was one of the great turning points in the Battle of the Bulge. This legendary event has often been described in histories of World War II, but there is a fascinating subplot to the story that is little known.

It took the 4ᵗʰ Armored Division five days of bitter, costly fighting to break the ring of German units encircling the 101ˢᵗ, but only six days before the linkup, elements of that same division had actually been in Bastogne on the day it was being encircled. In fact, during that earlier movement into the town, those forces had come within one kilometer of the same spot to which they would return six days later, after heavy fighting. How could this have happened?

To understand this enigma, we must go back to December 8, 1944, the day the 4ᵗʰ Armored Division was pulled back from heavy fighting after reaching the Maginot Line, at a point a little more than nine miles from the German border. It was time for refitting and rest

105

so that the division would be better prepared to cross the border and continue its assault to the east. The move to the rest area was not only welcome and richly deserved but necessary. The men of the division were exhausted after incessant fighting during the heavy, record-breaking November rains. The weather, the enemy and the gummy mud combined to make conditions deplorable and had taken a serious toll on the men and their tracked vehicles. Such extended breaks in the fighting were rare, and spirits were high.

At the time, I was serving with Combat Command "B" (CCB) of the 4th Armored Division, commanded by Brig. Gen. Holmes E. Dager, and its 8th Tank Battalion, which I commanded as a young major. During the division's rest period my command post was in Domnon-les-Dieuze, a tiny, wet, muddy and depressing French village about 40 miles northeast of Nancy. Almost immediately, the town became littered with tank parts and equipment of all types. Not knowing how long we would be there, the men wasted no time in tackling their tasks.

On the fourth day the troops were excited and energized by the visit of the Third Army commander, General Patton, who swooped in for a quick stop. He arrived at high speed in his jeep, with a wide, crooked grin and all his stars blazing. He was jolly, animated and interested in how we were doing. After jumping out of his jeep, he worked his way along the entire length of the small town. He stopped at every vehicle, talked with every cluster of soldiers and had something to say to each—a question, a word of encouragement or appreciation, a compliment, a wisecrack, a good-natured dig. He was a master at this kind of rapprochement. His visits were brief, and he kept moving. But in 30 minutes or so, he had worked his magic—he had "touched" virtually every man in that battalion.

We soon learned that the 8th Tank Battalion was the only battalion in the division that he visited. Although the troops had no inkling of the momentous events that lay just ahead, Patton was apparently aware that an attack might be in the offing. After visiting the three other divisions of the XII Corps that day, he wrote in his diary that he had decided to put the 6th Armored Division and the 26th Infantry Division into the III Corps because "if the enemy attacks the VIII Corps of the First Army, as is probable, I can use the III Corps to help."

December 18 is a day I will always remember as the most confusing day of the entire war. Early that morning I was told to attend a meeting at division headquarters, but before I left for the meeting it was called off. The previous day I had been told that a move was imminent and to have my troops ready to move on short notice.

At 10:45 AM on the 18th, CCB was placed on a one-hour alert. I continued with my preparations for the move the next day to the east, as well as the subsequent attack into Germany, by sending billeting parties forward to obtain billets for the battalion to occupy at the end of the march to the border.

At 5 PM the one-hour alert was canceled. Shortly afterward, I also received word the move to the east the next day was off. I recalled my billeting parties. With no order for the next day, the men settled in for the night after the evening meal.

Then, suddenly, at 11 PM the 8th was ordered by CCB to be prepared to move at once. That directive was quickly followed up with instructions to cross the initial point, or I.P. (as yet to be designated), at 12:50 AM and then move in a totally different direction—north! We would be moving to the III Corps zone (wherever that was) to assist in stopping a strong German counterattack in that sector.

The radical change in mission, the confusion that had preceded it, the lack of information, the uncertainty, the hasty departure in the pitch-dark and the highly unusual timing of the move—50 minutes after midnight—all combined to indicate we were involved in something serious. A cloud of apprehension hovered over the entire battalion.

As ordered, the 8th Tank Battalion crossed the I.P. at 12:50 AM on December 19. We had no information about the situation up ahead or about the enemy. CCB's orders were to move to an area in the vicinity of Longwy, France, many miles to the north. The 4th Armored Division, previously attached to the XII Corps, was now assigned to the III Corps.

Combat Command "B," with its 8ᵗʰ Tank Battalion out front, led the advance of the division. Combat Command "A" (CCA) would be the next to move out, nine hours behind CCB and along the same route. Thus, the 8ᵗʰ led the odyssey north into the cold, black night, reinforced with the half-tracks of the 10ᵗʰ Armored Infantry Battalion. At the head of the 8ᵗʰ was my tank, making it the lead element of the Third Army in its advance to the north.

Amazingly, the combat command had but one map, and that was with General Dagen. During our rapid movements across France that summer and autumn, we occasionally had to rely on Michelin road maps for direction. But to be completely without maps was a new experience.

Once the column was on the road, we rolled mile after mile into the unknown. I was guided and directed by General Dager in a variety of ways. He radioed instructions from his jeep, his staff relayed radio messages, he sometimes rode alongside to shout directions at me in my turret, and at tricky intersections he dismounted and pointed the way.

The hours and miles passed, and Longwy loomed closer. The end was in sight. But then our spirits were dashed. As we reached Longwy, we were waved on, and we rolled through the city without slackening our pace. Our tank guns were still pointed to the north, and now, for the first time in the war, we were in Belgium. We passed through Arlon and changed direction to the northwest, still with no reduction of speed.

We began our journey in darkness and were to end it in darkness, as night came upon us again. A difficult situation became considerably more difficult, since we now had to travel under blackout conditions, and our progress would be greatly slowed. On top of that we had absolutely no idea of what lay ahead, and we were expecting to be fired on by the enemy at any moment.

Neufchâteau, another milestone, came and went as we continued to roll, still without enemy contact. Again we changed direction slightly, this time moving to the northeast. Now we were on the Neufchâteau–Bastogne road, headed toward Bastogne, another unfamiliar town.

As we neared the town of Vaux-les-Rosières, we were at last told to stop for the night. Combat Command "B" moved into that location, which was west of the road. I selected a spot about two kilometers east of the road for our bivouac area (I would later learn that it was near a town named Nives). By the time we settled in, it was 11 PM.

Except for brief halts, and one longer one to refuel, we had been on the move unceasingly for more than 22 hours—half of one night, all day and half of another night under blackout conditions. Remarkably, we had traveled 161 miles over roads that were sometimes bad—without maps and without confusion. The fact that we arrived was a tribute to both our men and vehicles and spoke volumes for the work we had accomplished during the recent rest period. Most important, there had been no enemy contact.

That night none of us realized that we were the vanguard of what would later be called the greatest mass movement of men in the shortest period of time in the history of warfare. Patton's troops had been poised to attack the Saar to the east. Forced to abandon that plan, he ordered the major part of his Third Army to make a gigantic 90-degree wheeling movement and then drive north at full speed. Involved in the spectacular maneuver were thousands of men and vehicles operating in damnable weather, often over icy roads.

Once we reached the bivouac area, there was still no rest for many of us. Many of the men were exhausted, but as soon as we reached our position we sent forward some strong patrols of light tanks and armored infantry to detect any enemy movement from the north.

Early the next morning, December 20, I was, figuratively speaking, hit by a thunderbolt. General Dager called me on his radio and, without any preliminaries, ordered me to send a task force into Bastogne. I was stunned. I protested vehemently, reminding him that the situation up ahead was unclear, terribly confused, and that this was no time for a piecemeal commitment of my forces. To my great surprise, Dager agreed with me. He said that he had just made the same arguments in a tug of war with Maj. Gen. Troy H. Middleton of the VIII Corps. Middleton had ordered him to take all of CCB into Bastogne, and he had hotly resisted, insisting that Middleton wait until Gen. Hugh Gaffey arrived with the rest of the 4th Armored Division. Middleton finally agreed not to commit the entire combat command, but only after Dager conceded that he would send a task force instead.

As ordered, I formed the task force. It consisted of "A" Company, 8th Tank Battalion; "C" Company, 10th Armored Infantry Battalion; and "C" Battery, 22nd Armored Field Artillery Battalion. I placed in command of the task force Capt. Bert P. Ezell, my battalion executive officer. His force would henceforth be known as "Task Force Ezell." Ezell's mission was to report to Brig. Gen. Anthony C. McAuliffe, commander of the 101st Airborne Division, learn about the situation in Bastogne, receive instructions and render support if so ordered.

The task force moved northeast on the Neufchâteau–Bastogne road and reached Bastogne without seeing any enemy troops. Upon entering the city, Ezell was told to report for instructions—not to McAuliffe, but to Col. William Roberts, commander of Combat Command "B" of the 10th Armored Division.

Shortly after Ezell radioed me that he was in Bastogne and had made contact with their troops, I was astonished to receive an order from division headquarters to recall the task force to Nives at once. I immediately called Ezell, whose radio operator told me that he was out talking to a colonel. I shouted, "Get him!" I reached him not a moment too soon, for at that very instant Ezell had been receiving instructions for deployment from Colonel Roberts. When I told him to return, Ezell was dumbfounded. As was to be expected, he had a difficult time convincing Roberts that he had to leave with his force just after arriving in Bastogne. A short time later, just after noon, a delighted and vastly relieved task force was on the road again.

Seven hours after it set out for Bastogne, Ezell's task force returned to our bivouac area with many more vehicles than it had when it pulled out. The men were beside themselves, chatting and shouting excitedly. They had seen some strange sights—so strange that they had a difficult time explaining it all to the rest of us.

As the task force moved away from Bastogne, they had encountered an American 2-½-ton truck in a ditch on the right side of the road. The truck was barely damaged and its driver was still sitting behind the wheel. But the top of his head had been blown off above the eyes, apparently by an armor-piercing round.

Moving a little farther down the road beyond the ditched truck, the troops noticed tank tracks running across the asphalt pavement. They were much wider tracks than could be made by American tanks and must have been made by German Panther or Tiger tanks.

The task force then came upon another strange sight—about two battalions of U.S. artillery stopped along the road. The equipment seemed to be in good shape, but there was no sign of any troops. Some of the vehicles were still idling. It was not clear whether the artillery units had been attacked and their positions overrun, or if they had been spooked by the sight of German tanks crossing the road just to the north of them and had abandoned their guns and vehicles. Given the evidence they had seen so far, it appeared that a strong German force had moved rapidly west and cut across the Neufchâteau–Bastogne road while Ezell was moving toward Bastogne. Perhaps the lead German elements had been moving so rapidly that following forces had not yet caught up with the vanguard. Ezell's units had apparently managed to slip through a gap in the enemy echelons driving west. The task force hauled back as much of the abandoned artillery equipment as they could handle and encountered no resistance on the way back to the bivouac area.

As December 20 passed, events continued to move swiftly. At 2 PM, CCB was reassigned to III Corps with the rest of the division. The 8th Tank Battalion was ordered to retrace its steps of the previous night and move southwest to Neufchâteau, then southeast to Léglise. We arrived in the vicinity of Léglise after dark on the 20th. Shortly after, I

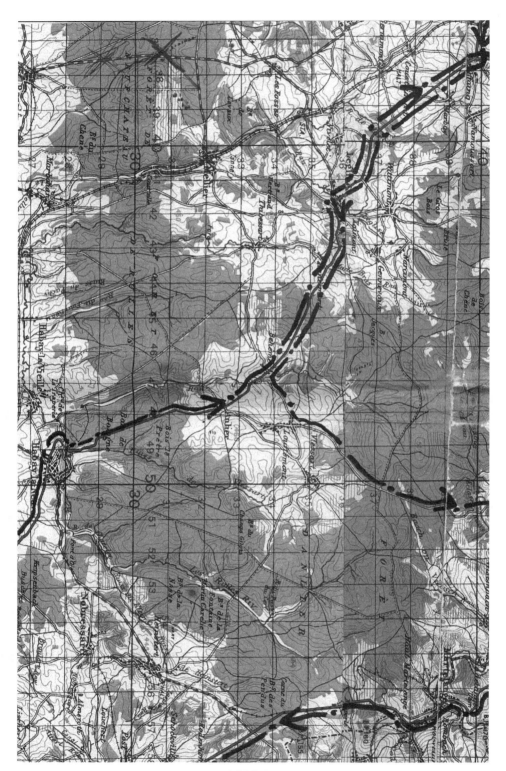

BASTOGNE

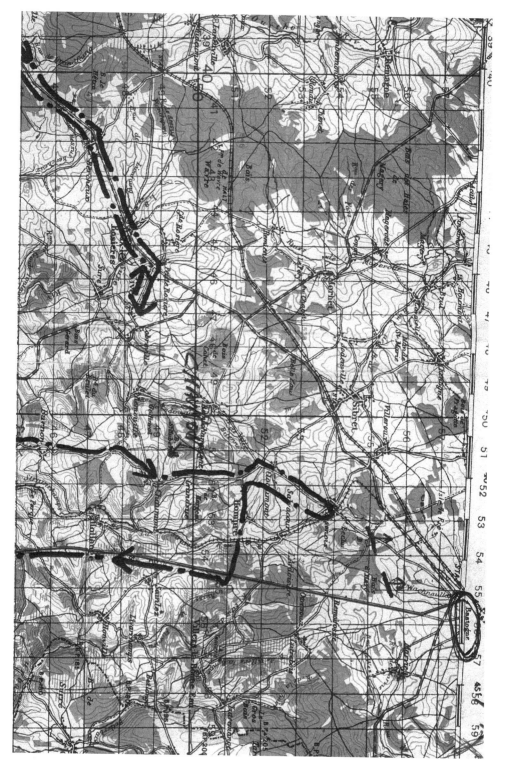

CHAUMONT

was surprised to learn that the rest of the division had remained in the vicinity of Arlon, and none of its units had made any attempt to close up on CCB. Only later did we learn why CCB had gone where it did and when it did.

On the 21st, I received my orders from General Dager at CCB headquarters for the attack that would take place the following day. I was also informed that during the previous night and early that morning very strong German forces had driven west and flanked the city of Bastogne on the north and south. The two forces had met west of the city and completely encircled Bastogne. Trapped in the city was the 101st Airborne Division, to which were attached elements of the 9th and 10th Armored Divisions.

This was shocking news, but Task Force Ezell had provided ample clues that the Germans had been on the move the previous day. What really was disturbing was the realization that the encirclement had been taking place while Ezell's group had been in Bastogne, and it had continued with unabated fury after the 8th Tank Battalion and CCB had left the area.

I could not help but think about what could have happened. If he had not been recalled by division headquarters, Ezell and his men might have been trapped in Bastogne along with Colonel Roberts' combat command of the 10th Armored. And what if General Dager had not won the day in his tussle with General Middleton? All the 4th Armored's CCB—if we had moved into Bastogne as General Middleton had originally ordered—might well be stuck in the besieged city.

We moved out of Léglise at 4:30 the next morning—the 22nd—so as to arrive at the I.P. at 6. The 8th Tank Battalion and the rest of CCB were part of the 4th Armored Division's attacking force, coordinated with the 80th and 26th Infantry divisions of III Corps. The 4th Armored was on the left flank.

We began our slow, difficult return to Bastogne. The following day, at Chaumont, the 8th Tank Battalion was on the receiving end of one of the most powerful tank-led counterattacks of the war, temporarily slowing its advance to Bastogne and inflicting heavy casualties. Ironically, the battle at Chaumont was fought just four kilometers east of the quiet bivouac area we had occupied at Nives just three days earlier.

It took five days of bitter fighting to relieve the 101st in Bastogne, but by December 28 the area had been cleared of the enemy, and all of our positions had been consolidated. When Captain Ezell walked into the 8th Tank Battalion command post in Assenois, he was just one kilometer southeast of where his task force had been eight days earlier as it rolled into Bastogne.

Those of us who participated in this confusing operation, as well as historians who have analyzed the Battle of the Bulge in the years following World War II, could not help but note the ironies and incongruities surrounding the battle. A number of questions have been raised about our mission:

- Why did CCB, whose original destination was the vicinity of Longwy, continue on alone until it reached a position in VIII Corps sector, only nine kilometers from Bastogne?
- Why did General Middleton of VIII Corps seem to exert "ownership" of CCB?
- Why did the rest of the 4th Armored Division not close up behind CCB instead of leaving CCB near Bastogne while the rest of the division assembled well to the rear, in the Arlon area?
- If General Dager had not protested dividing his command, what might have happened to CCB if it had rolled into Bastogne as ordered, on the day when the enemy was very much on the move?
- After moving into Bastogne, why was Task Force Ezell immediately and summarily recalled, especially considering that General Middleton had argued strongly for its presence there?

- After the elements of Task Force Ezell had returned to their parent units, why was all of CCB relieved from assignment to VIII Corps and withdrawn—back to the rear—less than a day after arriving in the forward position?

- Should commanders at higher levels have exploited Task Force Ezell's rapid progress to Bastogne once they knew the unit had entered the town without a fight and returned? And should General Middleton have been allowed to hold onto CCB and use it to try to keep the Neufchâteau–Bastogne highway open, possibly preventing the encirclement of Bastogne?

- Once CCB had moved into its bivouac at Vaux-les-Rosières, should the rest of the 4th Armored Division have capitalized on the situation, moving up to attack from the bivouac location only a short distance from Bastogne rather than consolidating for the attack farther south and then fighting its way north along the difficult forest axis from Arlon to the encircled city?

Among those who have answered "Yes" to the last two questions is Charles B. MacDonald, who stated in his book *A Time for Trumpets*: "If Middleton had been allowed to hold CCB and with it keep open the Neufchâteau-Bastogne highway, Bastogne probably never would have been surrounded. Even if the Germans had cut the Neufchâteau-Bastogne highway, the 4th Armored Division might have capitalized on the location of CCB and attacked from Vaux-les-Rosières instead of from Arlon. Which would have spared many officers and men of the 4th Armored Division a great deal of misery and, in some cases, death." The following additional information about the events leading up to the Battle of Bastogne provides answers to some of these nagging questions.

On December 18, Lt. Gen. Omar N. Bradley, commander of all U.S. ground forces, called off Patton's planned offensive into the Saar.

Without hesitation, Patton told Bradley that he would concentrate the 4th Armored Division in the vicinity of Longwy, pull the 80th Infantry Division out of the line and get the 26th Infantry Division moving within 24 hours. Much later that same day he issued the order that got CCB moving just after midnight.

General Patton met with his staff at 8 the next morning, December 19, as CCB was already well on its way to Longwy. His plan, he told his staff, was to strike due north and hit the underbelly of the German penetration where it would hurt. During the next hour, Patton and his staff planned, in outline, three distinct operations. Arrangements were made for a simple code to indicate, via a brief telephone call, which operation would be implemented.

Later that same day, Patton met at Verdun with Supreme Allied Commander Gen. Dwight D. Eisenhower and a distinguished gathering of senior commanders that some have called perhaps the most historically significant conference of the 1944-45 campaign. All agreed that there should be a counterattack at the earliest possible moment. Patton told the group that he could be ready to attack with three divisions of the III Corps on December 22. A stronger force, he said, would take several more days to assemble and would forfeit surprise. The group was astonished at his rapid response to the situation and was more than satisfied with his proposal. It should be emphasized that at this meeting Patton pledged a three-division counterattack with the entire 4th Armored Division as the key division in the corps. He was completely unaware that CCB was then on its way toward Bastogne.

Given the situation, it is absolutely inconceivable that CCB should have been sent on its merry way all the way to the outskirts of Bastogne and told to report to the VIII Corps. It turned out that General Bradley was responsible for that trip. Whatever the rationale for its mission may have been, the motivation for this decision is difficult to comprehend.

In his memoir *War As I Knew It*, General Patton wrote, "The next morning I arrived at Bradley's headquarters in Luxembourg and found that he [General Dager] had, without notifying me, detached Combat Command 'B' of the 4th Armored Division from Arlon to a position southwest of Bastogne. Since the Combat Command had not been engaged, I withdrew it to Arlon [not Arlon but Léglise]."

Historian Martin Blumenson, in the second volume of *The Patton Papers*, quotes from General Patton's diary entry of the same day, December 20: "In the morning I drove to Luxembourg, arriving at 0900. Bradley had halted the 80th Division at Luxembourg and had also engaged one combat command of the 4th Armored Division in the vicinity east of Bastogne [not east but southeast] without letting me know, but I said nothing."

General Patton then drove to Arlon, to the headquarters of General Middleton's troubled VIII Corps to get a firsthand picture of the situation in the Bulge. When he arrived, he found Maj. Gen, Hugh J. Gaffey of the 4th Armored Division, Maj. Gen. Willard S. Paul of the 26th Infantry Division, and Maj. Gen. John Milliken of the III Corps already there. There is considerable speculation and some difference of opinion about what actually took place during their meeting. However, subsequent events lead easily to certain assumptions.

General Middleton still must have been anxious to send CCB into Bastogne behind Task Force Ezell and surely requested permission to do so. Elements of his corps were already scattered, and his armor was especially fragmented. Middleton wanted to avoid more of the same. General Gaffey must have wanted his combat command returned. With a major attack coming up in just two days, he needed his division at full strength, and it would have been severely handicapped without CCB. General Milliken also knew that the key to his III Corps three-division attack was having the 4th Armored at full strength. He surely must have supported Gaffey's argument to have his CCB returned.

As events later developed, CCB shouldered an extremely heavy share of the 4th Armored's fight at Bastogne. The combat command acted as the powerful left flank, not only of the division, but also of the III Corps all the way to the encircled city. In retrospect, General Dager's resistance to committing CCB to Bastogne earlier surely saved the unit. If he had not protested, CCB probably would have been in Bastogne before Patton was aware that it had been given away by Bradley.

It was fortunate that Task Force Ezell returned unscathed from its fruitless mission. The loss of a tank company, an armored infantry company and an artillery battery would have considerably weakened CCB.

At the Verdun meeting, General Patton had committed himself to a coordinated attack with three full divisions. He knew that the situation in the Bulge at that moment was confused. That was not the time to reinforce a failing situation and risk having elements of the 4th Armored committed prematurely. Patton's decision was revealed when Task Force Ezell was ordered out of Bastogne shortly after noon and CCB was directed to move to the rear, which it began to do by midafternoon.

Patton chose as his ultimate course of action a well-planned, well-coordinated, orderly attack toward a known, specific objective. He jumped off from ground that was firmly in his hands. His planning and execution were sound and professional. Undeterred by the panic around him, he kept his eye on the ball.

Patton's counteroffensive not only broke the ring enclosing Bastogne but also destroyed a portion of the German penetrating force, eliminating hundreds of enemy vehicles and thousands of troops. Because of his rapidly organized and well-executed counterattack, he was able to snatch the momentum from the Germans and seize the initiative. He had done what he had promised his commanders he would do.

In the eyes of historians, the experience of Task Force Ezell is an extremely minor episode in the war in Europe. It did not have any significant impact on any campaign. But finding the answers to some of the more puzzling aspects of Ezell's mission helps to enrich our understanding of the Battle of the Bulge. It clarifies how the counterattack was planned and provides some fascinating sidelights on the men who made the decisions and brought about the dramatic linkup at Bastogne. No one who learns about Ezell's trip to the city during its encirclement can help but be struck by the story's ironies and might-have-beens. Although I was a participant in much that happened, I still find it a strange and fascinating tale. In sharing my own experience and research, my goal has been to shed a little light on an obscure, yet telling incident that had formerly been shrouded by the fog of war.

CHAPTER SEVEN

CHAUMONT

On December 19, 1944 as the 4th Armored Division led by Combat Command "B" was already rolling north, General Eisenhower had gathered at Verdun all his senior commanders for a critical, emergency meeting. All present now recognized that what they had initially thought was a minor incursion by the German Army in the Ardennes was a surprisingly massive attack that posed serious dangers to the American forces deployed in the area and to the region. "Stricken" best describes the atmosphere prevailing at the meeting. All present were stunned by the unfolding developments, and knew that an immediate, drastic response was required. Yet, at that moment, all seemed paralyzed by the enormity of the situation and challenges facing them. Finally, in desperation, Eisenhower asked General Patton if he had a suggestion. Patton immediately declared that in 48 hours he could have three divisions attacking the underbelly of the German incursion. For a moment there was a stunned silence, then snickering, and then even a hint of laughter from a couple of British officers. "What audaciousness," they muttered. Eisenhower was completely disbelieving. Patton insisted that he could do it. Eisenhower, clutching at every straw, then told him to go ahead, to do it.

Without any directive or instructions from the top, on his own and relying only on his sixth, his special battle sense, he had three divisions moving north—my 4th Armored Division, the 26th Infantry Division, and the 80th Infantry Division.

It was Patton who yanked back Task Force Ezell from Bastogne, and had CCB moved from the VIIIth Corps to the IIIrd Corps with the rest of the 4th Armored Division. He had promised Eisenhower a three-division attack, and he deemed it absolutely essential that the 4th Armored be at full strength.

On December 21, his three divisions were ready to move out the next day. He had already accomplished a miracle. He had turned his army, thousands of men and thousands of vehicles ninety degrees from east to north. Led by my tank and those of my tank battalion in gray, windy, bitter cold weather, and over treacherous, icy roads his Army traveled from deep in Lorraine to the environs of Bastogne. We had moved all one night, all the next day, and half the next night, this time under total blackout conditions, and because it was the great unknown out there we were expecting at any moment to be fired upon and attacked. The distance advanced was an amazing 161 miles.

President Nixon, a great admirer of General Patton, would later claim that it was the greatest mass movement of men in the shortest period of time in the history of warfare.

That was PART I. Now we would continue, this time embarking on what would be a most challenging, extremely dangerous, treacherous but epochal operation. It would be PART II.

On the afternoon of the 21st I met with General Dager, who carefully explained what would be next. The broad mission assigned was that CCB and the rest of the 4th Armored Division was to attack north to Bastogne in conjunction with the 26th Infantry Division, and the 80th Infantry Division to relieve the surrounded troops in that city. The 4th would attack with three combat commands abreast—CCB on the left, CCA in the center, and CCR (Reserve Command) on the right.

Then, Dager became specific. He said that, as always, the 8th Tank Battalion would lead the attack for CCB. Then he designated an I.P. (initial point), the axis of advance, and the time that the I.P. would be crossed.

I was awake at 3:00 AM. It was now December 22. The battalion moved out of Léglise at half past four until they reached the very tiny village named Beheme. My lead elements turned off the main road onto a dirt road that was too narrow and too primitive to be designated as a secondary road—more like a farm road or a logging trail. It ran almost due north to Bastogne, and it was my assigned axis to that city. When we left the main road, we entered what appeared to be a narrow bowling alley. We would have to ride this road all the way—there would be no deviating from it. We crossed the I.P. at the designated time, and were now headed north.

At 6:00 AM it was very dark. A low haze hung over everything and everyone; visibility was almost zero. The fields were packed with snow, and the road was icy. And it was cold! The days that followed would be the coldest on record.

As we began our advance to the north, the atmosphere was one that we had never experienced before. It was grim, foreboding, menacing, intimidating, ominous, and depressing.

We had experienced the lovely summer and perfect tank weather across France and the atrocious fall and horrible tank weather in Lorraine. We were about to experience something totally new and different—a winter in the Belgium Ardennes. In fact, winter officially began the day before.

The tanks advanced slowly and cautiously, for even though daylight had come, visibility was still very poor. It was still dark, gray, and hazy, with the ceiling just an arm's length above us. And who knew what was out there?

We advanced safely along three kilometers of fairly open ground, when we entered the extremely tight confines of the huge Foret d'Anlier. Here the opening was just a little over one tank wide. The forest closed in tightly on both sides of the road.

The forests of France were nothing like this. Here the trees looked like huge evergreens—the tallest, thickest, most majestic, most imposing ones that I had ever seen. The branches were wide, thick, luxuriant, and seemed almost to interlock. The trees had grown together so tightly that the forest seemed almost impenetrable.

The only consolation was that if there was enemy resistance, it had to come from the very edges of the forest. Deeper in the forest,

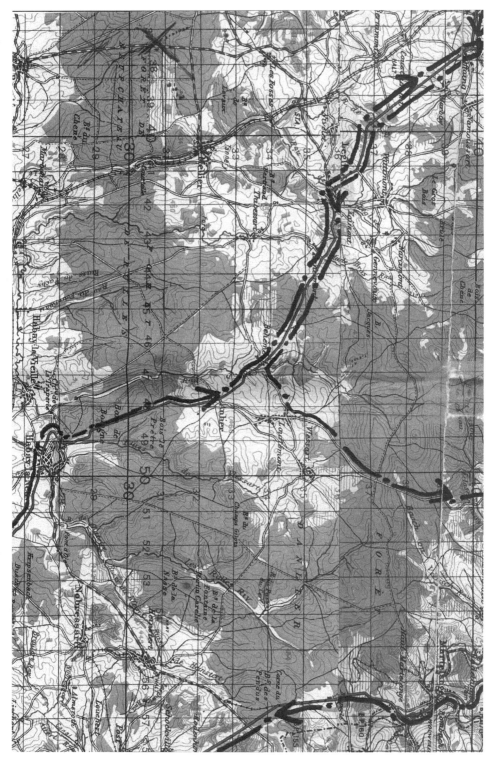

BASTOGNE

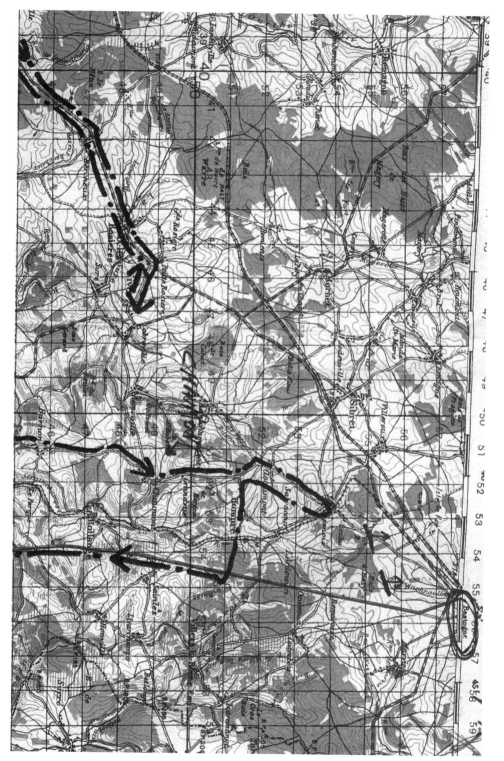

CHAUMONT

there were no fields of fire for them. The advancing tankers did not hesitate to fire at anything that looked the least bit suspicious. It was what we called reconnaissance by fire.

While holding our breaths, expecting a blow to land at any moment, my force advanced cautiously but steadily. We continue to persevere along the narrow passage, and put yards and then kilometers behind us.

Finally up ahead there became visible an apparent patch of brightness. Sure enough, it was the light at the end of the tunnel. As we emerged from the Foret d'Anlier, I estimated from my map that we had traversed nearly six kilometers through that truly ominous patch of Belgium. Up ahead about a kilometer away, I could make out our first objective—the sizeable town of Fauvillers. The terrain was now more open and visibility had become better. Still not knowing what to expect, we, nevertheless, moved aggressively to, and then without hesitation through, the town.

Up ahead were more woods—this time the Bois Habaru—and a stream called the Troquebou Rah. From my map I concluded that the woods were not nearly as thick, or as close to the road, and not anywhere near as extensive as the one we had just passed through. The stream appeared relatively innocent. So now we pushed ahead more aggressively and confidentially. Sure enough, we successfully negotiated the woods and the stream, and advanced through the small towns of Hotte and Menufontaine. We now knew that the enemy was lurking out there. Since leaving the large forest, we had begun to receive scattered, harassing, hit and run fire. It was not threatening, as the positions available for the defenders did not give them much of an advantage over us who were doing the attacking. Every time there was enemy fire, my tanks quickly returned it—with interest. Thus far, enemy resistance had not appreciably slowed our advance.

But halfway between Menufontaine and the next town of Burnon our advance came to an abrupt and grinding halt. For the first time my lead elements came under heavy enemy fire just north of Menufontaine. My tanks of "A" Company immediately deployed to the left of the road and began pouring direct fire at the suspected enemy locations. Fortunately, there were no woods here, so my tanks had clear fields of fire. A swollen stream flowed parallel to the road on the right, and prevented deployment in that direction.

The heavy outpouring of fire from "A" Company seemed to quiet the enemy, so the tanks again pushed ahead aggressively. But their advance was short-lived. To their crushing disappointment they were forced to halt again. About halfway between Menufontaine and Burnon, the swollen, fast moving La Sûre River flowed across their path, and the bridge over the river had been destroyed. As they neared the river, the tanks continued to pour fire across it. I moved up, took a quick look, and immediately realized that we could not cross it without a bridge. There was no way around it to the right or left; the river was too deep, too wide, and too swift flowing to even to attempt to ford it. Without further hesitation, I sent word back for the engineers to come hurrying forward to install a bridge.

Now for the first time since moving out, I had a requirement for artillery. I called a request back to my supporting artillery, the 22nd Armored Artillery Battalion. I asked them to deploy immediately, and to begin dropping 105-mm rounds on the bridge site and the area around it. From fire received from the enemy, I knew that they were located on the high ground to the north and northeast of the bridge site, and they would be subjected to artillery fire, as well. When I received word that the 22nd was ready to fire away, I pulled the tanks back a short distance so that the fire could drop in unhindered. The artillery was prepared to continue to pour fire on the area until the engineers would close in.

However, at that point, I ordered the artillery fire to be lifted. In order to have reasonable safe conditions under which the engineers could work, we needed to secure a bridgehead on the north bank of the river. Accordingly, I pushed my tanks and the supporting 10th Armored Infantry back close to the bridge so that they could continue to pour out supporting fire. As the engineers were closing in behind us, two platoons of "C" Company of the 10th were given the most difficult and unenviable job of moving into the icy Sûre River, somehow negotiating it and clambering up its northern bank. Once on firm land, soaked as they were, they had to push out to widen the bridgehead. They did all this in about an hour and a quarter, for the engineers arrived at about 3:45 and immediately began to work.

It was quickly obvious that Company "B" of the 24th Armored Engineer Battalion was another experienced, well-trained, dedicated unit of the 4th Armored Division.

With absolutely no wasted motion, no slippage, and completely ignoring the fact that as they worked they were extremely vulnerable to enemy fire, they quickly, professionally, quietly and expertly installed a 36-foot treadway bridge over the raging river. Extra bridging had been required because of the width of the river and its soft banks.

Darkness had descended upon the bridge site during the final stages of its installation. It had already been a very long day, but it was far from over. The infantry from the 10th were poised and prepared to rush across the bridge the moment it was declared "in." They dashed across and quickly went about the job of widening and deepening the bridgehead. "A" Company tanks, likewise, were assembled so that they could quickly, one-by-one, move across the bridge, and join and strengthen the infantry. While the remaining elements of the 8th and 10th continued the slow process of easing across the bridge in the dark, two platoons of the 10th moved into Burnon. They were greeted by heavy machine gun fire, which they suppressed along with the capture of 19 Germans. In less than an hour, the town was clear.

Now the 8th and 10th, at strength and assembled, fanned out north of Burnon, and were poised to continue the attack to the north. Just up ahead was Chaumont. We had hoped to reach that village before sunset. Had we done so, we would have advanced this day over half the distance to Bastogne. The blown bridge had prevented that.

Things had settled down sufficiently so that I was able to report my current situation to CCB. That headquarters immediately came back with instructions to secure what I had, and to stop for the night.

Shortly after, they reported to me that CCA had considerable difficulty in the vicinity of Martelange, with extensive demolitions, a blown bridge, and a huge crater. CCB also sent information that Reserve Command would be attacking the large town of Bigonville in Luxembourg way to our right at first light in the morning. CCB indicated some concern about my present position. For the moment CCA was bogged down in Martelange, and the three combat commands were severely echeloned to the right. Even though we had been delayed by the blown bridge, CCA was about 10 kilometers southeast of my force, and Reserve Command another 9 kilometers or so southeast of CCA. That meant that my 8th of CCB was way out in front, and was sticking out like a sore thumb, almost inviting someone to give it a painful nudge.

Even with our day's difficulties, at our present rate of advance we were only about another day from our objective, Bastogne. However, we knew that the closer we got, we could expect heavier and more determined resistance. As we closed in upon the city so far out front of the other elements of the division, we could expect to draw plenty of attention.

I now turned my priority from tactics to administration. Now that the day had ended, and not knowing what lay ahead, it was essential to be full up with gasoline and ammunition, so I ordered the supply trucks forward to service our tactical elements. To ensure their safe arrival, I sent back to the rear some light elements—light tanks, elements of the reconnaissance platoon, and some armored infantry. Their purpose was to secure the sides of the road, and to escort the supply trucks. As we had moved forward, the enemy could easily have sneaked back to the edges of the woods along which we had advanced.

The trucks arrived safely and were still in the process of resupplying when we were hit by a thunderbolt. This one was a lulu. It stunned and staggered all hands. They were just in the process of settling in for the night when CCB sent me a simple, terse order: "Move all night." CCB was quick to explain that the order came from higher headquarters. "Higher headquarters" would soon be known and, as expected, was General Patton, himself.

Apparently, the excellent progress of CCB that day had gotten him fired up and his juices flowing—he could almost smell Bastogne, about a day away. So, figuratively, he was using his spurs and riding crop to get there "firstest and the quickest." At this point he had already made believers out of Gen. Eisenhower, and his fellow senior generals. He wanted to finish it off in grand style. It was later learned that Patton had ordered the night move, completely out of character with his principles, with the very optimistic, but completely unrealistic belief that when daylight came, he would have forces in Bastogne.

So at midnight it was, "hit the road again, Jack." These were the guys who had made that difficult, trying, exhausting 161-mile, forced march. They had been on the move patrolling, outposting, and had gone in and out of Bastogne. They had moved back to the rear, and had been up since 3:00 AM fighting all this day and early night. As they were moving out again, it was almost the exact hour merely three days before when they departed from Domnom deep in Lorraine. Unbelievable! How much can you squeeze into seventy-two hours? How much can a man endure? How long and how far can you drive him? That all remained to be seen.

So, as ordered, we moved out just after midnight. The terrain on the left was open, and sloped gently downward to the west. To our right, it was a completely different story. Starting about 500 yards from Burnon and extending to the north was the very deep, long and most forbidding Fôret de Lambaichenet. This would provide ideal locations from which the enemy could operate at night—a real threat.

It was dark; there virtually was no visibility. It was bitter cold. Commanders in the tank turrets of their medium Shermans could see practically nothing. So I pushed out better eyes and ears—elements of the 25th Armored Cavalry, and right with them light tanks from my "D" Company. Following was a medium tank company, and an armored infantry company mounted in their half-tracks. The night with its swirling snow was as miserable as one could get.

As we advanced and as we expected, we drew small-arms fire from the woods on our right. With the Germans protected by the darkness, we had to settle for raking the edges of the woods with our fire. Panzerfausts claimed a couple of the armored cavalry's jeeps. Our force continued to move at a slow but deliberate pace. As the lead elements were about a half kilometer from Chaumont, the night was breaking and daylight began showing.

The jeeps of the 25th and the light tanks moved closer to the outskirts of the village. Just as they reached the point where the woods peeled away, and the road took a slight jog to the right to begin its slow and gradual descent to the main part of the village, the Germans who lay in wait launched a stiff counterattack. This was the heaviest resistance encountered on this operation. Several German 75-mm self-propelled assault guns (Stu G III's) hit the lead elements of the column instantly knocking out three of the 25th's vehicles and a light tank from D/8. As this was happening, the Germans brought down artillery fire in support of the attack, and paratroopers armed with Panzerfausts were taking shots from some distance at our vehicles. At the first sound of enemy fire, Shermans moved forward and immediately took the German 75s under fire. They quickly knocked out one of them, while the rest were chased off, as well as German paratroopers who were seen dashing back to the woods.

The tanks by their continued fire stopped the counterattack from moving closer. As we later advanced, I was able to note that the tank fire had caused heavy German personnel casualties.

I would sadly learn that three of the four tank crewmen of the light tank that had been knocked out were killed, and its commander, Lieutenant Day, was wounded and evacuated.

The counterattack sobered and forced reality upon me. I was now convinced that we had either hit the edge of the German's organized area, or, as I had feared, were rushing forces forward to blunt the advance that was threatening them. I now realized that Bastogne had suddenly become farther away than one day. It appeared that from now on we would have to fight for every yard.

After the counterattack was repulsed, our advance continued. Sporadic fire continued to be received from the enemy. Even though it was daylight, visibility remained poor. By noon we controlled the ground southwest of town. However, the enemy had demonstrated that he was present and prepared to fight.

Now sitting on the high ground and from my tank turret I looked out as far as I could see and made a visual reconnaissance. However, bad visibility clouded and obscured objects farther out.

I knew that I had to attack and seize Chaumont. There was no way that I could bypass it either to the right or left. My route to Bastogne would force me through that little village, and on to the next small town, Grandru. There was another and very important reason to have a clear road. Once we reached Bastogne it would become a critical artery. Ambulances removing casualties from the city, and supply trucks going into it would make it a very busy road.

Because of his strong early counterattack, the enemy had clearly demonstrated that he was out there in some strength. The message that I received from him was that it would be dangerous and foolhardy to continue advancing in column down into town on the narrow, restricted, descending road. Chaumont, in addition to having just the one road through it, presented another problem. It sat on low ground pretty much like being on the bottom of a saucer. Once committed there was only one way for the forces to go—down and through the town.

As I looked at how the road descended into town, I was reminded somewhat of Vœllerdingen, which we had recently traversed on the way to Singling. The road down was not quite as steep, and Chaumont was a much tinier town. However, as in Vœllerdingen, once the tanks got down into town, they were totally committed and super vulnerable.

After considering all factors, I was convinced that although it would force a bit of a delay and might prove not to be necessary, the situation required a coordinated attack on the town using the whole battalion, that of the 10th AIB, and my supporting artillery.

Once I had developed my plan, I sent for my key commanders. Radio orders were not the answer this time. I decided to have "B" Company attack the town by driving down into it from the high ground. Because they were so vulnerable moving down into that saucer, I wanted them protected from both sides—east and west.

"C" Company with their eleven tanks would operate on the left. They would be driving over wide-open, frozen, relatively level ground, and would operate close enough to support "B" in town, but yet far enough out, so that they could ward off an attack from the woods to the left.

To my right a long ridge looked down upon Chaumont from the north and east. The top of the ridge was open, while the forward slopes were dotted with trees (the back side of the ridge was more heavily forested). If the enemy occupied this ridge, they would have an excellent view of any forces advancing north up the main road into Chaumont. More importantly it would provide them with dominating terrain and good fields of fire from which to hit those advancing elements. Securing this ridge, unquestionably, would be a major priority. Recognizing this, I assigned the ridge to "A" Company and its nine tanks. If "A" Company controlled it, I was confident that "B" would be protected from the right.

The primary attack would be made by the eleven tanks of "B" Company. They would have to move straight down the road into Chaumont. Infantrymen of the 10th would initially approach the town mounted on the tanks, but soon would have to dismount, for they could expect "close in" fighting, as well as house-to-house battling.

I felt very confident that I had developed a sound plan for the attack. I had instructed "C" and "A" to move out when "B" did, and to keep abreast of "B's" progress, and to coordinate their support. I informed my commanders that I would be with "B" Company when they started their attack.

However, before commencing the attack, I requested an extensive preparation from my 22nd with heavy salvos dropping into the heart of Chaumont, hitting the woods west of "C"/8th's axis of advance, and particularly heavy barrages on the ridge to the northeast. It seemed that in a minimum amount of time, my tank company commanders and their infantry counterparts were ready. With that, I ordered the artillery fire to be lifted, and the medium Shermans of the three companies moved into the attack. It was about 1:30 PM. "B" had started moving down the road to Chaumont, and on the flanks "C" and "A" were simultaneously moving. The resistance from Chaumont appeared to be light and scattered, a good indicator that the artillery had done some good. All at once, I received a radio call from Lieutenant Stephenson, the "C" Company commander. He had startling, astonishing news that was difficult to believe. He said that the wide-open and solidly frozen ground was not frozen solid after all. His lead platoon of five tanks had bogged down on that "frozen solid ground," and were mired so deeply that they were unable to move. They were sitting ducks—absolutely useless and vulnerable as hell. Stephenson held back the rest of his tanks, and now all of a sudden our left flank would not have the security for which we had planned. I had often discussed the "imponderables of the battlefield." This had to be a classic example. It would turn out to be one of the coldest winters ever recorded, and without question the ground would have been expected to be frozen solid.

I quickly reached for my 1/100,000 map, and there it was—a faint, blue, west-east line that went into the town. It was so inauspicious and innocent appearing that under the circumstances, I had paid no attention to it. I would later learn that there was marshland in the area with flowing water that would never freeze, and that was the answer to our riddle.

My other tanks were advancing. Surprisingly, an armor-piercing round came out of the hills and hit one of "B's" leading tanks. As the crew was evacuating it, it was hit again, causing an explosion that totally destroyed it. As the "B" Company tanks edged closer to town, the infantry jumped off the tanks so that they would be ready to clear the houses. They were suddenly hit with surprisingly heavy resistance. It appeared that the Germans had decided to make a real fight of it, which the infantry later declared was some of the heaviest opposition they had yet encountered. After the hard fight, two companies of the 10th supported by tank fire from "B"/8th carried the day. As the battle was ending, the infantry rounded up the last of the Germans numbering about 100 members of the 14th FJ Regiment. With the village clear of the enemy, the infantry and tanks continued moving slowly through it.

I was down in town in my command tank with "B"/8th. Now that I knew that Chaumont was firmly in our hands, and since there was still enough daylight to continue the advance, I ordered my lead elements to move along the main road that turned to the north, and to move in that direction to the next town, Grandru, which I hoped that we would reach before dark.

I was on my radio instructing my elements to get on the road behind "B" when it happened. Without any warning, seemingly out of nowhere came the frightening, demoralizing, intimidating, unreal sounds, screeches, and screams that can only come from incoming rounds of high explosive, armor-piercing shells that were hitting, crashing, exploding, and ricocheting all around us. What is happening? It shook, staggered, shocked, and instantly unnerved the men. It had occurred so suddenly, so unexpectedly, that for a brief instant there was panic. German troops had jumped off assault carriers, and were rushing into town, and "B" company tanks were being hit. Now there was stark realization that this was a heavy German counterattack. The fire was so powerful, and we were so vulnerable that the initial, overriding question was—is this doomsday, a wipeout?

Even with the initial shock and the confusion and chaos, professionalism soon settled in. Each tank had been responding, as it had been trained to do. They began moving and shooting. They moved as best they could within the narrow confines of the town shooting in the direction of the heaviest fire. But the stuff was coming in much faster and more furiously than it was going out. It was perfectly obvious that we were outgunned and outnumbered—and could be overwhelmed. The enemy fire was aimed right down the alley from the high ground to the north, and particularly from the northeast of town. Under the worst possible circumstances there was no panic. Tankers blown out of their tanks without weapons withdrew methodically and in very many cases heroically. As they headed for the security of the ridge to the south, it was anything but every man for himself. The tankers now withdrew as "medics." Every one of them dragged back with them wounded infantrymen, and shielded them as best they could. There was no panic. This was as orderly a withdrawal as could be performed under such chaotic circumstances.

My tank was down in town at the back end of "B" Company. We were still down in that saucer, were a prime target, and although not yet hit, could be goners in seconds. It was vitally essential that we move and keep moving. But the only place to move to was back up the road out of town. There was no place to turn. Even if there had been it would have been suicide to be churning around in one place. We had to keep moving, but the only way was backward. So the tank continued backing in the direction from which it had come. My gunner and loader were working furiously, pouring out fire at suspected targets. I was like the man who was trying to juggle six balls with one hand. I was trying to spot targets, direct the fire of the tank, give directions to the driver who could not see to his rear, talk to "B" company, which was literally fighting for its life, and coordinate the actions of "A" and "C" Companies.

My tank slowly, but successfully, continued backing up while the guys in the turret kept pouring out the fire. But as we left town, the road began to rise and bend. It was now impossible to continue backing with all eyes looking forward toward the little village. So I ordered one final burst of fire, and then traversed the turret 180 degrees. Now the front of the tank, its driver and bow gunner were still facing the town. The gun was now pointing up the hill with the back of the turret facing the town. Now I was able, on my tank intercom, to give explicit directions to the driver. Even though the tank was still backing up the hill, it was able to pick up speed. From the very outset we had moved, and had never stopped moving because a moving target is more difficult to hit. The tension had crackled. Each member of the crew knew that at any instant the blow could come. Now we were out of town, progressively opening up more distance from the enemy guns. Just as I had begun to breathe a bit easier, the one that we had been expecting, dreading finally found us. There was a low, loud, deafening, ear-splitting sound followed by a terrible, horrible blow! The tank was shoved violently backwards. It was as though it had been hit by a huge sledgehammer, and picked up and thrown backward by a huge, superhuman hand.

The three of us in the turret were tossed and bounced like rag dolls. Stunned and dazed, we quickly untangled ourselves, and got back on our feet. That was not easy. While lying on the turret floor, we had been part of the clutter and utter chaos of the tank.

The large, heavy tank gun rounds, which had been clamped upright, were now strewn like huge match sticks on the turret floor. Every item in the tank had seemingly been picked up and pitched. It was as though a giant hand had grabbed everything in the turret and tossed it violently about. Not a single item was near its original resting place.

For a moment the tank was stopped. The crew looked at one another—shocked, stunned—with stricken eyes. What happened? What was it? I quickly regained my composure and shouted, "Keep moving!" With the range locked in for the enemy, a second round would surely, quickly follow. As though nudged by a prod, the tank moved and picked up speed.

"What was it?" I asked myself again. I looked behind me to check where the blow may have come from, and to my utter amazement and astonishment, there near my radio was a vertical crack in the turret. *A crack in the turret!* Unbelievable. Yes, a seam of light was showing. Without question something big had hit the turret, had violently pushed the tank, and had cracked its turret. We had dreaded it, feared it, and it had happened. We had been hit!

After we had calmed down, and moved out of range, we tried to come up with a solution to the puzzle. Why did that round not blow us to smithereens? Why was the tank still able to move?

From the magnitude of the blow, the round that hit must have had great power, and it surely was traveling at super speed. *Why did it not penetrate the turret?*

Each man in that tank recognized that whatever had happened, each had been spared, each was alive, and the tank was, basically, intact. I was convinced that it was a minor miracle—that each of us had been spared and uniquely blessed by the Supreme Being.

We finally reached the ridge, and were out of direct fire range. Now my immediate concern was to reorganize my forces. The elements of my task force not hit or bogged down had been withdrawing in an orderly manner. The enemy counterattack had been stopped, for there was no indication that they were in any way advancing. There could have been several reasons for that. We had no idea of how many casualties were inflicted upon the enemy by the fire from "B" Company's guns in the saucer before they were put out of action, and from the fire of my own tank gun. "A" Company had occupied portions of the same ridge as the enemy and had poured fire in their direction. "A's" aggressive fire now seemed to be serving two purposes—protecting the withdrawing units and holding back the enemy. Also, the enemy was aware that our forces would soon be holding dominant terrain, and it was now becoming dark. So for whatever reason, the enemy chose not to follow up their attack.

As our units withdrew, they quickly established coordinated defensive positions on the high ground south and southeast of Chaumont, which we had earlier occupied, and from which we had launched our attack upon the village. Gathered in defensive positions were elements of our 25th Cavalry Reconnaissance, my light tanks, units of the 10th Armored Infantry, and my surviving Sherman tanks. Our artillery was right behind us and intact. Because the enemy and we had been so closely intermingled during the battle for Chaumont, we could not use our artillery. So all in all, although we had been hit hard, and suffered personnel and vehicular casualties, we had never panicked, and were now an organized, still potent force.

Once I was satisfied that the task force was in the best possible defensive positions, which we would continue to improve and adjust throughout the night, I got busy on my radio reassuring my commanders, assessing just what had happened, and receiving reports on the status of my battalion and the supporting forces.

In our present positions we already had numerous advantages over the enemy. We were on dominating terrain. Our defense was well coordinated. The terrain that we occupied provided us with excellent fields of fire. The enemy no longer had surprise and momentum, which they had already expended. If they chose to do so, they had the disadvantage of having to expose themselves, as they attacked uphill in the face of our deployed and well-positioned forces.

For the moment the pressure was off. As I relaxed a bit, I was suddenly aware of a painful throbbing of my right hand. I was wearing a mitten on it. The palm and thumb were cowhide; the back and long gauntlet with the strap at the wrist were of a GI colored fabric. What caught my eye and to my great surprise—for during all the excitement I had felt nothing—was that the mitten was soggy with blood. I looked closer and saw that the thumb and area around it seemed to have been sliced and mangled and blood was still oozing through. The initial numbness must have left me, for I was now well aware that something had nicked me. I could feel the damp, squishy blood inside the mitten, and the thumb, particularly, was throbbing painfully. I well knew that it was not cause for alarm, and that the best thing that I could do at the moment was to leave the mitten as is, so that the blood might coagulate. I would visit my aid station a bit later.

Now that our situation seemed under control, I had a burning desire to try to satisfy my curiosity. Why did the high velocity, powerful armor-piercing round from the German tank not penetrate the turret of my Sherman? It was just barely light, and I climbed out on the back deck, before the soon arriving maintenance crew would get their hands on it. A quick study provided me with the amazing, unbelievable, incomprehensible answer.

Jutting out innocently and inconspicuously from the turret was an insignificant, nameless object that had saved my life. I was frank to admit that it was so innocuous that I had never noticed it before. Why should I? It served no useful purpose that I could tell. Facing the rear of the tank it was located to the right of the antenna well, and was positioned on the turret almost directly behind my back, as I stood in the turret. The object, at best an appendage, was a stubby jutting piece of steel about five inches wide, four inches high, and six inches deep. The front was cut and sloped at a rather sharp angle. And, of all things, this is precisely where the round hit. Even though the powerful round was armor piercing and traveling at a speed of hundreds of feet per second when it hit, it just could not penetrate the additional six inches of steel. With the front angled as it was, the round ricocheted, and went screaming off into the wild blue yonder. But the impact was so massive that something had to give. It was the turret. It was so stressed that it just had to crack. I was shaken and sobered by the realization that if the round had hit a couple of inches up or down, right or left it could easily have penetrated the turret, blown me to smithereens, seriously damaged the tank, and undoubtedly hurt or killed the other members of the crew.

The man upstairs controls the inches, and that day had them working in our favor. Never a day passes without me thinking of that moment at Chaumont.

Now that night had come, and only sporadic fire was to be heard, I leaned back in my tank and reflected upon the long day of vicious fighting. What had originally appeared to be a successful and satisfying capture of a heavily defended and critical objective on the way to Bastogne, found us not only stopped dead in our tracks, but pushed back to where we had started the attack. Who was it that had fought us all day unsuccessfully only to catch their second wind, and hit us so very hard as the day was ending?

Of course, as I asked myself those questions, I knew that I did not have the answers. Now, over the years, some of those questions appear to have been answered.

When we reached the outskirts of Chaumont early on the morning of December 23, we were quickly hit by direct fire rounds coming from Stu G III's. They were elements of the 5th Parachute Division (5th FJ Division). How many were on hand we would never know, but it was they that gave support to the paratroopers, who would be fighting as infantry. The Stu G III's were 75-mm self-propelled assault guns. Their direct fire cannons were capable of disabling our Sherman tanks. These were the elements with some artillery support that were defending the village and who we would fight all day and finally overcome.

The 5th Parachute Division was commanded by Generalmajor Ludwig Heilmann. He was elsewhere on the 23rd, and was not a factor in the Chaumont battle.

However, a Generalmajor Heinz Kokott is an entirely different story. He is undoubtedly the key factor in the change of our fortunes that day.

General Kokott commanded the 26th Volksgrenadier Division. His command post sat directly on CCB's axis of advance, and was located in the tiny town of Hompre, just about two miles north of Chaumont. Technically speaking, this placed him in the zone of the 5th

FJ Division, whose mission was blocking to the south. Kokott himself was facing north to Bastogne. He was well aware of the American 4th Armored Division's drive to the north, and recognized that it was a real threat to his rear. If they continued advancing, the Shermans could well run over his command post. With General Hellmann at Lutrebois, he was now much closer to the point of danger, and he knew that this was no time to be concerned about division boundary lines. So he took charge of the German battle for Chaumont.

He gathered up the paratroopers who had not been killed or captured, but who were pushed out of Chaumont, and sent them back into action along with some units and officers from his own 26th Volksgrenadier Division.

Then, at the most critical time and right out of the blue, came a completely unexpected windfall, a definite *game changer*. Another imponderable of the battlefield.

That afternoon without any warning, without notice whatsoever four Jagd Tigers were unexpectedly dropped into General Kokott's lap. No one knew where he was supposed to have been going, or where he had come from. But here he was. An unknown major presented this totally unexpected gift. Now that he had them, General Kokott did not know exactly what they were. But this was completely understandable, for such brand new Jagd Tigers had not yet made a combat appearance in the European battle.

They represented power at its best. Amazingly, they carried a 128-mm cannon. Without any hesitation, General Kokott rushed them to Chaumont, where they were quickly positioned on the dominating ridge as the fight in Chaumont was ending. Immediately, they became the decisive element on that little battlefield. Our Sherman tanks tightly constricted down in the village with their low muzzle velocity 75-mm guns had no chance of outdueling those monsters. There is absolutely no question that the Jagds brought a new dimension to that battlefield, and they were unquestionably the ones that turned the tide.

Their participation in the Chaumont battle answered the question of what it was that had hit my tank. It had been accepted that because of its muzzle velocity and range, a Stu G III did not have the power to cause the massive hit to my tank. The Jagd Tiger, with its 128-mm cannon, certainly could have done it. Thus, unquestionably, it was the one.

On this day, after a fine offensive effort, just as we were about to score a touchdown, we were tackled viciously below the knees. There is no question that we had received the heaviest, most massive, concentrated, and powerful counterattack of the war. As our forces withdrew, there were flames in Chaumont with hardly a building left undamaged, graphic testimony of the intensity of the battle.

For the first time in the war "B" Company, which had come close before, was now stripped of its tanks—naked. The other two medium tank companies did not fare much better, with one having seven left, and the other with six. When my tank was repaired, it would give us fourteen Shermans with which to continue our attack.

Even though that attack had been momentarily halted, we had suffered numerous personnel and vehicular casualties, and Bastogne had been pushed back, a bit farther out of reach, I believed that under the circumstances we were still a formidable force to be reckoned with. Despite the abruptness and power of the attack, our forces had never panicked; there had never been any sign of a rout. Conversely, those troops had withdrawn in an orderly manner, quickly resumed control of the high ground south of Chaumont, shifted and improved their positions, and immediately began reorganizing their units.

Although we had been delayed, our mission was still the same, simple one—get to Bastogne as rapidly as we could. We would use the night to reorganize, regroup, resupply, so that by first light we would be as combat ready as our resources would permit.

Although General Dager at CCB headquarters had received a running account all day of the action from my operations officer in his S3 half-track, I felt strongly that I should provide him with a firsthand report of all that had transpired, and the current situation, as well as my plan for the next day. So in the darkness, with an armed escort, I made the hazardous journey back to his headquarters.

He was waiting for me, and I immediately gave him a detailed description of the day's operations, and the situation existing at that moment. He listened with deep concern, and at the end of my portrayal, he fully endorsed all that we had done, and was pleased with the current situation, despite the day's heavy blow.

Then he informed me that CCA had had a host of problems and a most difficult day, which held them to an advance of a mere 3 kilometers. Reserve Command, inside Luxembourg, had attacked Bigonville. They had encountered icy roads, heavily mined approaches, and anti-tank fire, which prevented them from seizing the town.

The upshot of all of this was that CCA was still echeloned at least 9 kilometers to the southeast of my position, and CCR another 5 kilometers beyond that. Realizing that, it is little wonder why the heavy counterattack had been directed at us. Neither General Dager nor I had any doubt that because we were out in front of the pack, the enemy had decided that they just had to blunt our attack. Consequently, Dager instructed me to stay put the next day, so that the forces on my right could catch up. The day could profitably be used to get into the best possible shape for the resumption of the attack on Chaumont the following day. It might also provide an opportunity for the near-exhausted men to get some rest.

Early on the 24th I was awakened by the sun, an element not seen for several days, but which kicked off the day on a high note. After many days of wretched weather, the sky, except for moving, fleeting clouds, was clear. A remarkable, reassuring change.

Late the day before, while we were hard at it, our supply trucks, moving up from the rear brought us more than gas, ammo, and rations. This time they also delivered to each trooper a small card—business card size—along with their rations. On one side was a Christmas message from the Army Commander with a familiar signature—G. S. Patton, Jr.

On the reverse side was a prayer requesting help from the Almighty during the strenuous days ahead. It is difficult to describe the emotions of the men who were astonished to receive such a most unusual card under such atrocious conditions. They were deeply touched and moved. All who served in the Third Army that day still remember that little gift from their commander. Many still have the card and treasure it.

That day, the 24th, was Christmas Eve. There was quick evidence that things would be different and better. Very early, friendly fighter aircraft were already aloft. As they flew over us, they dipped their wings in a gesture that told us on the ground, "Hey, guys, we are with you today." They would prove later in the day that they meant exactly that.

My tank was back and I was in it. The maintenance crew had welded tight the crack in the turret, the guns and radio had been checked, and my tank crew, despite the darkness, had somehow brought order out of chaos, and the tank was again shipshape.

As has been mentioned, my plan was to consolidate the ground just south of Chaumont, and to be reorganized and ready to move as the columns on my right caught up. Much to my great chagrin, the enemy would not let me alone, as he, too, had plans, which he quickly began putting into effect. Starting early on, he became a troublesome nuisance all day. Since I was forced to react, it would turn out to be busy and hectic day.

Very soon patrols with Panzerfausts probed and probed, and attempted to infiltrate our position. Elements of the 10th AIB and the 25th Cav were busy repulsing the pesky, determined paratroopers.

Then there appeared to be a significant change in strategy. The large patch of woods just southeast of Chaumont had been an irritant. Ever since we had been in the area, we had received harassing fire from that location. The enemy would move to the edge of the woods, do some hasty firing, and when we returned fire, they would melt deeper into the woods. The 25th Cav had been particularly active in keeping our flank safe from them. But now, surprisingly, artillery, mortar, and machine gun fire began coming in. Soon there was an unexpectedly

heavy engagement with enemy forces, who had been firing and trying to slip out of the woods towards us. The cavalry had a hard fight, but successfully held off the enemy.

That did it for me! I had my artillery support working all day hitting suspected targets. Now I called upon them to concentrate their fire, and to pour it on the area that had been so troubling and could become a very dangerous right flank. Just as the artillery had done their characteristically good job, I received a totally unexpected and royal bonus. For many, many days we had not been able to receive any air support. Not long after the artillery fire had lifted, eight P-47s zoomed in and bombed and strafed the areas where the enemy had been most active. That did it. The combination of heavy fire from the artillery and air almost simultaneously effectively cooled off the Germans. Elements of the 10th moved right in after the fire, mopped up the area, and by 2:30 declared it clear. That flank was no longer a threat.

Then late in the afternoon CCB called with an early Christmas present for me. It was so surprising, so unexpected, that it was almost unreal. It seems that some astute, perceptive individual on up the line must have realized that with my losses of men and vehicles my capabilities had definitely been markedly diminished, while the toughest going to Bastogne was still ahead. A decision had been made to do something to make me more effective. The answer was on the way, and was to arrive sometime during the evening. It was a whole battalion of straight-legged infantry. To be attached to me was the Second Battalion, 318th Infantry Regiment of the 80th Infantry Division. This was an absolutely fantastic development.

With a whole new battalion at my disposal and available to be committed the next day, I immediately grabbed my map to analyze again the ground over which we would be operating the next day. I was quite excited to have this extra muscle, so I made a substantial revision to my next day's plan.

I was well aware that General Dager must be anxious to know how I intended to use my reinforcements, so I hightailed it back to

CCB headquarters with my revised plan, which he quickly endorsed. With a "good luck" he sent me on the way to meet my attachments. Sure enough, at about nine o'clock out of the darkness came a most welcomed sight. From the shadows in tight formation on the narrow road came what appeared a vast number of walking men. As they eased up closer, they were halted, given a command, and immediately, as if on signal, they slumped to the ground. Without doubt, they were not only walking men, but very tired walking men. They faced a very tough day coming up.

Someone found me in the dark, and announced, "There's a Lieutenat Colonel looking for you." I was soon guided to a tall, fine-looking, fresh-appearing individual wearing silver leaves. After a brief warm greeting, I gave him instructions about deploying his men for the night.

It was about eleven o'clock when I was finally able to get all my key commanders together, including the new addition to our team. At this meeting, I presented my plan, and instructions for the next day's operation.

In many ways, this was a most significant gathering. Present were my tank company commanders, the CO of the 10th AIB, the CO of the 2/318th, the CO of the 22nd Armored Field Artillery Battalion, and the commanders of the engineer and cavalry units. By any measurement this was, despite our losses, a strong brigade-sized unit. Heads together, we huddled in the dark, with only one flickering light to aid us.

My day was not done until about 12:30, when I was finally able to stretch out in my tank. Before sleep came, I sadly and nostalgically recognized that at that very instant Santa was streaking through the skies, climbing down many chimneys, and filling a multitude of stockings for very many children in many lands. With those thoughts it was difficult to comprehend that my Christmas Eve was spent planning and preparing for a life and death struggle when daylight emerged to once again free Chaumont and its neighboring Grandru from the invading Germans.

Shortly after first light, we moved into the attack. The Germans remaining in Chaumont—there had been no sign of the Jagds since the counterattack—knew that we were coming, and were ready for us. They greeted us with fire from the woods in all directions.

I had organized our main elements into two task forces. One would consist of the tanks of "C" Company and all remaining elements of the 10th AIB. The other would have the tanks of "A" Company and the infantrymen of the 2/318th. The artillery was loaded for bear. Theirs would be marching fire above the two elements. They would have their 105-mm shells dropping on suspected targets just in front of our forces, and would move them forward as the two teams advanced.

Both teams moved out quickly, decisively, and aggressively. By 9:55 all woods were clear, and the right flank was secure.

Now it was time for another coordinated attack on the tiny village that had proved to be such a troublesome roadblock on our thrust to Bastogne.

The team of "C" Company and the 10th AIB attacked to flank the town on the right, while Company "A" with the attached 2/318th made the very necessary frontal attack down into Chaumont. Both attacking elements immediately received artillery and mortar fire. "B" Company was out of action, and what was left of it was in Battalion Reserve awaiting reorganization. The force advancing on the east flank made slow but steady progress, and by 1:40 PM had a platoon across the stream northeast of Chaumont. However, the elements in town were still receiving considerable resistance. But the attackers continued pouring out heavy fire, they moved aggressively, and succeeded in pushing back the determined enemy. The team on the right seized objectives northeast of town, and gained positions east of Grandru. By 7:15 PM it was over at last. Chaumont was finally cleared of all enemies. Both forces outposted for the night the positions for which they had fought so hard all day to reach and had finally won.

So that is how I spent Christmas Day 1944. And yes, I had received Christmas presents—if you could call them that. We had recaptured Chaumont and had recovered seven of my tanks. These had been damaged and disabled, but my talented maintenance crew could get them combat ready. Still another gift had been the arrival of the 2/318th. Someone, somewhere deserved a big "Thank you" for his great foresight. They had provided the added muscle that I needed, and it was that element that helped tip the balance.

BURNON AFTERTHOUGHTS

Many times over the years, I have thought about a "what if." What if the bridge at Burnon had not been destroyed, forcing upon us a delay of several hours during the middle of the day? With our already aggressive advance, would we not have reached Chaumont well before darkness? Would there have been an element of surprise? How heavily would Chaumont have been defended? Would it have been an easier and earlier fight, without the reinforcements that might later have been brought in because of our bridge delay? Under these circumstances, could we not have moved through Chaumont much earlier on the 23rd?

Even with the bridge delay, we had captured Chaumont late on the 23rd. We had defeated the forces defending the village. It was forces that came from the outside who reinforced the defeated German troops and launched the counterattack. In this case it was the delay at the bridge that certainly enabled the Germans to mount the counterattack.

I have always maintained that time is one of the most valuable commodities on the battlefield. The Germans are masters at utilizing time to reorganize forces quickly. I believe that this was one such prime example.

If the bridge had not been blown, could we possibly have been in Bastogne at the end of the day on the 24th? We had advanced halfway on the first day; could we not have finished the other half on the second day?

We can speculate, but we will never know . . .

CHAUMONT

The first time that I remember seeing the name Chaumont was the afternoon of December 21, when General Dager assigned to me my axis of advance to Bastogne. As I looked at my map, I saw up ahead of me settlements named Fauvillers, Hotte, Menufontaine, Burnon, Chaumont, Grandru, and on to Bastogne. At that moment, I could not possibly comprehend that the hours that I would spend at one of the places on my axis would prove to be one of the most defining periods of my life.

I was there as a 27-year-old youth commanding a brigade-sized task force. It was at Chaumont on December 23 that our attacking force suffered a massive German counterattack. Many men were killed and wounded, and tanks and other vehicles were disabled or destroyed. The greatest challenge that faced me under those most difficult circumstances was gathering and holding together my forces, so that they would resume their offensive action two days later. During those most hectic hours, my own tank was hit by a German tank, and I was wounded, and to this day I find it difficult to understand how we survived that hit.

Two days later, I spent Christmas Day 1944 in a life and death struggle to recapture Chaumont, which we accomplished successfully.

My time in Chaumont was undoubtedly the most difficult period of my life. I was sorely tested. By a miracle I survived the battle. Hardly a day passes when I do not think of that little village just south of Bastogne in far-off Belgium.

On Christmas Day each year, as festivities swirl about me, I endeavor to move to a quiet place, so that I can momentarily relive my Christmas of 1944.

Chaumont, yes, I surely do remember you.

Beech Tree

Because of the fury of the initial Chaumont engagement, it was little noted that vehicles were knocked out and men were wounded and killed at the base of and opposite a tree. A tree? From our breakout in Normandy until that action, we had passed thousands of trees. For our deeply involved troops that tree was just another one of many trees.

The years passed and the branches of that scrawny beech tree grew in all directions, and it has become large, beautiful, imposing. Over time to the residents of the community it has become a solemn, regal presence, for they are aware that it was "The Silent Witness" to the beginning of the Chaumont Battle.

In 1984, crews were at work in the area. On their schedule was the cutting down of the beech tree. Most fortuitously in the area at that time was Mr. Pierre Eicher. His family home in Marnach, Luxembourg was hit by a German rocket on December 16, 1944, the first day of the Battle of the Bulge. It was totally destroyed, as it burned to the ground.

He possessed an awareness of the significance of the beech tree. He went to the mayor of the small community, and convinced her that the tree should be saved, and she agreed. It was Pierre Eicher who saved the tree.

Today the beech tree is the well-recognized *symbol* of the 1944 combat that took place around it. At its base is a stone monument. Recently erected is a large information board which explains in three languages to all visitors what occurred there in 1944. Those are man-made monuments.

At that site men died. It is hallowed ground. God also has a monument. It witnessed the action there, has watched over it for 65 years, has grown into an imposing presence, seems indestructible, should be there for the ages. It is *The Beech Tree*.

CHAPTER EIGHT

URMITZ

R EMAGEN: On March 7, 1945, U.S. forces in Europe and citizens all over America received electrifying news. The last many weeks had been difficult ones in Europe. Winter doldrums had prevailed. The cause may have been the aftereffects of the Battle of the Bulge; terrible winter conditions; spirited defense by Germans who, among other things, controlled the Siegfried Line and the east banks of the raging Our and Sauer Rivers; and virtually no sign of any offensive action by U.S. Forces. Then, suddenly news that instantly made headlines everywhere. Elements of the American 9th Armored Division had *seized a bridge over the Rhine River and U.S. troops were scrambling across it.*

Yes, it happened. A railway bridge across the Rhine connecting the villages of Remagen and Erpel was captured that day. Although it had been damaged, not only soldiers but also tanks and trucks with supplies were able to traverse it. The bridge had been named the Ludendorff Bridge, but henceforth would be called the Bridge at Remagen.

While American troops continued to move across it, the Germans took all possible violent action including V-2 bombs, sent by Hitler himself, to destroy it. It had been wired so as to be completely blown, but by some fluke critical portions were saved. The fluke, it would be later learned, were two Polish engineers from Silesia who were conscripted into the Wehrmacht, and who had cut several of the fuses of explosives. Then, absolutely amazingly, ten days later the bridge suddenly collapsed into the Rhine.

For days up until then, headlines all across America would continue about Remagen. The Allies called the capture, "The Miracle of Remagen." General Eisenhower declared it, "Worth its weight in gold." Thousands of words have been written about it, hundreds of books tell its story. It has earned for itself a very well-established niche in the history of the war in Europe

Urmitz

Two days (March 9th) after the bridge was seized at Remagen, an event took place at a location on the Rhine just about 18 miles upstream from Remagen. This was not just an event—it was one of great, most significant historical import. Yet, because of the great attention paid to Remagen, it rests in obscurity. Historians seem unaware of it, or believe it of little importance, as few words have appeared about it, and little mention is made in history books. Ironically, the few words that have appeared about it are distorted and inaccurate.

The purpose of this paper is to, finally, tell the Urmitz story. It is written not by a historian, but by a participant—one who played a leading role in the events, who saw up very close with his own eyes all that will here be described.

Background: Between 1916 and 1919 bridges were constructed at Remagen and at a place called Urmitz. The bridges were built to facilitate transport to the Western Front, to improve rail links between Germany and France. The bridges were 325 meters long with two rail lines and a walkway. Both bridges were similar in appearance, as they had twin towers at each end.

At the time of the capture of the Remagen Bridge, it had been claimed to be the only remaining bridge that led over the Rhine River into Germany's heartland. INCORRECT.

On March 7, the day of the capture of the Remagen Bridge, it had been claimed that aerial reconnaissance that day confirmed that no bridges remained intact over the Rhine in the U.S. Third Army sector. INCORRECT.

The Urmitz Story Background

I commanded the 8th Tank Battalion of the 4th Armored Division. That division was General Patton's spearhead all across Europe. We were the ones who made the spectacular, history-making sweep across France in late August of 1944. Many weeks later it was that division as part of Patton's Third Army that attacked the German underbelly in the Battle of the Bulge, and relieved the surrounded 101st Airborne Division at Bastogne. Some days later, on January 10, 1945 in a determined effort to end that battle by cutting off the Germans at the neck, a three-division attack was launched. The 101st Airborne Division, the 6th Armored Division, and the 4th Armored Division were successfully pushing back the Germans.

In the midst of the battle the 4th Armored Division received a stunning order. It was directed to execute one of battle's most difficult maneuvers to disengage from a fight and withdraw immediately. Early the next morning, the division, after having obscured all markings and operating with radio silence, streaked from Belgium to Luxembourg. Apparently senior intelligence officials having been badly burned by being totally surprised by the German Ardennes attack on December 16 did not want to be surprised again. They must have had some kind of indicators that another counterattack was planned, this time to hit Luxembourg. At any rate, theirs was a great overreaction to their information, for the Germans did not make another offensive move.

Now we of Patton's Third Army were stopped in Luxembourg, during what continued to be a deadly, vicious winter. His infantry was deployed along the Our and Sauer Rivers. Their job was to establish a bridgehead across the rivers so that a bridge could be installed to enable the tanks to cross. This was well nigh asking for the impossible. There was sleet, snow, bitter cold winds; raging, swollen rivers; and the most formidable German-held defensive positions. Virtually all the artillery that could be mustered fired over our infantry and into the ranks of the Germans. The only elements in my battalion that could assist were my

assault guns, and I sent them forward to augment the artillery. As for my tanks, there was no place to go. So we sat impatiently, despondently, eagerly awaiting the call to "go!"

After over a month, the call finally came. We had no warning, but in a minimum amount of time my tankers were fully loaded and ready to go. It was on February 22 that we crossed near the junction of the Our and Sauer Rivers, and for the first time set foot in Germany. As I crossed, I marveled at the courage and dedication that had been required for the doughboys to provide us with such an easy and safe passage.

I quickly learned that the bridgehead was not very deep. I was not too far east of the river when my battalion went into its first bivouac. Weather conditions had not improved, and were as fierce as ever. Worst of all the fields were muddy bogs, reminiscent of what we had faced in November and December. Once again the tanks would be severely restricted, and would have anything but freedom of movement. And the enemy was out there very close, and appeared ready to contest us for every yard.

Up until this point in the war, tanks had always led the fight with the infantry supporting and always doing their best to close up and clean up behind us. Now the roles would be reversed. It would be the infantry leading and the tanks supporting. For the first time in the war, I would not operate as a tank battalion. Instead, my tank companies and platoons would be attached to infantry elements. The fighting would be done by many small units scattered over a wide area. These actions would be slow, hard going and time-consuming.

How slow, how difficult? Our gains would not be measured by miles as in the past. Now it was yards and kilometers. It took six days to wrest from the enemy the 25 kilometers from our first bivouac area to that initial, very important objective, Bitburg. On the first day of March my battalion was occupying Rittersdorf, 2½ kilometers northwest of that important city. We pushed out aggressively from it, and were able to fight our way to the Kyll, and to gain and hold defensive positions along the west bank of the river from Fliessen to Irsch.

On March 2 we stayed put, and continued to hold those positions. The day brightened for us when we learned that discussions were taking place between senior commanders of our division and the 5th Infantry Division, with which we had again been working. It was agreed that the 5th would attack as soon as possible, get troops across the Kyll River and establish a bridgehead. This was exciting news, for we knew that once a substantial bridgehead had been established, our division could pass through it, and break out in true Armor fashion, as we had done so often before.

The 5th Infantry chose midnight of the 3rd for their assault. Diversionary fires would be launched at 11 PM in which we would fully participate. The attack was successful, but did not proceed quite as rapidly as we had hoped. Nevertheless, the long awaited order that cut us loose finally reached us. We were given the word "move out," and we did!

It was early on the morning of March 5 that the 4th Armored Division with Combat Command "B" (CCB) leading began crossing the Kyll, and without delay began attacking to the northeast through the 5th Infantry bridgehead. Combat Command "A" (CCA) led by my battalion followed CCB. The two combat commands advanced in one column to Metterich, where they split, with CCB attacking to the left toward Baden and CCA attacking toward Gondorf.

CCB on a major, red-dotted road hit its first resistance north of Baden. They then drove with such speed through Meisburg that many of the enemy and much equipment was captured. The tankers of CCB destroyed four German tanks on the way to Wallenborn, and seized many wagon trains and miscellaneous vehicles in that town. This was a sensational early outburst. It was shades of France in late August, and was a good Armor day's work. Starting this day, it would no longer be yards, kilometers gained but miles once again. CCB's advance had been a surprising, most impressive initial thrust that gained for it a substantial twenty miles.

CCA, after splitting from CCB at Metterich and confined to a small, narrow, secondary road with deep, muddy terrain on both sides, quickly captured a sizeable number of the enemy. Disappointedly, my force was soon halted by a blown bridge, for which there was no readily available bypass. Despite the most difficult terrain conditions, my tanks vigorously pushed to the bank of the river, plunged into the water, and successfully forded the stream.

But now I was faced with a real dilemma. Should I stop now with my attack barely underway and wait for the engineers to close up and bridge the stream so that I could move forward with my entire force intact? Or should I exploit the mobility of the tanks and retain the momentum by shoving off with my tanks alone?

I had high hopes of bursting out of the bridgehead and gaining considerable ground on this first day. Thus, not wanting to be halted so quickly and to have my attack sputter, I chose the latter course, and attacked with my tanks toward my first objective—Gondorf.

The tanks of "C" Company in the lead received enemy tank fire from the woods northeast of that town. "C" quickly took the tanks under fire, and knocked out four of them, as well as some miscellaneous equipment during the brief engagement. However, "C," too, had losses—one tank due to tank fire and one damaged by a mine south of Gondorf.

The tanks entered the town wiping out small arms resistance, and destroyed two more tanks on the outskirts. Without delay, the attackers pushed on to Oberkail where they found the bridge over the Kyll River destroyed. Once again a tank engagement ensued. Tanks from other companies moved up to assist "C" Company which lost two more tanks—one to enemy tank fire and the other from a Panzerfaust. Small-arms fire and Panzerfausts were overcome; the town was cleared and outposted. The objective, Gondorf, had been seized.

Thus far, this had been a most unusual day and a most uncharacteristic operation. After fording the stream, the tanks had plunged forward on their own. There was nothing behind them, no armored infantry, no cavalry, no engineers. Those in wheeled vehicles and even half-tracks had not only advanced as far as they could, but many vehicles, particularly the infantry half-tracks, were completely bogged down and unable to move. Tanks had to be diverted from their primary mission of attacking forward to extricating the half-tracks from the unbelievable, sticky mud. This just had to be one of combat's most exasperating situations. Tanks were fighting to their front, while others were hauling out bogged-down vehicles to their rear. Tanks were operating in opposite directions.

As soon as I was informed that CCB had cleared Metterich, I ordered the half-tracks and wheeled vehicles back to that town to pick up the good road that was being used by CCB to Baden and beyond. The day for me had been weird and exceptionally frustrating. The axis that had been assigned to me for my advance was in absolutely no condition for wheeled vehicles to negotiate. The roads were bad, and the terrain on each side, even worse, well nigh impassable. Although in their advance the tanks had already seen considerable action, it was not enemy resistance that had slowed or delayed our force, but the bad road, blown bridges, and the very muddy terrain so reminiscent of November in Lorraine. Despite all the difficulties, problems, and frustrations the tanks had gained over six miles, which put them well out of the bridgehead.

That evening I conferred with the Commander of CCA, Col. Hayden Sears. We both agreed that it was completely unprofitable and actually foolish to try to keep plugging on my assigned, almost impassable axis, when to our left just three kilometers away was the road over which CCB was making good progress.

So the next day the elements of CCA remained in position until all of CCB had cleared Orsfeld. The tanks sideslipped the three kilometers to their left, while the half-tracks and wheeled vehicles already on the road closed up. At that point the lead elements of CCA (my tanks) were right behind the rear units of CCB. That meant that CCA would follow CCB in a column of combat commands. Although unusual, this formation made great sense. For the past many months the 4ᵗʰ Armored Division had operated habitually with its combat commands widely spread, covering wide areas, as it endeavored to seize ground as rapidly as possible and to destroy the enemy and their equipment along the way.

However, this situation was different. The mission of the 4ᵗʰ Armored was to get to the Rhine as soon as possible. In the process it would have to overcome the very difficult and treacherous Schnee Eifel. Any deployment of forces would be difficult, and under these circumstances might not be required. The most rapid and efficient way to advance is in column. As long as CCB was making good progress, why not hook up and follow them? If CCB should hit serious resistance, CCA could certainly, at any time, break out and resume attacking on CCB's right or left, as was so often in the recent past, making that two combat commands abreast.

Early on the morning of the 6ᵗʰ, CCB shoved off aggressively, and in rapid succession advanced through a series of German towns all the way to Ulmen. During their rapid advance, the force at times received harassing artillery, mortar, and rocket fire from both flanks, and there was at least one roadblock in each town that had to be destroyed. Results, in some instances, bordered on the spectacular. Best evidence that the advance of CCB was, indeed, rapid was the surprising capture of the command post of the Thirteenth German Corps in the vicinity of Neunkirchen, which was overrun with the commander, Lt. Gen. Edwin Graf von Rothkirch und Trach and his staff still in it. Not long after CCB's forces entered Ulmen, they captured a large quartermaster depot brimming with supplies and equipment.

The 7ᵗʰ dawned extremely cold and with limited visibility because of falling snow. *It was sometime during this day, not too far to our northeast, that elements of the 9ᵗʰ Armored Division were seizing the Remagen Bridge.*

CCB again continued its rapid advance. It entered Buchel without opposition, and then it was on to Kaisersesch. Closing in on the town, there were indications that there would be resistance. So upon reaching the outskirts, the command employed a new tactic. They brought forth a loudspeaker system, and over it delivered an ultimatum for the town to surrender or be destroyed. The enemy immediately gave in. At least 200 prisoners were taken, and approximately 300 Allied prisoners and slave laborers of many nationalities were freed. Continuing its advance, the force hit organized resistance at Kehrig. The town was defended mainly by an antiaircraft regiment, which poured out heavy fire. After a considerable fight, the town was captured, and then in a valley beyond, the antiaircraft guns were knocked out at a cost of two tanks lost—one to antitank and the other to Panzerfaust fire. At Ochtendung, two enemy trains and columns of troops were caught attempting to flee the town, resulting in serious German losses, and the town was taken just before darkness settled in. Remarkably, with all the fighting they had to do, the force had advanced 26 miles. Again this was reminiscent of the heady days of the summer before, during the sweep across France.

CCB of the 4th Armored Division had advanced so rapidly and aggressively that the Germans were scattered and running in all directions without the ability to put together any semblance of an organized defense. The best evidence that the Germans were losing heart—their will to fight—were the long lines, the hundreds of Germans shuffling to the rear. It was now becoming commonplace to watch the Germans in their ankle-length gray coats—stricken, defeated faces, and hands clasped over their heads—on the road going back, while our tanks were moving relentlessly forward.

And now the excitement began to mount, not only because of the successes of the past days, but because at Ochtendung the 4th Armored Division was not more than nine miles from the Rhine River—that tremendous objective that had been in their hearts and minds for those many weeks. Now it was out there, almost within easy reach and less than three days after crossing the Kyll. So there was unbounded euphoria up and down the long column.

My battalion followed by the rest of CCA's elements closed up on CCB, spread out, and my lead units soon occupied the high ground south and east of Ochtendung and the towns to the south, Minklefeld and Waldorferhof. This now put us on line with CCB.

The three days just completed had been exciting, extremely rewarding, and exhilarating. After many frustrating, insufferable days marking time in Luxembourg, the 4th had finally been unleashed. They were back in the saddle again. Now they had just done exactly what they had been designed, created, and trained to do. Their great mobility, plus firepower, once again equaled shock action. They had advanced rapidly and aggressively, disrupting and scattering the enemy and getting into his rear areas in typical Armor fashion.

The division had advanced 65 miles in three days. More accurately, because of twisted roads, it probably advanced closer to a hundred miles, and it was not three days but 58 hours after leaving the Kyll. This feat was bound to electrify all the forces in Europe, as well as at home. The winter had been a long, stagnant period, when any gains were measured in yards. Suddenly, almost out of nowhere, here was a 65-mile leap in a minimum amount of time. And it was through and over the extensive, treacherous, and almost impassable Schnee Eifel range.

Almost hidden behind this epochal advance was the destruction and devastation left behind. The Eifel was littered with hundreds of vehicles of all kinds and equipment of all descriptions. The number of prisoners captured was in the many hundreds. This action by the 4th Armored proved to be one of the turning points in the final phase of the war in Europe. This was a remarkable advance—at times 60 miles long and 75 feet wide—and proved that lightning warfare of those summer days in France was not dead yet. It had come back to life.

The moment he had heard of this great success story, Gen. Omar Bradley was, likewise, euphoric, and was reported to have exclaimed that the 4th Armored Division "had staged the boldest, most insolent armored blitz of the Western War."

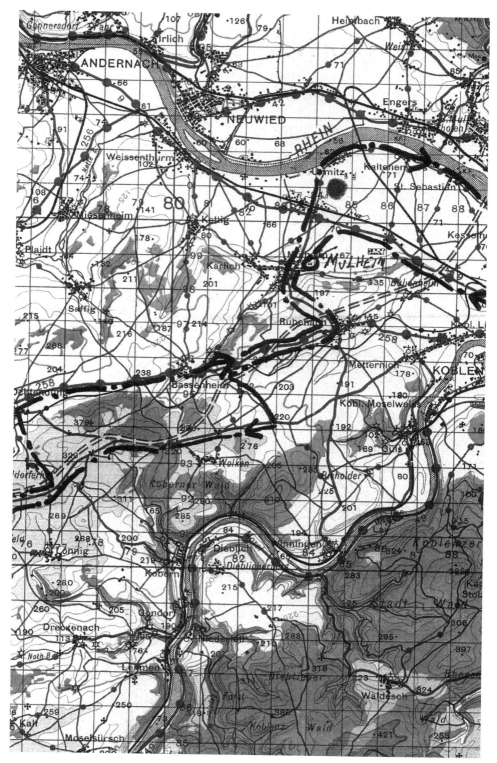

URMITZ

Now came March 8th. Little did we realize that the excitement was far from over, and that this day and the next would provide us with not only severe challenges, but also mind-boggling battlefield confusion, and a staggering, unbelievable, gruesome spectacle.

The day started with both combat commands making a push to the Rhine River. CCB on my left had assigned to it Saffig and Ketting as its initial objectives. During their advance, they received artillery, small-arms, and Panzerfaust fire, as well as encountering some scattered mines. Nevertheless, the attacking elements made steady progress, and captured still more Germans. They entered Ketting late in the afternoon, which put them about a kilometer and a half from the river. Advance elements proceeded through the town and took up positions on the high ground overlooking the main highway from Andernach to Koblenz, which ran parallel and very close to the Rhine River. From their positions they found that enemy convoys moving toward Koblenz were within range, and made excellent targets. Consequently, many motorized vehicles and horse drawn wagons were destroyed.

My 8th Tank Battalion and the supporting 53rd Armored Infantry Battalion moved out and attacked abreast of CCB. Our elements were cross-reinforced. (They had tanks of mine, and I had some of their infantry). My battalion seized Bassenheim, while the 53rd took Wolken. Then we were ordered by CCA to launch a simultaneous attack on Karlich and Mulheim. As we advanced, we received direct, artillery, mortar, and sniper fire, particularly heavy from the direction of Mulheim. We were able to overcome all resistance, and by late afternoon we had seized both towns. My battalion suffered some casualties, and lost three tanks, one of which was recoverable.

While my force was clearing Mulheim, I pushed my own tank along the high ground just south of it. I was impatient to see what lay to the east. I reached a modest promontory, looked out in front of me, and just could not believe all that I was seeing. What an incredible sight to behold! There unfolding before me was an absolutely unbelievable, startling, spectacular panorama. Sitting there so close that I felt that I could simply reach out and touch it was the Rhine River, about which I had read so much, heard so much, and thought so much.

As I quickly swept it with my eyes, it more than lived up to its advanced billing. In the late afternoon light, it was not the brilliant blue that I had halfway expected, but more of a gray-green. The river was very broad, and lovely to look at. It was majestic and regal. It was perfectly obvious why it was one of Europe's famous, historic rivers, and one of the world's great ones.

Although fascinated by it, I was even more greatly tormented by it. I was staring at an imposing, frightening, super-difficult obstacle that somehow very soon would have to be conquered. So it, too, was the enemy.

My look at the river and reflections took but an instant. With that first glance I also saw an astonishing, incredible, totally unexpected sight, one that was unbelievably exciting, exhilarating, and which instantly rushed my adrenalin to its absolute peak. I was looking at a structure, which if soon conquered, would itself be the tool we required to conquer the Rhine. *I was looking at a bridge over the Rhine that was intact, undamaged.*

This is from a single-page document recently uncovered by myself, and on which there is no indication of source. Thus, unfortunately, attribution cannot be paid. The words shown below are particularly pertinent to this story, and are quoted:

As aerial reconnaissance confirmed that no bridge remained intact over the Rhine in the U.S. Third Army sector on March 7, the 4th Armored Division halted just under cover of the reverse slope of the last high ground short of the river at Urmitz. Because of haze, the actual bridge was not visible but the suspicions of the Americans were aroused when they saw that Germans were still retreating towards the bridge area. Reports from civilians were contradictory, some saying the bridge had been destroyed and others that it had not. Combat Command 'A' made ready for an attack before daylight on the 9th, but then General Bradley ordered the Third Army to turn southward across the Moselle. Unaware that the bridge was no longer an American objective, German Pionierkommando blew it shortly after daybreak using a cutting charge a third of the way along the main open span and the three lattice spans were also dropped.

That bridge was directly in front of me and not more than 2½ kilometers away. An amazing, incomprehensible, totally unbelievable sight unfolding before my eyes was graphic testimony that the bridge was intact, undamaged. That bridge was teeming with traffic desperately moving across it to the east. Vehicles, wagons, horses and men were jammed together. The Germans were fleeing in from all directions, frenzied, in great panic to get over the one bridge available to them before the Americans caught up with them.

URMITZ THE BRIDGE

Even more startling were the roads leading to the bridge. These were jammed tightly with vehicles of every size and description, men riding and walking, horses loose and pulling guns and wagons with not a space or gap to be seen. A main road went south from Andernach to Koblenz. It was jammed as far as the eye could see in both directions. Traffic moved at a snail's pace southeast from Andernach, and northeast from Koblenz. There was a road that went directly east from my position at Mulheim, crossed the Andernach/Koblenz highway, and continued to the bridge. That road was the only way to get to the bridge. So what I was seeing was traffic tightly entwined from Andernach, snaking along and then turning to the bridge on the Mulheim road, and traffic tightly entwined from Koblenz, snaking along, and turning to the bridge on the Mulheim road, with both trying to merge together at that intersection for the one kilometer drive to the bridge. Merge was not the word. Fighting desperately, even violently to squeeze in was more accurate. It was an almost impossible situation, a huge mixing bowl of humanity and everything with wheels and tracks in the German military inventory. It was a game of musical chairs with ten individuals scrambling for the one chair remaining.

After fighting through the intersection, the battle had only begun for that last kilometer. It was as though rams had locked horns, and fought each other all the way to the bridge.

The bridge that they reached was a two-track railroad bridge—certainly not designed to accommodate wagons, trucks, and tanks. Because these were successfully crossing, planks must have been installed over the tracks. Whatever the solution, it was working—up to a point. The traffic was having some difficulty negotiating the bridge, for when it moved it was frustratingly slow. Obviously, those fleeing hoped for haste, but gained only frustration.

Between my position and the river, the terrain was like the lowlands beside any significant river. There were no trees to hide behind, no ridges for defiladed positions and protection. It was as flat and level and open as a tabletop.

Never before in the war had there been anywhere near such a vast array of lucrative, tempting, mouthwatering targets. It put Coney Island to shame. Here was an intact bridge over the Rhine with hundreds of men with their hundreds of vehicles and wagons, helplessly bogged down, defenseless, and out there for the taking.

Even with the day fast fading and the light ebbing, I knew that an opportunity like this would never again present itself. It was a one-time deal. The prize out there was so huge, so critical that I could not delay taking a crack at it. A usable bridge over the Rhine at this stage would revolutionize our efforts, shorten the war, and save many lives. So I alerted two of my companies to get ready to make a charge over the open ground, to try to seize the bridge at Urmitz.

Shortly after, I ordered, "Go!" No sooner had the tanks begun their advance, and had barely stuck their noses out, when they received a murderous volume of fire. Such an immediate and deadly response emphasized that the Germans, too, knew the immense value of their bridge, and were not going to give it up lightly.

Apparently, emplaced at the bridge site and other nearby locations were dual-purpose 88s. They had obviously been installed to protect the bridge from air attack. The guns were primarily powerful anti-aircraft weapons, but they possessed great flexibility. They could easily be depressed, and become potent, direct-fire, high-velocity, tank-killing guns. That was the role that they were now playing. This was the most concentrated 88-mm fire that we had yet experienced. The close ones and the terrible noise from ricochets at Fresnes-en-Saulnois in Lorraine could not hold a candle to this.

In that first instant there was no question that, even with that lucrative objective, that jewel out there in front of us, it would have been absolutely foolhardy and suicidal to attempt to cross that 2½ kilometer tabletop in the fading light with the guns now zeroed in upon us, and without an adequate artillery preparation. I also knew that the bridge could be blown at any moment, now that the Germans knew that the Americans were so close. Moreover, each minute that passed meant that some military equipment had successfully gained the east bank of the river.

I conceded that regardless of how aggressively and courageously my tankers charged toward the river, my losses would have been severe, and the undertaking from the very beginning in doubt. So, applying that old saw about discretion being the better part of valor, and husbanding my troops to fight another day, I, with great reluctance, had quickly pulled back my tankers to safety, as darkness began to settle down around us.

Even as the tanks were settling in, our ever-alert artillery had the range and direction of the 88s, and began firing upon them, as well as pummeling those many hemmed-in, lucrative targets. Artillery fire would continue unabated, causing flames and explosions all through the night.

Early that evening I had a meeting with Colonel Sears, at which time he directed me "to be prepared to drive at first light to the Rhine River, and to seize the bridge over it."

At 5 AM I received orders to stand fast, and not advance, as ordered earlier. Between six o'clock and half past eight, heavy concentrations of artillery fire from several battalions continued to be poured down on the suspected locations of enemy guns, and on vehicles on the roads near the Rhine.

During the brief period of waiting, I had the rare and fabulous opportunity of hurrying to and climbing the steeple of a church close to our position, just after the early morning fog had lifted. I gained a spectacular view of the bridge that we would be attacking with its teeming, congested humanity and vehicles. I could see clearly in all directions the disorganized remnants—an every-man-for-himself struggle for survival—of the rotting of a once proud army. Yet, I knew that a large, hard core of fanatics would be awaiting me as I pushed out into my attack.

Now the time had come to make our move. My tanks with infantry mounted on them, and with artillery rounds roaring overhead and exploding up ahead, moved out aggressively, but each of us cringed a bit in expectation of that first incoming 88 round. Astonishingly, as we advanced, there was none. We were already on the flat, open terrain, and began picking up speed. We had still not been fired upon. The only possible answer—our artillery must have done a real bang-up job.

My lead elements continued to move, unimpeded by enemy fire. Nothing now was holding them back; they were gaining on the big prize—the Holy Grail was now almost within reach. Excitement increased, and so did the speed of the tanks. We were now about halfway to the bridge, AND THEN SUDDENLY, IT HAPPENED!

From the moment we moved out, I, up in the turret of my tank, had my eyes glued on the bridge. While staring fixedly at it, it abruptly came to life. There was dust, fire and amazingly, unbelievably a high, wide, bizarre, grotesque arch over the bridge. Incomprehensibly, making up that arch and floating high in the air were bodies of men, horses, motorcycles, wagons, light trucks. At a lower level, because of their heavier weight, were bigger trucks, and beneath them, barely above the ground, were tanks—a huge, massive collection of human and vehicular debris. A split second later came the sounds. First were thunderous, horrendous, earth-splitting, ear-shattering explosions, followed by a whole series of loud, lesser explosions. To be sure that this would not be another Remagen, the Germans obviously had collected, installed, and detonated a powerful and massive amount of explosives. How else could the huge arch and the elements that made up that arch be explained?

Our tanks in an instant stopped, were frozen, unable to move, for its crew members were horror stricken, and also were frozen in disbelief. Our priceless objective, our goal—the bridge—was blown to smithereens. For me it was a totally shattering feeling.

But then came shock and revulsion with the realization *that the long bridge, loaded and jammed with Germans, had been blown up by Germans!* I had heard and read about carnage; this day I saw carnage in the most basic, literal, hideous, most raw form.

My men and I in our tanks remained motionless, stunned. I now recognized and saw graphically that the highest priority of the Germans was to deny the bridge to the advancing Americans; nothing was more important. And the cost was tremendous, not only for those caught on the bridge, but also for all those trapped on the west side of the Rhine with no place to go.

I had some solace. It was now perfectly obvious that if we had attacked and advanced the previous day, the bridge would have gone up then, after I had perhaps fruitlessly sacrificed some tanks to the ready and waiting 88s. I consoled myself by recognizing that under no circumstances could we have seized the bridge intact, for even then there were alert German hands at the ready prepared to push the plungers.

Trying to overcome my disappointment, I gave the word to my tankers to move forward. They advanced rapidly toward the river and the blown bridge. Knowing that the jig was up, definitely, German soldiers—drivers and passengers of the stranded vehicles—came streaming toward the advancing tankers in droves with their hands on their heads. They did not want to be anywhere near their vehicles, which were already being methodically destroyed by the Americans.

When I arrived at what had once been the bridge, I saw sights that I could never adequately describe, and would forever be etched in my mind. No Hollywood director, regardless of how imaginative, or "way out," could ever recreate the scene.

There was utter, total destruction, desolation, and chaos in all directions. Then, from my position on the bank of the Rhine, I saw in it what could best be described as the flotsam of the explosions, the floating debris. Entwined in the twisted remains of the bridge were parts of trucks, wagons and other vehicles. Humans had just vanished. Cluttering up all the nearby roads were now abandoned enemy vehicles and equipment. Engineers would be busy all night destroying them, and in the process would run out of every demolition item that had been available to them.

I glanced back and forth once again at the gruesome scene. There was an air of absolute finality about it. It was over—all over. With nothing more required for the moment, I had my forces withdraw, and we began moving back to the environs of Mulheim from where we had started that morning. We had been stunned, stricken, momentarily paralyzed by a sight that was so awful, so terrible that it was beyond human comprehension. Now, and for years to come, we would ask ourselves, "Did we see that? Did it really happen?" We were returning completely changed individuals.

AFTERWORD

The Urmitz Bridge was blown on the morning of March 9, 1945. It was the last bridge to be destroyed over the Rhine.

The name of the bridge was the Crown Prince Wilhelm Bridge, more accurately the Kronprinz Wilhelm Brücke.

It was constructed along with the Remagen Bridge between 1916 and 1919.

Royal Engineer Port Construction units of the British 21st Army Group began clearing work on June 25, 1945. A channel in the Rhine was open to traffic on September 1.

In 1947, work was started to build a new box-girder bridge, which was opened in 1954, first as a single and later as a double-track railway.

The Remagen Bridge was not rebuilt. A pair of surviving towers of the old bridge remain and now house a museum.

Although the events at Urmitz were for the Germans an incredible disaster, they were successful in greatly slowing the momentum of Patton's Third Army, forcing Patton into needless fighting a considerable distance to the south, and delaying him by many days from finally getting on the east side of the Rhine, poised to continue his fight through the German heartland.

After the Urmitz bridge was blown, and not knowing that it was the last, the 4th Armored Division, still hopeful that an intact bridge might be found at Mainz or even Worms, continued to push south. There was no bridge at Mainz. It was then that Patton faced the inevitable. Now he recognized that the only way for his forces to cross the Rhine would be over a bridge that he, himself, would have installed. So it was that on March 22 elements of his 5th Infantry Division, loaded on assault boats, successfully crossed the Rhine and developed a bridgehead on the east side of the River. That enabled the engineers to start immediately installing a pontoon bridge across that challenging obstacle.

It was on the morning of September 24 that elements of Third Army led by the light tanks of my 8th Tank Battalion began crossing the Rhine at Oppenheim.

Final thought: Will the action at Urmitz ever become even a footnote in the history of World War II in Europe?

This incredible article was discovered just before going to print.

Tuesday, 13 March, 1945

GERMANS FIRED ON OWN MEN

From SAM WHITE, Special Correspondent of THE ARGUS,
with Lieut-General Patton's Army Near Coblenz.

The Germans blew up the Kronprinz Wilhelm Bridge across the Rhine, near Coblenz, while their own troops were moving across it. They then raked the survivors with machine gun fire as they swam about in the river.

This has just been revealed by an imposing collection of eye-witnesses, including a German Army captain and three Luftwaffe pilots. Although they appeared to be at a loss to explain the Germans' action, it seems clear that the purpose was to keep the troops in the Rhine-Moselle triangle fighting for as long as possible by cutting off their only escape route. It is known that the troops who held the machine gun posts on the other side of the river were SS troops.

The action occurred on Friday, shortly after a long convoy of horse-drawn and motor vehicles was ambushed as it was moving through a narrow lane along the Rhine by the fast-moving artillery of one of Patton's armored spearheads. The first shots knocked out the leading vehicle, and this, combined with panic among the horses, threw the entire convoy into confusion. Some of the vehicles managed to break loose and make a dash for the bridge, only about 200 yards away. They were jammed tight along the entire stretch of the bridge, when suddenly a great explosion threw the men, machines, and horses high into the air.

When the smoke of the explosion cleared it was seen that the center span of the bridge had collapsed, and that dozens of men were threshing about in the water. Many were obviously wounded and were crying out for help, while others were trying to gain the east bank.

It was then that calculated and deliberate machine gun fire was opened up on survivors. All the witnesses say it was an unforgettable, horrible sight, as the cries for help mingled with the relentless bursts of machine gun fire. Wounds, fatigue, and panic must have resulted in the death of all who survived the explosion.

The scene where the convoy was trapped is ghastly. I have seen nothing like it since the slaughter at Falaise. For about two miles, right up to the approaches of the bridge, the road is blocked with the bodies of men and horses and the wreckage of 137 trucks, thirty-eight staff cars, thirty-six 88mm guns, sixty-nine 20mm AA guns, twenty-five half-tracks, three Tiger tanks, and a huge pile of small arms.

Out of the entire convoy the Americans captured 1,771 prisoners.

# # #

CHAPTER NINE

OHRDRUF, THE FIRST

T
o its great frustration, my 4th Armored Division, which had been and would continue to be Gen. George Patton's spearhead all across Europe, upon reaching that major, long sought after objective, the Rhine River, and "riding" its west bank to the south, found all bridges over the river destroyed. Now to cross it required a pontoon bridge that would be installed, as many before it, by our army engineers. However, before the installation could begin, a bridgehead across the river had to be seized and secured. That mission was assigned to the 5th Infantry Division. That outfit, without delay, moved up, and using assault boats to cross the river on March 22 and 23, established that bridgehead.

At 0900 on the morning of the 24th, the light tanks of my 8th Tank Battalion began moving across the bridge. The tanks of my battalion would be the first Third Army elements to cross the river. It was this crossing of the Rhine by Third Army Infantry and Armor that enabled General Patton to gleefully proclaim that he had beaten his disliked and discomforted rival, Field Marshal Bernard Law Montgomery (Monty) across the Rhine River.

Once out of the bridgehead, our forces moved aggressively to the northeast. We soon developed crossings over the Main River, and advanced through Hanau, thus outflanking Frankfurt 17 kilometers to the west. Our division had made a swift, historic sweep across France in August, but had been badly bogged down by atrocious weather and deep, clinging mud in November and December. Now in late March the terrain was much drier; we picked up speed, and began a charge that was reminiscent of that historic sweep across France during the last two weeks of August.

By the last day of March, the 4th Armored was east of Bad Hersfeld alongside an autobahn that went east to the next major city, Eisenach. Interestingly, after the war and during the occupation of Germany, those two cities would be split by the East/West German Border that would be better known as "The Iron Curtain." Across that border from Bad Hersfeld all during the "Cold War" would lay what became East Germany, and the Russian zone of occupation.

Eisenach was a very historic, old German city on the northwestern edge of the Thuringian Forest. It would soon, in a sense, become the gateway to East Germany. The mission assigned to us when we reached the Bad Hersfeld area was to continue our aggressive assault to the east with our initial axis of advance the major cities of Eisenach, Gotha, Erfurt, and Weimar. We were totally unfamiliar with those names.

We moved out early on April 1 and headed to the northeast. We recognized that up ahead was a major obstacle, the Werra River, which we hoped would not delay us. Our goal was to seize a major crossing about 5 kilometers northwest of Eisenach. For the last few kilometers we moved parallel to and hugged the Werra, which flowed south of us. When we reached our planned crossing site, it was again shock and dismay. The bridge had been blown. Now, as at the Rhine, we immediately searched desperately for an intact bridge, but there was none. All apparently had been wired with demolitions, and hands had been at the ready to push the plungers. Now, again as at the Rhine, we would have to install our own bridge.

As daylight was ebbing, we settled on a place named Spichra to be the site of our bridge. It was about 9 kilometers slightly northwest of Eisenach.

By the time it was daylight again our forces were already hard at it. But April 2 would turn out to be a most difficult, taxing, frustrating day. To our great surprise there was a quite remarkable resurgence, at this late date, of German military strength both on the ground and

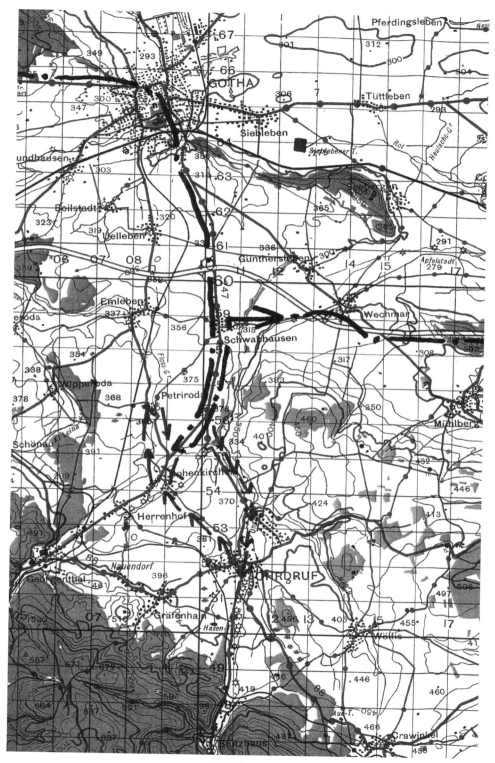

OHRDRUF

in the air. It appeared that they were absolutely determined to keep us from crossing the Werra. Their ground elements strongly resisted our attempts to establish a bridgehead. After some heavy fighting, we prevailed, and the engineers were furiously at work installing the bridge. Then, to our great astonishment, the German Air Force, which had been relatively dormant for the last few days, suddenly appeared out of nowhere in surprising strength. Fifteen planes bombed and strafed the Spichra bridge site, which resulted in some damage and caused delay in its construction.

That day they threw at us all they could muster to keep us from making that crossing. However, we were even more determined than they. We were successful in completing the bridge, and before it turned dark, my entire battalion had crossed the river.

By first light on the 3rd we were already rolling. The route that I had chosen would encircle Eisenach by going directly east out of the Spichra bridgehead, then to the southeast. At a point ten kilometers southeast of Eisenach the route intersected with the Bad Hersfeld/ Eisenach Autobahn that continued directly to the east. Although moving along the autobahn made us extremely vulnerable, I decided to use it, as it was the most rapid way for us to advance to the east. We were anxious to get it over with. The next major city on our axis of advance was Gotha. By moving along the autobahn we would be 5 kilometers south of that city as we bypassed it. My tanks were soon rolling east along the widest, smoothest, firmest road yet encountered, and faster than we had in a long time.

We had not covered many miles when our advance came to a screeching halt. We had to jam our brakes, dig in our heels. The road had suddenly ended. There staring at us was a yawning chasm. A huge overpass had been blown. We had nowhere to go, so we began to turn around. At that point the enemy lowered the boom. We received fire, and received vehicular and personnel casualties from the howling, frightening, screeching German 88s, as we desperately evacuated the area to get out of the range of the guns.

After backing away, we moved north for 5 kilometers to the main road leading to Gotha. There would be no bypassing the city, and it was now readily apparent that we would have to fight for it. The day was now spent, so we settled in for the night.

It was now April 4, 1945. I was the commanding officer of the 8th Tank Battalion, Combat Command "A" (CCA) of the 4th Armored Division. It was a warm, sunny, pleasant spring morning. But I was greatly puzzled, for the day was already well advanced. For the past many days by first light, which came early, we were well down the road. Now I was still awaiting orders to move. I could not help asking myself, "What's up? What has happened, why are we still here?" A message from my CCA commander, Col. Hayden Sears, soon provided me with the answer. We all knew that our next objective, the impressive city of Gotha, was a large built-up area with a critical bridge. If the city was heavily defended and the bridge blown, it would seriously delay our advance and impede our momentum. Our division commander readily and alertly recognized what was facing us. Accordingly, he had earlier sent an ultimatum to the city's burgomeister, the lord mayor, informing him that if he did not surrender his city by 11 AM that shells from the guns of several battalions of artillery would rain down upon and destroy the city.

The burgomeister must quickly have decided that our commander meant business, for his answer soon came. His message read that he would surrender the city by 10:30 AM, thirty minutes before his ultimatum.

My battalion, which had been at the "ready" for some time, was ordered to move out immediately, and we did so without delay. Our advance was without incident, and it was a bit before 12:00 when we entered the outskirts of the city. White sheets were hanging from the buildings along the street. This meant that my tanks could continue their brisk advance along an open main street, across an intact bridge, and on to our next objective.

However, as I neared the center of the city, much to my astonishment, Colonel Sears was waiting for me and waving me down. I stopped my column and clambered down from my tank so that I could confer with him. For the past days we had been advancing aggressively and successfully directly to the east, and I had expected to continue to do so. With his first words, Colonel Sears abruptly changed that, and I was extremely surprised at the instructions that I now received from him. As was our custom, our division operated with mission type orders. So, as expected, my instructions were brief and to the point. He informed me that intelligence had been picked up by higher headquarters reporting that somewhere in the vicinity of a town called Ohrdruf, about 14 kilometers south of Gotha, was located a huge underground communications complex. It reportedly had extensive radio stations, cables, and switchboards in deep, concrete rooms. The reports indicated that the installation was built for the German army headquarters in the event it was forced to retreat from Berlin.

The mission given to me by Colonel Sears was to move south, seize Ohrdruf, and to endeavor to locate and uncover the huge underground installation. So I had my battalion supported by the division's 53rd Armored Infantry Battalion make the 90-degree turn and head directly south. Shortly after 1 PM, my tanks moved out, broadly deployed.

The medium Shermans were assigned the job of attacking, seizing, and securing Ohrdruf, while my light tanks operated on both flanks, providing security to the attacking force.

The tanks had only advanced a short distance when they began to receive enemy resistance, which grew heavier as they moved ahead. The force initially received fire from shoulder-held Panzerfausts, which were targeting the tanks and attempting to destroy them. Then came heavy small arms and mortar fire, as well as an occasional artillery round. The deployed tanks immediately poured out heavy fire, and continued to move ahead. When they reached a road junction about 4 kilometers from the town, resistance became considerably heavier, but the charging tanks overwhelmed the enemy forces and it was not long before they were in Ohrdruf. They soon were in full control of the town, and elements of the battalion fanned out in all directions, taking control of the roads leading into town, and outposted the area. I had been constantly on my tank radio, fully involved in maneuvering my units and receiving reports from them. Now that the fight was over, we controlled not only the town, but also would soon control wide areas in all directions out from the town. I was expecting a call at any moment from one of my units reporting the discovery of that underground communication complex, but none came. If it was big, if it was out there, we surely would have found it by now. (Later, the complex was discovered. It was located at a sizeable town called Arnstadt, about 15 kilometers directly east of Ohrdruf.)

Preoccupied with thoughts of the communications center, I suddenly remembered that during the heavy fighting near Ohrdruf, radio traffic had been interrupted with reports indicating that "some bodies had been discovered." At the time, involved as I was with the battle, those reports made no impact upon me. Now that things were quiet at last, I decided that it was time to check out those reports.

I got back on my radio, asked questions, and began receiving some answers from my "D" (light tank company) company commander. He informed me that he had been in contact with the lieutenant platoon leader of the light tanks that had been operating along the extreme left flank. Apparently his tanks, led by a tank commanded by S.Sgt. Lester Guidry, and which included Orville Pirtle, driver; Joseph Robbins, bow gunner; and Raymond McMillan, gunner, had in the late afternoon unexpectedly and most surprisingly overrun a large area and installation with "bodies." The tankers were stunned, staggered.

My first question was "What kind of bodies?" The answer that spewed forth was most confusing, convoluted. The tankers who first came upon the site had reported, "We don't know what it is; we never expected to see anything like this; the worst sight we had ever expected to see." Then words like "ghastly," "dastardly," "gruesome" gushed out.

The tankers seemed tongue-tied, inarticulate, desperately seeking words that were not in their dictionary to describe what they had uncovered.

When I ended my tank radio exchange, instead of receiving a clear-cut answer for which I had hoped, I was totally and completely confused. I, too, asked myself, just what is it?

Some weeks before, I had heard what appeared to be a vague rumor about the Russians overrunning some sort of a bizarre complex. But that was in far off Poland, so what I heard made no impact upon me. We tankers were totally involved in combat, and thus were not exposed to subtle rumors that emerged in some parts every now and then that such installations might possibly exist. The words "concentration camp" were not yet in our lexicon. So it was perfectly understandable that none of us recognized it for what it was. It was sometime later that we would know and understand the magnitude of our discovery. It would be acknowledged as an eye-opener of shattering proportions, a blaster of rumors into fact, and something of tremendous historic significance. Thus, it was that late on the afternoon of April 4, 1945 the 8th Tank Battalion supported by the 53rd Armored Infantry Battalion, Combat Command "A" of the 4th Armored Division in General Patton's Third Army OVERRAN THE FIRST CONCENTRATION CAMP LIBERATED BY THE ALLIED FORCES.

Compared to later camps liberated, the Ohrdruf Camp (also referred to as Ohrdruf-Nord and Nord Stalag III) was a small camp. It was located on the outskirts of the very pleasant, pretty, and prosperous town of Ohrdruf. Although the camp was small, it represented and displayed all the elements of Nazi madness. Bestiality and sadistic natures were fully exposed here. It was confirmation of Hitler's great atrocities.

Of course I, like everyone in the task force, was dumbfounded and disbelieving. I just had to see it for myself. At the very first opportunity, I left my tank, hopped into my jeep and headed for the forested area. During the short drive, I gritted my teeth and steeled myself for the worst. I left my jeep at the edge of the woods, and began walking with considerable trepidation the short distance through the trees. I emerged into a small clearing that at first glance looked a bit like a small parade ground. My eyes were quickly drawn to the center of the clearing, and I recoiled in horror. I was totally unprepared and dumbstruck by what I was seeing. There, not too far away in an irregular, elliptical circle, were about 75 bodies. I was shocked, stunned. My feet seemed leaden, but I moved the short distance to the bodies and when I reached them, I gasped. The bodies were gaunt, emaciated, starved, skeletal from which remnants of clothing hung. There were massive bruises on arms and legs that must have come from beatings. What really shattered me was to note the way each had died. It was obvious that these individuals had been too sick to walk. Each had a small red spot on his forehead or throat. They had been dispatched by a single shot from a pistol. The pistol that had executed them could not have been a large one that would have blown a hole through their heads or necks. The small pistol that was used was large enough to do the trick. Each had slumped or fallen backwards, so most feet were pointing toward the center of the circle. At that point, it was obvious that the poor guys had little blood left, but somehow some oozed out and stained the ground around them.

As I would subsequently note upon investigating the rest of the camp, the guards must have left in great panic. There was no attempt made to tidy up the camp, to hide or bury the dead. I can only surmise that as we advanced from Gotha toward Ohrdruf, someone, somehow along our axis had gotten word to the camp that the Americans were on the way. The guards well knew that the poor souls were in no condition to be moved, so it was bang, bang, about 75 times—summarily dispatched.

Staggered though I had been, I soon regained my composure. Little did I realize that the shocks and surprises would continue to come. For the first time, I noted a small cluster of buildings at the edge of the woods to my left. These resembled sheds or very large sized outhouses. As I walked toward the first building, the camp odor became much stronger, somewhat suffocating. I reached the latch, opened the door, and once again I recoiled in absolute horror at the sight and smell. This was such a shock that it was a moment before I could move. There, from floor to ceiling, stacked like cordwood, piled one on top of another, were grotesque, naked bodies, whose arms and legs were stiffened at every conceivable angle.

What I stared at were virtual skeletons with very little flesh clinging to their bodies. Those bodies were covered with lime. The lime, however, did not cover the massive sores and bruises left by disease and brutality. Nor did it obscure the telltale, stifling, indescribable stench of death. It was an awful, unbelievable sight combined with a horrible odor. I stepped back, slammed the door shut, finally took a deep breath, and moved away.

I was not yet finished, but I was already benumbed. It was not over; there was more to come. I circled the bodies on the ground, and entered the woods on the opposite side of the clearing from the buildings. After a short walk, another small clearing and another staggering shock. How long could this continue?

In a minimum amount of time I had reached the highest plateau of shock, disbelief, disgust, revulsion—nothing more could rock me. So when I reached what I quickly learned were the disposal pits, all I could do was stare. The very first thing that my eyes focused on was a deep, over a block long trench filled with skeletal bodies similar to those that I had just seen at the shed. They were also sprinkled over with lime. There must have been more than 200 corpses, perhaps even a greater number, if the trenches were deep. This undoubtedly was the next destination for the bodies that I had just seen stored in the sheds. Then I caught sight of what just had to be the centerpiece of the activity at this camp. It appeared to be an extremely large hamburger grill fashioned from cross rails. Scattered all around the grill and some distance away was gray bone ash that was almost knee deep. Lying on or poking out from the ash were unburned skulls and bones of every size and description. Yes, this was the disposal pit. Cadavers would be stacked high on the grill with spruce branches and pine logs underneath. Details of firemen would keep the flames of the pyre red hot. The guards who fled at our approach did not have nearly enough time to fire up and dispose of the bodies in the trench.

I had been in combat since late July. I had seen the most horrible of wounds, soldiers on both sides killed, dismembered. I had watched helplessly as German and my own tankers perished as flames engulfed their tanks after being hit. By this time, I believed that I was somewhat hardened, and understood deaths on the battlefield, but the examples of the deliberate and bestial suffering and death, which I had just examined, was far beyond my comprehension. As I stared at the Nazi slaughterhouse, I just could not accept that human beings could have such utter and total disregard for other human beings, and would callously, methodically, unemotionally *exterminate* them. What depravity!

A division medical officer who would later visit the site exploded, "I tell you," he said to no one in particular, "that German medical service is nil. This is how they have progressed in the last four years. They have now found a cure-all for typhus and malnutrition. It is a bullet through the head."

I was overwrought with emotion. I had never before been in such an agitated state. I had enough; I just had to get away; I was definitely not interested or in the mood to explore the rest of the camp. I would leave that to others.

As I left the Ohrdruf concentration camp, I knew that what I had witnessed that day would remain with me for the rest of my life. The mental pictures of that experience continue to pop up from time to time, and remain vivid and troubling.

I would learn that not long after my visit, as a group of my soldiers moved about the camp in silent horror, a collection of skeleton-like survivors emerged from the woods. They had lived because they were able to move in the hurry, confusion, and desperation of the evacuation. Now as they emerged and saw American soldiers, they instantly pleaded for food. The G.I.'s quickly gathered what they had. These items, of course, were field rations, not nearly conventional food. However, it did no good. The undernourished, starving, emaciated wrecks of men were not able to tolerate the food; it was too rich for them to keep down, basic as it was.

The survivors were Belgian, French, Russians, Serbs, Poles and from other ethnic groups. They described how S.S. guards had brutally murdered and burned over 4,000 of the camp's inmates since December. That certainly explains the mounds of bone ash.

Two days later, on April 6, my combat commander, Col. Hayden Sears, had gathered and transported to the camp 30 of the leading citizens of that strongly pro-Nazi town. Sears wanted these well-dressed burghers to have a close-up view of the gruesome, grisly, and ghastly sights, so he personally and forcibly escorted them around the camp. They stepped carefully and gingerly about the bodies with expressions of disgust, disdain, and distaste written on their faces. Although the camp was only a short distance from the center of Ohrdruf, they feigned total ignorance of the existence of the camp. They declared that what happened there must have been the work of very few people, and that they were in no way responsible. At least the mayor (burgomeister) turned out to be honest. He made a tangible confession. He and his wife hanged themselves that night.

Now it was time for us to continue attacking to the east. However, we would have to wait patiently for the infantry to close up, and relieve us in place. While we waited, we would learn more about the camp that we had just liberated.

There were reports that at Ohrdruf (S III) on April 2, a telephone conversation was held between the Weimar (30 miles northeast of Ohrdruf) Police President S.S. Colonel Schmidt and Heinrich Himmler, the feared and despised S.S. leader, at the urging of the Ohrdruf camp commandant, S.S. Captain Oldeburheis. On the basis of that phone call, whatever action was required at the camp was left to the discretion of the commandant. Thus, the conditions existing at the camp when we arrived were undoubtedly based on his decisions.

The camp at Ohrdruf had been created in November of 1944. This concentration camp was occupied by forced slave laborers, who apparently worked on the construction of the underground communications complex. They were guarded by S.S. personnel.

By March of 1945, the camp had its peak population of some 11,700 who lived and slaved from there. Apparently, once the inmates were no longer able to work, they were executed and burned. When word filtered in that the Americans were getting closer, the guards hurriedly began evacuating individuals from the camp by marching them out primarily to the large Buchenwald Camp, of which Ohrdruf was a sub camp. These were called death marches, because when an individual could no longer march, he was executed on the spot.

On April 7, we received information of a completely different kind. On that day, a very bold, risky, and extremely foolhardy venture was undertaken by a small group of military personnel, who moved east out of our secure area on their own, without coordinating with anyone, to try to find and inspect the German communications installation which we had been unable to uncover. The group included the 4th Armored Division signal officer and his driver, and a very high-ranking intelligence officer who served on General Patton's staff, and who had been a distinguished Washington correspondent.

Word somehow was received that they had been ambushed by German soldiers and civilians near a town named Neudietendorf, which was 9 kilometers northeast of Arnstadt, the supposed location of the communications complex. A task force was immediately sent out in an attempt to rescue them. The force located the area, and found an enlisted man alive, and the body of General Patton's communications officer. The remaining members of the party were missing.

After a totally unexpected and protracted delay, the 4th was finally completely relieved by elements of the 80th and 89th Divisions on April 8 at 1400. Three days later, on the 11th, we once again moved out aggressively and advanced steadily. We were on a secondary road parallel to the autobahn, and reached a small town named Ichtershausen, which was almost directly south of the very large city of Erfurt. At that point we were a mere 4 kilometers north of the large town called Arnstadt.

That brought us head to head with a great irony. That town, as has already been mentioned, was the site of the underground communications complex, which we were charged to uncover around Obrdruf on April 4, and which we did not succeed in doing. Now we were only 4 kilometers from that facility, but would never see it. Moreover, that such an installation existed has long been forgotten.

Conversely, that small, until then unknown, camp which we had unexpectedly, surprisingly, and astonishingly stumbled upon has made an indelible mark in history. Graphic evidence of that occurred on April 12. On that day we of the 4th Armored were miles east of Ohrdruf and still advancing. We would later hear that on that day our little camp would receive national and international exposure. General Patton escorted General Eisenhower, General Bradley, and a very large collection of senior officers around the camp. General Eisenhower initially had no intention of visiting the camp, but an insistent aide convinced him that he needed to see the camp. Once he made the decision to go, he sent out for all available war correspondents and cameramen to join him. He wanted not only for them to see, but to record what they were seeing. He believed that it was urgent to "get it on the record" because he feared that somewhere down the road of history some bastard would rear up and declare that it never happened. Their tour revealed all that I have described in this text. We learned that General Bradley was so shocked that he could hardly speak. General Patton, that hardened warrior, refused to look inside a shack with the stacked bodies for fear of being sick. Nevertheless, it was still too much for him, and he rushed behind a building and vomited. As for General Eisenhower, throughout his visit his face was stern, grim, frozen. Before leaving, he ordered his aides to send word out to all units to have every soldier not otherwise occupied to visit the camp. He said, "We are told that the American soldier does not know what we are fighting for. Now, at least, he will know what he is fighting against." As soon as he was able to, he sent a cable to Gen. George Marshall, President Roosevelt's prime WWII advisor, with the words, "The things I saw begged description." Marshall, by cable, described Eisenhower's experience to Winston Churchill, the British Prime Minister.

Because of General Eisenhower's visit, and the news media that accompanied him, the word was out, and the significance of Ohrdruf spread in all directions. For the first time there was clear evidence that the Germans were guilty of unbelievable atrocities on a large scale. The camp would always be remembered as the first camp that included the frail, emaciated, starved, beaten corpses, as well as individuals who somehow managed to survive. The revelations of those horrors would serve to mark the loss of innocence of the entire world.

And how prescient was General Eisenhower! What he had feared and worried would happen *is happening* years later. Declarations that it never happened are being received from surprising and frightening sources. During recent days, the United Kingdom removed the word Holocaust from its school curriculum because it offended the sensibilities of the Muslim population, which claims it never happened. A well-established, influential Catholic bishop proclaimed categorically that the Holocaust never happened. He caused the Pope great anguish, and the pontiff was forced to go to great lengths to apologize for and to discredit the bishop's words.

I was there! I saw it! It happened!

CHAPTER TEN

THE "NAME ENOUGH" DIVISION

*Written by Brig. Gen. Albin F. Irzyk. Reprinted with permission
from* ARMOR *Magazine, July-August 1987.*

O ther divisions were acquiring nicknames, and Maj. Gen. John S. Wood, commanding the 4th Armored Division, was pressed to come up with one for his. He was so sure of the future greatness of his division that he declared, "The 4th Armored Division does not need and will not have a nickname—They shall be known by their deeds alone." Those words, from that day forward, became the division's famous motto and the reason it was so often referred to as the "Name Enough Division."

At Utah Beach, as my tank prepared to roll down the ramp of the LCT that had carried us across the English Channel, the British skipper shook my hand and said, "Good luck." I was so sure that great things were ahead for us that, as I mounted my tank, I called to him, "You'll be reading about us. Remember, it's the 4th Armored Division." He laughed and shouted back, "Oh, you Yanks are all alike." Not quite, for I knew even then that we were something special.

When we landed in France, the *esprit de corps* of the troops matched the supreme confidence of the division commander. He had taught us to believe in ourselves, to feel that we could do anything, that we were the very best, a different breed. We all felt that we were destined for greatness, much the same feeling that a college football team must have when it senses the national championship, even before the first game has been played.

In the weeks ahead, authoritative, confirmatory voices began to be heard:

Gen. George S. Patton declared, "The accomplishments of this division have never been equaled. And by that statement, I do not mean in this war; I mean in the history of warfare. There has never been such a superb fighting organization as the 4th Armored Division."

Freed American POWs reported, "The 4th Armored Division is both feared and hated by German frontline troops because of its high combat efficiency."

G.I.s themselves said, "It is the best damned armored division in the European Theater of War."

But before we learn too quickly what this division became, let us first examine how it all started.

The 4th Armored Division was activated on April 15, 1941 at Pine Camp, NY. For nearly a year and a half, the division trained hard all day, even conducting schools at night. During the winter of 1941-42, it experienced intensive cold weather operations.

By early fall of 1942, it was time to move on, and so we cut our ties to Pine Camp and headed for maneuvers in Tennessee. While there, General Wood was reprimanded, ridiculed, and rebuked during weekend critiques of those maneuvers. His superiors told him that he had moved too fast, too far. They informed him that he just could not do it in combat with the enemy shooting, fighting, and attacking, so why was he doing it in Tennessee? He stood his ground and quietly told them, "We can do it, and we will do it." (And we did!)

From Tennessee, we crossed the continent to the Mojave Desert, and its wide-open, unlimited spaces for moving and shooting. Our training was imaginative, realistic, and daring. Who else but the 4th would put a company of tanks in a wadi against another company of tanks, both firing live .30 caliber machine gun rounds at one another? Everyone else might be satisfied with a moving target that was a wooden frame on a sled, but not the 4th. It used a real, honest-to-goodness moving tank at which we fired live .30 calibers.

Then it was on to the shimmering heat of Camp Bowie, Texas, with its great firing ranges, and an opportunity to sharpen our marksmanship with all the weapons in our arsenal. Shortly after our arrival at this Texas base, a 1st Sergeant—apparently jaded by what seemed endless training—was heard to say to a company lieutenant, "I'll bet three months' pay that the 4th Armored Division never sees combat. Damned if we're not running out of places to maneuver."

It was at Camp Bowie that the 4th went through a period of reorganization and become the first light armored division. By this time, too, a unique bond had developed between the members of the division and its commander. The men recognized that they had a very special leader who was deeply and emotionally involved with them. There has never been a division commander before or since who loved every man in his division as he did, and who in turn was loved by every man in that division. No other division commander saluted his men before they had a chance to salute him. This mutual and competitive saluting had a great deal to do with the extraordinary spirit which developed.

Still another important factor in the development of the division was the constant requirement for the division to send out cadres to new units in our ever-expanding army. We moaned at the time, for we had to send out some really top people. But also, and more importantly, we used the cadres to weed out. Providing these cadres gave us an opportunity to sift, cull, refine, polish. When we finally sailed overseas, our barrel was filled with big, red, shiny, juicy, firm apples, with not a rotten one in the bunch.

We said at the time that the 4th would go into battle "a division of non-coms." Because of extensive training, intensive schooling, and opportunity to cadre, many privates also knew the jobs of their corporals and sergeants.

Later, as combat thinned the ranks of officers and non-coms, these individuals would step forward and keep the division going with undiminished efficiency.

We were finally in England, but the training continued unabated on the fields, downs, and lanes of Wiltshire. It was during a dawn attack on the Salisbury Plain that we first heard and then saw the returning, damaged, aerial armada overhead. We knew instantly that the invasion was on and that we would soon be in France. It took time to extend the Normandy bridgehead, but we finally landed at Utah Beach 36 days after D-Day.

It was not long after, in Normandy, that the 4th Armored won its military immortality. It slashed rapidly and aggressively out of a depressingly stalemated situation to seize the tactically and strategically important city of Avranches, a decisive objective that gave access to Brittany on the south and west and to Le Mans, Chartres, and Paris on the east. For us, the action in Normandy was strongly reminiscent of Tennessee. We shouted excitedly at one another, "Just like maneuvers!" (except that our ammunition was live, the incoming fire was real, and the prisoners did not have aggressor armbands, but strange uniforms). The 4th spearheaded the main effort of the VIII Corps, and indeed, all of the U.S. ground forces. The U.S. Army Official History was later to say, " . . . the sensational success of General Wood's 4th Armored Division had exploded the nightmare of static warfare that had haunted the Americans so long in the Cotentin." *(Normandy was a part of France's Cotentin Peninsula.—Ed)*. Despite General Wood's protest that the enemy was to the east, where the war was to be won, his division was ordered SOUTHWEST to seize the Atlantic ports of Lorient, Vannes, and St. Nazaire. The 4th Armored burst out of Avranches and swept across Brittany like the hordes of Ghengis Khan. The Army's Official History later put it most succinctly: "A naturally headstrong crew became rambunctious in Brittany." Wood had already reached the outskirts of the Atlantic ports and had lost much valuable time before he was finally ordered to turn around.

Once the division headed east, it began what was to be an epochal sweep through France. As if to make up for lost time, one combat command left Lorient and moved 264 miles in 34 hours. From that point on, General Patton plotted the strategy and General Wood executed it and became the architect of the rampage through France. For weeks, as the 4th Armored went, so went the Third Army. Wood's vision set the pattern for armor operations in Europe.

His division, operating like cavalry, slashed and sidestepped with speed and surprise. It was confident and cocky, and demonstrated a daring, audacious, hard-riding, fast-shooting style. The 4th bypassed strongly held positions with rapid flanking movements and deep penetrations. When towns or strongpoints could not be bypassed, they were taken in stride with sudden, headlong assaults, bruising power, and violent fire, which broke the enemy. The division wasted no time in rebuilding blown bridges, but found other river crossings instead. It had a restless ardor for pursuit of a defeated enemy. Its outstanding characteristics were its ability to move and shoot, but above all to move. Movement became its middle name, constant momentum its trademark. A German colonel captured during this period, an officer who had commanded units in Russia, exclaimed, " . . . To know the commander of this armored division would explain to me how this army managed to achieve such a speed of advance, which in many instances caught us completely unprepared." During the sweep across France, the Third Army was the south flank of the entire Allied Expeditionary Force; the XII Corps protected the south flank of Third Army, and the 4th Armored was the south flank of XII Corps. There was nothing south of the 4th Armored. General Wood never worried about his flanks; he echeloned in depth. He also developed a long, amazing, unique, and lasting relationship with the Thunderbolts and Mustangs of the XIX Tactical Air Command, which not only supported his operations, but watched his flanks. The teamwork between the XIX TAC and 4th Armored was probably closer in spirit and superior in quality to that of any other operation in WWII, and was not to be equaled again until the Vietnam War 20 years later.

During this period, we moved too rapidly and were too widely scattered for the conventional gathering of commanders for the typically detailed, specific orders. General Wood resorted to oral or "mission-type orders." We received these by radio, or on overlays jeeped in or flown in by artillery spotter planes. The orders consisted of a line of departure, a broad directional arrow (axis of advance), a goose-egg (objective) and the terse order to "get going at first light." That's all we had; that's all we needed. And once when we ran out of maps and orders, all General Wood needed to say was, "Go East!"

After nearly seven weeks of rapid movement and sensational and unprecedented success, the 4th was hit an anvil blow which staggered and slowed it. On the morning of September 19, German armor in two main columns attacked the vanguard of the 4th Armored around Arracourt. Hitler had been trying to accumulate and concentrate armor in front of Patton. He now had the reconstituted Fifth Panzer Army, into which a great portion of German tank production had been poured. The German attacks and counterattacks, which were to be known as the Arracourt tank battles, would for the next nine days result in the biggest tank battles U.S. forces had yet fought in Europe. More than that, it would prove to be a supreme test for General Wood's superbly aggressive division. Could it fight and defend as well as it could raid and pursue?

The furious attacks and counterattacks by the Germans should have been no contest. They were equipped with the new, powerful, sleek, huge Panther tanks. The American low-velocity, 75-mm Shermans were just no match for them.

But tankers of the 4th had already seen serious fighting, honed their skills, acquired experience, and developed outstanding teamwork. They had learned their lessons well and quickly. They exploited their edge in maneuverability to take the Panthers in the side or rear; they fired at tracks to immobilize them; and they used their superior turret power traverse to get well-aimed shots off quicker, better, and faster. On September 19, one combat command alone reported 43 German tanks, mostly Panthers, destroyed or damaged as against losses of five Shermans and three tank destroyers.

By the time the dust had settled at Arracourt and environs, the Germans had suffered a mortal blow. In the most formidable tank attacks since the battles against the British at Caen, the 4th Armored definitely proved itself as admirable a group of warriors in hard, defensive fighting as in the racing pursuit.

Not long after, in a message to General Wood, General Eddy, XII Corps commander, stated, " . . . the Germans are frightened by your superior equipment, frightened by your skillful tactics, and above all, frightened by your magnificent courage and will to win." Soon the rains came to France—constant, heavy rains. Streams and rivers flooded their banks. Water saturated fields became bogs with deep, sticky mud. The 4th Armored Division entered a completely new phase of operations. The division held back initially, pending an exploitation situation, but was quickly committed when the infantry bogged down. "Penny-packet" tactics now replaced massed armor employment. Because of the rain, mud, and terrain, the division had to operate almost on a one-tank front. It was subjected to continuous fighting under almost impossible conditions for armor. The division took its lumps, but amazingly—even with a seriously reduced tank complement and heavy losses among experienced personnel—it continued to grind ahead slowly but steadily. Even under these conditions, captured Lieutenant-General Fritz Bayerlein considered the northward advance of U.S. tanks (4th Armored, XII Corps, Third Army) as a masterpiece of tank warfare, perfectly directed and executed.

Then, without warning, the division received a devastating blow that left it stunned, demoralized and reeling. Word spread like wildfire to all corners of the division that General Wood was relieved of his command. We were told that he was tired and sick and was being sent home for a rest, and that he would be replaced by Maj. Gen. Hugh J. Gaffey, Patton's chief of staff. It was difficult to comprehend that, after all we had been through together, the men and their beloved division commander had parted company. With heavy hearts, we continued to slug it out.

Already beyond exhaustion, but with its nose in the Maginot Line, the 4th was finally relieved by the new and fresh 12th Armored Division to rest, refit, and reorganize. It was not long after, with broken tracks and tank and vehicle parts scattered in and around tiny, French farm villages, and with the rest, refitting and reorganizing still incomplete, when the "fire call" came. We were alerted for a move north where, according to confused reports that reached us, some sort of a German breakthrough had occurred. We rapidly put our vehicles and tanks back together again, packed up, and were soon moving toward a confused situation and parts unknown. Except for brief halts, the lead combat command traveled unceasingly for over 22 hours—half of one night, all day, and half of another night—under blackout conditions. Remarkably, they had travelled 161 miles over frequently difficult roads, without maps and without confusion, to the environs of a city called Bastogne. Such endurance was a tribute to both men and vehicles.

The 4th Armored was the vanguard of what President Nixon, a Patton admirer, later called the greatest mass movement of men in the history of warfare. Patton's troops had been poised to attack the Saar. He then abandoned this plan and ordered the major part of the Third Army to make a gigantic 90-degree wheeling movement and then drive north at full speed. Involved in this spectacular achievement were probably a quarter of a million men and thousands of vehicles, operating in damnable weather over often-icy roads, led by the 4th Armored Division.

There followed five days of bitter fighting. The 4th Armored Division fought day and night; fought German tank counterattacks and fanatical defenses; and even fought snow, ice, and bitter cold. And just before dark on the day after Christmas, 1944, elements of the division succeeded in making contact with "the beleaguered, battered bastards of Bastogne." The dramatic link-up of the two forces, an emotional, historic moment, broke the siege of Bastogne and was one of the great turning points in the Battle of the Bulge and of the war in Europe.

Shortly after, General Patton wrote to General Gaffey, the new division commander, "The outstanding celerity of your movement and the unremitting, vicious, and skillful manner in which you pushed the attack terminating at the end of four days and four nights of incessant battle in the relief of Bastogne, constitute one of the finest chapters in the glorious history of the United States Army."

And from the commanding general of the 101st Airborne Division, Maj. Gen. Maxwell D. Taylor, came these words: "It has been an honor and privilege for this division to serve alongside the 4th Armored Division. If we are ever in a tight spot again, it is our hope that the 4th Armored Division will be sent to get us out."

For three more weeks the division was engaged in operations against fierce German resistance to reduce the Ardennes salient.

Another possible German counterattack was feared, so the 4th was moved south into Luxembourg, where it remained for an extended period of time. When it was thrust back into action, the division embarked on a whole new phase of spectacular achievements that won it even greater glory. It crossed into Germany and quickly made its presence known.

On February 23, 1945, the division helped seize crossings over the Our River in the vicinity of Vianden, and breached the Siegfried Line. Shortly after, it began a drive toward the city of Bitburg. The attack went well and by the end of the month the division had seized the high ground north of Bitburg and occupied the west bank of the Kyll River. Once again the division's advance was so rapid that many prisoners were captured and large amounts of equipment seized.

On March 5, the 4th crossed the Kyll River and in actions so reminiscent and so characteristic of its performance during the early weeks in France, spearheaded the Third Army's advance to the Rhine. This river was reached north of Koblenz on March 7, a distance of 55 miles covered in 48 hours. As a result of this advance, enemy resistance north of the Moselle and west of the Rhine was thoroughly disorganized. At that point, the division was the easternmost unit on the Western Front.

It had come farther and faster to the Rhine than any other outfit. The division's feat electrified the Allies. After a long winter of bitter struggles for gains of yards, the division's 65-mile sweep from Bitburg demonstrated graphically that the lightning warfare of the past summer was still possible. A captured German general, Edgar Rohrich, was heard to say, "I'd ask nothing more of life than a chance to command a division like this 4th which I see here."

On March 15, the division passed through bridgeheads over the Moselle in the Trier area and in 36 hours reached Bad Kreuznach, a distance of 40 miles, thereby outflanking the Siegfried Line, covering the Sarre, and threatening the entire German defensive position in the Palatinate. Shortly after, the division reached the outskirts of Worms, thereby cutting the vital Frankfurt-Sarre lines of communication.

On March 17, General Bradley sent these words to General Patton: "This is the second time in two weeks that this division has broken through the enemy's defenses and contributed so materially to cutting them to pieces. They have both been magnificent operations."

Virtually without halting, the division passed through bridgeheads over the Rhine in the Oppenheim area, and by March 27 had seized bridgeheads over the Main River at Hanau and Aschaffenburg. Still without pause, the 4th continued its dynamic thrust northeast and ever deeper into the heart of Germany. Major General Hoge, who had recently succeeded Major General Gaffey as division commander, received a message from General Eddy, his corps commander, which read, "Your immediate smash beyond the Main, one hundred miles to the northeast into central Germany, proceeded to open the way for a sweeping corps advance and to electrify our nation at home."

Much of the time, during this period, the situation map at General Eisenhower's headquarters showed a finger bulging forward of the front lines. That finger was the Third Army and its tip was the 4th Armored, still the spearhead. Although the terrain, the weather—in fact the total environment—was now vastly different from that of France in the summer and fall of 1944, the rapid movement, the aggressive slashing, hard-riding, fast-shooting, shock-action style of the 4ᵗʰ continued unabated.

As it spurred on its advance, town after town and city after city were left behind—Hungen, Grunberg, Ulrichstein, Schlitz. When the division passed Bad Hersfeld, it moved into what is now East Germany, and in its headlong dash to the east either overran or bypassed a series of major German cities whose names are no longer familiar to Americans. First it was Eisenach and then Gotha. And south of Gotha was Ohrdruf. It was at Ohrdruf that the men of the 4ᵗʰ had an experience that will be imprinted in their minds for the rest of their lives. Elements of the division liberated Ohrdruf-Nord, or North Stalag III, on April 4, the first concentration camp to be liberated by U.S. forces. By this time, men of the 4ᵗʰ were hardened warriors. They had seen death many times, in many different forms, as well as every imaginable type of wound. But what they saw here shocked, stunned, and silenced them. They saw at first hand the brutal evidence of the bestiality of man, and now had a clear vision of the terrible, inhuman Nazi beast that they were fighting so hard to defeat.

With renewed determination, it was time to move on. More major cities fell in their wake—Erfurt, Weimar, Jena, Gera and finally on to Chemnitz (now Karl-Marx-Stadt). As the lead elements of the division were approaching the environs of Chemnitz, the reins were suddenly pulled back tight and they came to an abrupt stop. Unknowingly, in their zeal to keep advancing, they had passed the "restraining line" which had been agreed to by the highest of councils. Ironically, after months of pushing hard, they were now told they had gone too far. Members of the 4ᵗʰ were then at the easternmost point reached by U.S. forces. Here, the command, "Go East" would no longer be given to them.

So after a brief pause—and with the German populace, because of their fear of the Russians, pleading for them not to leave—the division pulled back and then made a 225-mile forced march to the south, skirting the Czech border all the way to a location on the Danube River. From that point, the division attacked to the northeast, through mountain passes, through the Sudetenland, and well into Czechoslovakia. They were stopped once again for political reasons, something the enemy had never been able to accomplish, and this time they finally stopped for good. It was the final stop, for VE Day came soon after. Elements of the 4th met elements of the Russian Army, and subsequently moved to their occupation areas. Thus ended an amazing 10-month odyssey.

A group of ordinary men had done some most extraordinary things. They had led the breakout in Normandy, captured Avranches, swept across Brittany to the Atlantic, turned around, set the pattern for armor operations in Europe, rampaged across France, won one of the great tank battles of the war, made the reckless, wide-open, headlong dash to Troyes, slogged through rain and mud to the Maginot Line, pulled back and made the "fire call" to Bastogne, Belgium, relieved the 101st Airborne, moved back to Luxembourg, spearheaded the Third Army's advance to the Rhine, breached and outflanked the Siegfried Line, liberated the first concentration camp, swept deep into central Germany and reached Chemnitz, the easternmost advance of Allied forces, moved south to the Danube River, pushed aggressively into Czechoslovakia, and met the Russians. No other division moved so fast, ranged so far, or covered so much ground. Three thousand miles were registered on the mileage meters of the 4th Armored Division's forward echelon vehicles, which only moved from one division command post to the next. Combat miles covered by the battalions in the 295 days from Normandy to Czechoslovakia were nearer double the 3,000. The combat troops had an unsurpassed and unforgettable tour of Europe that could never be matched.

In ten months, the division took 90,364 prisoners, killed 13,641 of the enemy, wounded an estimated 30,000 more; destroyed or captured 847 German tanks, 3,668 other vehicles, 603 artillery and anti-tank guns, 1,192 horse-drawn wagons, 103 locomotives; shot down 128 Nazi planes; took scores of major cities and hundreds of towns and villages. The 4th's losses were 1,519 killed, 5,029 wounded and 270 missing. A total of 418 tanks were lost.

Members of the 4th won more than 4,000 individual decorations. Three were Medals of Honor, and there were 34 Distinguished Service Crosses, 802 Silver Stars, 3,031 Bronze Stars, 88 Air Medals, 11 Soldiers Medals, 92 Croix de Guerre. Forty men received battlefield commissions as officers and nearly 6,000 received the decoration grimly known as the "German Markmanship Medal"—the Purple Heart.

The division compiled a record unsurpassed in results achieved as compared to casualties taken. Perhaps there has never been a division that inflicted such discrepant losses upon an enemy. Statistics portray a graphic, remarkable portrait of the division's achievements. Yet, numbers cannot depict the full, complete picture. There is absolutely no way to calculate mathematically the paralyzing effect and the consequences of one of the many armored breakthroughs produced by the 4th. There is no equation yet developed that determines the value of an important piece of ground that has been overrun or a strategic city or bridge that has been captured. Add these elements to the cold statistics and the total reflects a most imposing record.

The Third Army and the 4th Armored have always been mentioned in the same breath. One final, revealing statistic confirms that relationship. Of the Third Army's 281 combat days, the 4th was in Third Army for 280 of them, more than any other division.

Earlier, it was mentioned that the 4th Armored had no formal nickname. Newspapers and magazines had a field day, however, and applied an almost endless number of monikers in their published accounts of the division's exploits. Among the most frequent appellations: "Patton's Best," "Breakthrough," "Patton's Favorite Spearhead," "Crack," "Ubiquitous," "Irrepressible," "Phantom," "Invincible," "Immortal," "Fabulous," "Hard-riding," "Romping."

All of these prompt the inevitable questions: "Why all the accolades?" "Why was this division so different?" and the most often asked, "What made the 4th Armored Division great?"

There are so many intangibles that the answer still remains difficult to box in. Of his men, General Wood said, "I have seen nothing like them in the three wars I was part of, in my time." Yet in 1960, a few years before his death, General Wood himself had difficulty finding an answer to the question. He stated, "I wish I were able to draw up a set of rules for developing a fighting unit like the 4th Armored Division. I am convinced that it was almost unique in its fighting characteristics and esprit, but it did not conform to the rules. In fact, that is perhaps its most outstanding characteristic. Outsiders could never understand what made us so different nor just how we operated." He continued, ". . . But for the production of a fighting organization like the 4th Armored Division, it would be like giving an artist a set of draftsman's rules and a color chart and asking him to produce the Mona Lisa. There is very little science in command—it is merely the most difficult of arts, done with the lightest of touches!"

Although I was a member of this division, the question of greatness has long puzzled me, together with other soldiers, correspondents and historians. What combination of what ingredients gave this division its greatness?

The personnel of the 4th had the same geographic and ethnic mixes, the same age group, the same educational and economic levels, membership in the same strata of our society as all other divisions. Nothing different—no advantage here.

However, I do believe that there were some ingredients that were peculiar to the 4th that gave us a big edge over other divisions. The first of these was training. We were provided with the time and the places. The division had the blizzards of northern New York, the spaces and sand of the Mojave Desert. In between were the rivers, streams and valleys of Tennessee, the great firing ranges at Camp Bowie, and the opportunity for the final tune-up on the Salisbury Plain of England. No division had been exposed to more different facets of training in such a wide variety of locations. By the time it crossed the English Channel, the division was superbly trained, already seasoned, and honed to a razor's edge. No unit could have been more ready for combat than we.

The second ingredient was the demand and requirement to send out cadres. This turned out not to be a disadvantage, but a great advantage, for the division was left with quality troops throughout; individuals who from top to bottom were knowledgeable, experienced, dedicated, professional.

The third ingredient we had that no other division had was Major General John S. Wood. This was a unique, unusual, and truly great leader—undoubtedly the greatest division commander of World War II. Liddell Hart, the eminent British historian, military writer, and critic, referred to him as "The Rommel of the American armored forces . . . one of the most dynamic commanders of armor in World War II and the first in the Allied Armies to demonstrate in Europe the essence of the art and tempo of handling a mobile force." General Wood believed deeply in sparing the men he had the honor to lead unnecessary hardships and useless losses, and possessed the willingness and desire to share their hardships and face the same dangers. The men knew that he referred to them as "my people." His was leadership at its absolute best. He was not only loved and admired, but today is idolized. As Gen. Jacob L. Devers simply stated, "They would follow him to hell today."

The fourth important ingredient that I am sure of was our Army Commander—General Patton. He was the right one for us, and was daring, imaginative, audacious, visionary. But to be successful, he needed the right tool—the 4th Armored. Patton plotted the strategy and Wood executed it. Patton and the 4th—the perfect combination.

Suppose our army commander had been Monty. He would have told us to move three miles and we would have moved three miles in a day. The world would never have known that we could have moved 20, 30, or even 50 miles a day. General Devers knew we could, for he said, "You were always on my left, but we knew you were at the front of Third Army. You did not stop at 5 or 15 miles a day, but went 70 or a few miles less." So we had the right army commander to pull the best out of us—to send us on impossible missions, which we made possible. The fifth ingredient that we had was people. We had Creighton Abrams—"Abe"—who was the hero, the architect of the victory in the tank battles at Arracourt and whose tanks were the first to link up with the 101st. He became the number one soldier in the army, its Chief of Staff, and the one for whom the current main battle tank is named.

There was Bruce Clarke, who left his post as division chief of staff to distinguish himself as a combat commander in the sweep across France. His exploits were rewarded with a promotion and transfer to the 7th Armored Division, where he gained fame in his tenacious defense of the St. Vith area during the Battle of the Bulge. He later became the commander of the United States Army in Europe.

The division had one Lt., (later Capt.) James H. Fields, who won the first Medal of Honor to be awarded in Third Army—"He gave himself first aid by cramming the compress from his first aid packet into his mouth. Holding another compress over his right cheek, he continued shooting with his left hand. When three Panther tanks moved up, Fields shot the tank commander of the lead tank left-handed . . . ."

And who but a cocky member of the 4th would have the audacity, the effrontery—with Germans prowling around him in all directions—to boldly, recklessly announce, "They got us surrounded again, the poor bastards!" Sgt. Constant A. Klinga uttered what was to be an oft-quoted 4th Armored battle cry just outside Avranches. He said it for the last time in Germany, as he was killed beyond the Seigfried Line.

People. Yes, people—thousands of them who were inspired, dedicated, who did everything that was asked of them and more. People who had an easy confidence and were a bit cocky; who took savage satisfaction in their expert use of the shock power given to their division; who turned over at least three times in critical slots and continued to operate with undiminished efficiency; who were motivated always by the highest esprit de corps. People—yes, outstanding people—all of them.

The final two ingredients that the division possessed were spirit and a soul. Early on, the division—because of the attitude and actions of its outstanding leader—developed an indomitable, unquenchable spirit that persisted until the end of the war. It began simply with pride in saluting and from then on manifested itself in every word, move, action. With spirit came a soul. That soul had élan, aggressiveness, the will-to-fight, dash, confidence, audacity, and a debonair, reckless, but ordered, discipline. The soul of the 4th Armored will march forever and will never die.

The ingredients unique to the 4th Armored mentioned above partially explain the question of its greatness, but because of intangibles, speculation among students of World War II will persist and the answer will probably never be fully developed.

We came to one last unique aspect of the division. After significant achievements in the battle across France, General Wood began to receive recommendations for the award of the Presidential Unit Citation for platoons, companies, and battalions that had distinguished themselves during the weeks of combat. He refused to approve any and declared that he would not single out any unit within his division. He said if such an award were to be granted, he would wait until the entire division, as a unit, received it. He showed great prescience and faith in his division.

On March 28, 1945, the *Stars and Stripes* carried a five-paragraph story that stated, "The War Department, by direction of the president, has cited the entire 4th Armored Division for 'extraordinary tactical accomplishment during the period from December 22 to March 27, inclusive'." No one in the 4th saw the story, because the division was then roaring northeast into Central Germany after crossing the Main River.

Nearly three months later, the troopers of the division were dressed in fresh-pressed ODs instead of battle-stained combat jackets, and wore lacquered helmet liners instead of mud-spattered tank helmets. They stood proudly in rigid ranks in Landshut on captured German soil, which they had played such an important role in seizing.

They shivered with emotion as they heard the language of the Presidential Citation echo across the German field. Then, with eyes glued to it, they watched the red and green colors of their beloved 4th Armored Division dip while the four-star general tied the blue streamer of the Distinguished Unit Citation to the staff and then saluted it.

They listened as Gen. Jacob L. Devers, the former commander of the Armored Force, say, "I am proud to present this citation to the 4th Armored, and I say this with a great deal of ego, for I feel I had a part in the training of this division."

So on June 14, 1945, at Landshut, Germany, the 4th Armored became the only tank division and the second entire division in U.S. Army history to be so decorated by the order of the president.

They now stood ready for their finest and last review together. It was to be the first division formation since Camp Bowie, Texas. Once again, they rose to the occasion. After ten months of combat, they were now momentarily parade soldiers again. As the band moved out, unit after unit passed the reviewing stand tightly dressed, in step, with chests fully extended. They marched well and impressively, like the proud veterans they now were. As they left the field, they knew this would be the last time they would be together, that the division would soon begin breaking up. However, they were consoled somewhat by the knowledge that they were marching into the pages of history and would one day occupy their rightful places in the pantheon of combat heroes.

CHAPTER ELEVEN

TANK VERSUS TANK

Reprinted with permission from Military Review: *A Monthly Review of Military Literature from the Command and General Staff School at Fort Leavenworth, Kansas, Volume XXV, Number 10, January, 1946.*

"T he American tank is not nearly as good as the German tank." "Next to the German and Russian tanks, the American tanks are the best in the world."

Quotations, opinions, and comments similar to the two above, which have been widely publicized and which have caused widespread discussion, have been made by various individuals. Because they have, to a certain degree, jumped to hasty conclusions, and because they have helped fashion many erroneous conceptions, I shall attempt in this article to present considerations which they have apparently overlooked, and which may change the outlook of many on American tanks.

In making those statements, what standards did the persons involved use? What were the items and factors that they utilized in making their comparisons?

If they used simply the gun, the weight of the tank, and the width of the track and thereby the flotation of the tank as a criterion, as I am sure they did, then I heartily concur with them that the German Tiger tank is unquestionably superior to the American Sherman tank. The German 88 *is* more powerful than any American tank gun used during the course of most of the war. The German tank *is* much heavier and, therefore, its armor is much thicker than that of any American tank. The tracks of the former *are* much wider, with perhaps a less vulnerable suspension system than that of the latter. If I stop here, as I am convinced so many have, there is no question but that the German tank is a much better one than our own. In this paragraph there is material, indeed, for sensational headlines in newspapers in the States.

Today, however, let us not stop here. Let us go on! What is the fuel capacity of the German Tiger tank? How long and how far is it able to run on a tank full of gasoline? Does it burn much oil? What is the composition and life of its tracks? How many rounds of ammunition is it able to stow? What is the life (discounting its being hit in action) of a Tiger tank? Is its engine comparatively free of maintenance problems? If maintenance problems occur, are they easy to remedy? How long and how much skill is required to change an engine? Is the German tank able to move for long distances and continuous periods at a steady rate of speed? How is its endurance? Could fifty-three Tiger tanks, for instance, move from the vicinity of Fénétrange, France, in the Saar, to an area near Bastogne, Belgium, a distance of 151 miles, in less than 24 hours to answer a fire call as did tanks of the 4th Armored Division? Could a German Tiger tank be used for weeks of training in England, land in France and fight across the widest part of that country to the German frontier, race back to Belgium, retrace its steps again to the German border, and fight its way well into that country before being replaced? Could the German tank roll for several hours at a speed of 25 miles per hour in exploiting a breakthrough?

Did it occur to the critics of the American tank that perhaps questions like those listed above, the answers to which will all heavily favor the American tank, should be considered before a decision is reached? Obviously not. I say most emphatically that such factors *must* be included before a thorough, honest, and fair comparison can be made and a sound and intelligent conclusion reached.

In addition to those just cited, items to be remembered, as well, are tactics employed and required respectively by the Germans and Americans, missions involved, and number of tanks on hand for the operations. To create a true picture of the weaknesses and strengths of the tanks being compared, those things take their places in the line of factors necessary to be examined.

On June 6, 1944, and for many days afterward, while the Germans had the Mark V Panther with a 75-mm gun and a Mark VI Tiger with an 88-mm gun, the American army was equipped with the M-4A1 tank, or the Sherman, as it is popularly known. It will be unnecessary in this article to list all the specifications of that tank except to say that it weighed approximately 30 tons and had a 75-mm gun. Its tracks were narrow and consisted of three different types: steel, flat rubber and rubber chevron.

During the initial period in Normandy just after the invasion, when engagements were toe-to-toe slugfests, battles with tanks fighting tanks were common. Soon, however, the deadlock broke and American tanks streaked to and through Avranches and hustled across Brittany. Without stopping for breath, the tanks continued on their way across most of France.

In order to keep rolling over hot roads for long, dusty miles for days on end, a light, mobile tank was needed which the terribly extended supply line could adequately furnish with precious gasoline. To withstand the terrific beating the tank was taking hour after hour, it was necessary for it to have a simple yet tough and efficient engine and mechanical system. The fact that the American tanks rolled with but few maintenance problems, and those rapidly attended to by the tank crew alone or by company, battalion, or division maintenance, all of which were close enough behind to repair the vehicle rapidly and send it immediately back into action, testifies to the excellence of the tank. Thus, tank units were still at full tank strength and functioning efficiently when they reached as far east as the Meuse River early in September after moving and fighting consistently day after day from the Normandy peninsula. They stopped then only because they had moved too fast and too far and were forced to wait a few days until their supplies could reach them in large enough quantities to send them ahead again. During that phase of operations, a group of tanks had made a forced march of 258 miles in 38 hours and arrived in good enough shape to have continued on had the situation warranted it.

In discussing tanks, many forget that the tank is *not* a vehicle built primarily to fight other tanks. Rather, its mission above all others is to get into the enemy's rear areas, to disorganize him, to destroy supply and communications, and generally to wreak havoc there. This is done mainly with its .30 caliber machine guns, especially the one mounted coaxially, and with high-explosive fire from the tank cannon. The tank cannon's chief function, however, is to protect the tank while it is disrupting, exploiting, and destroying the enemy. Of course, very, very often a few well-placed shots from the tank cannon will be much more effective than the .30 caliber machine guns, and therefore the cannon is used very frequently in offensive action.

The tank served its primary mission gloriously in that dash through France. Its opponent was dazed, disorganized, and on the run. Most of his equipment was "thin skinned," and was "duck soup" for our tanks. The .30 caliber fire and 75-mm high explosive fire, for good measure, was plenty good enough to leave much of the German army equipment and personnel strewn by the wayside.

A factor rarely considered, yet on occasion vitally important, is the type of bridge that a Sherman can use to cross a stream or river. Many bridges that are adequate for the American tank would pose a knotty problem for the German tank. The bridge would have to be much wider and much stronger, and would require a great deal of time and more facilities to construct. Many bridges intact and able to accommodate the lighter American tank would deny passage to the heavy, lumbering Tiger.

Hardly a critical word was heard concerning the American tank in those days. The reason obviously was that it was plenty good for the task at hand. The tank was accomplishing an ideal tank mission in a superior fashion, and it seemed to have been built for just that kind of job. During the summer and fall of 1944, the Sherman performed to perfection and brought the Allied armies within scent of the German frontier.

It was late in 1944 that the American tank became the target for taunts and criticism. Forgotten quickly were the results it had gained just a month or two before. In October, November, and December the ground became a sticky morass; the war was stabilized and no great advances were being made. The war was bloody and difficult, slow and discouraging. For every yard wrested from the enemy, tremendous effort had to be exerted.

During this stage of the war, the tanks could not perform as they had earlier. Rather, they were forced to fight tank versus tank. Here the German had a tremendous advantage. He was fighting defensive warfare. The terrain was admirably suited for him. It was rough, and this enabled him to pick the key terrain features on which to post his men and vehicles. The ground was so muddy that advancing, attacking elements could not maneuver, could not outflank. They had to slug it out toe to toe, face to face. Without a doubt the tank of the Germans was ideally suited for such a fortunate turn in the war for them. The tank could pick dominating ground, and with its huge gun and thick armor proved to be a roving pillbox par excellence. On many occasions it picked off American tanks as they floundered in the mud in an effort to gain valuable ground and dislodge their adversary. It was during those trying days that many an American tanker and those that observed him began to lose faith in the Sherman. The tanker was forced to move very slowly because of the muck, and very, very often he spotted a German tank, fired first, and scored a hit only to see his 75-mm shot glance off the enemy tank, causing absolutely no damage to it. The 75-mm gun proved to be comparatively ineffective during this chapter of the war. At 1,000 yards to 1,500 yards it could be effective, and a single tank has knocked out five Panther tanks with six shots. Yet to get that close to a German tank made the Sherman vulnerable indeed. Many tanks were lost in endeavoring to get in close, which was necessary in order for them to strike a telling blow. The absence of an effective armor-piercing shell proved to be a terrific handicap, as well. Thus, during that siege, the American tank was impotent when running into the German tank head-on. As a result, many a Sherman was lost even after it had shot first and scored the first hit. That was when the seeds of dissatisfaction in the American tank were sown and when much faith was lost.

It must be remembered that the German tank had everything its way. It was fighting a defensive game, the terrain was in its favor, and the wet ground played into its hands.

Still, it must not be forgotten that though the cards were stacked against the American tank, it defeated the enemy and gained the desired ground. Though the Shermans were easily bested tank for tank, they could always bank on a numerical superiority, which fact was considered in tactics and strategy employed. By banding together and maneuvering, they were able to dislodge and knock out the heavier German tank. Even during those days, one German tank knocked out for one American tank was a poor score. It was in most cases three to one, four to one, and five to one in favor of our side.

One must not forget that the German requirements and our own were totally different. They were fighting a slow war, a defensive war where they picked their spots. They had fewer tanks than we, so their tactics, of necessity, had to be different. We were fighting an offensive war, we were hurrying to get it over with, we wanted to shake loose, and we had many tanks with which to do it. Virtually never did a scrap take place with fifty German tanks against fifty American or twenty against twenty. The proportion was usually five American to one German, even ten to one, rarely if ever less than two to one. So it must be made clear to anyone comparing the tanks of the two nations that, as I said before, throughout the campaigns the requirements and needs were different. We could not use nor did we want a lumbering, heavy, mobile pillbox type of tank, and we could not have done what we did if we were so equipped. Then again we had numbers upon which to fall back, and we considered that in our tactics. Mechanically we had a tank that performed superbly, and after groaning and grunting through heavy, sticky mud for weeks on end, it still was running at the end of this phase.

There is no denying that in those hectic days a tank such as our newest Sherman with a wider track and a more potent gun would have saved many American lives and tanks and would have knocked out more enemy tanks, and more quickly, too. During that period, and that period alone, the American tank was discredited, criticized, and found lacking. The situation was hastily remedied, but for many it was a little late.

The closing days of 1944 and the early part of 1945 found a new type of Sherman joining the ranks of American tanks and replacing its tired brothers. Although it has no additional armor and weighs but a ton or two more, it arrived on the scene with a potent, long-tubed 76-mm gun with muzzle brake and high muzzle velocity that makes it effective at much longer ranges than the 75-mm. As a result, it is not necessary for the new tank to get as close in as the old tank before becoming effective. A new type of high-velocity, armor-piercing shell was added for the gun and gives it far greater penetrating qualities.

The new tank has an engine with a higher horsepower, which, in addition to an increase in power, makes it capable of higher speeds. Its track is much wider and has a new type track suspension system, which gives it more stability and cross-country mobility with which to combat adverse ground conditions. The tank has the traditional endurance of American tanks and rolls consistently for endless miles. It goes ninety miles and often more on a tank full of gasoline.

The tank is characteristically simple, as such equipment goes, and the tank crew alone is able to maintain its vehicle for long periods. New men in tank crews catch on to their jobs quickly, which is one important factor in making our tank crews superior to those of the Germans and explains why our armor operated most of the time at topnotch efficiency. One last advantage, though minor in discussion, was extremely valuable to the tank crew—the turret with two hatches. Also, the new Sherman, like the old, had the potent .50 caliber antiaircraft gun, which proved so effective against enemy planes and which played havoc with dug-in Germans.

All in all, the new type Sherman is a marvelous tank. It answered the prayers of the tankers and was on hand to drop the curtain on one of the dirtiest and hardest phases of the European war. It was the new tank with all the advantages of the old one and many new qualities that did the racing in Germany, Austria, and Czechoslovakia, and finished the war in a blaze of glory. Mounted in that tank, no American tanker was afraid to take on any tank that faced him. If only the new type of tank could have been produced and brought to the front lines sooner!

German tanks, on the other hand, are not what they are cracked up to be. Their heavy armor was a hindrance rather than an asset. The tanks could not carry on the same kind of offensive warfare that our tanks did. With their heavy armor and complicated mechanism they were tank destroyers and not tanks.

Even though the German tanks were much heavier and thicker than ours, their armor was centralized. Most of it was on the front slope plate and turret. Sides and rear were often vulnerable, and how we capitalized on that!

The armor on German tanks was generally poor. It often cracked on impact, leaving ragged, gaping holes, whereas the holes in our tanks were clean, circular, and easily repairable.

The Germans developed a gun with a high muzzle velocity and an effective armor-piercing projectile. To do this they sacrificed space in the tank, for they had to increase the size of the shell and thus could not stow many rounds.

It must be mentioned that once again the Germans lost sight of the purpose and function of a tank and thought primarily of destroying other tanks. Still, though our muzzle velocity was less than theirs, our high-explosive fire was just as effective. Of the two, the high-explosive fire was for us the more important consideration.

Mechanical advantages of the German tank over our own were few. The interiors of their tanks were not nearly as well equipped as ours, and it took altogether too much maintenance to keep a German tank rolling.

Still another item often overlooked is that it was necessary for us to carry an adequate basic load of ammunition and gasoline in our tanks, for to replace what we used we had to call upon trucks that had to travel over a long, dangerous supply route. The Germans, on the other hand, sat close in many of their defensive positions to their ammunition and other supply. It might astonish some to know that prisoners of war claimed that some of their large tanks had a running time of a mere two and a half hours on a full vehicular load of gasoline. Thus, the tanks did not have the endurance nor the cruising ranges of our tanks. Therefore, in many instances they had to be transported by rail virtually to the front lines, unloaded, and put into the battle. How far could we have gone with our tanks if we had had to follow a procedure like that?

Not yet mentioned is the power traverse with which American tanks are equipped. It is one of the very important reasons why so many of our tanks bested the German tanks. Of course, it may have been that our gunners and car commanders were superior to the Germans, and that the excellence of our tankers provided us with the upper hand. We agree to that, yet it is felt that of inestimable advantage to our tankers was the distinct handicap under which the German tankers labored because of a lack of a 360-degree power traverse comparable to ours. Because of that important disadvantage, they were slow firing and in many cases got off one round to our three or four. Instances have occurred where a Tiger tank lay hidden, waited in ambush, and fired the first shot at advancing American tanks and missed! The mistake was fatal, for American tanks maneuvered about it and with their rapid fire destroyed the German tank.

By means of the 360-degree power turret traverse with which all our tanks are equipped, a tank gunner is able to swing his gun in any direction in a second or a fraction thereof. The average American tank gunner can lay on a German tank, is able to get the first round off, and can usually score the first hit. The power traverse enabled American tanks to move down roads at high speeds shooting from one side of the road to the other. In this manner enemy infantrymen and bazooka teams were killed or pinned down as the tanks rolled by. The power traverse has been such an advantage and of so much importance that it is immeasurable.

At the moment, virtually every tank battalion is nearly completely equipped with the new type Sherman tank technically called the M4A3-E8. Of all the tanks operating today, that one, in my estimation, is the best there is. I would choose it above all others. Many, many experienced combat tankers feel exactly as I do. The tank will go faster and will live longer than the German Tiger. The Sherman burns less gas and oil and, as a result, is able to go much farther on a tank full of gasoline. Its maintenance problems are few and far between and are easily remedied. It is an easy matter to change an engine, which takes little more than four hours and which beats all hollow the best time for the Germans. It has a good gun, and good ammunition for it. It does not take much to tow one of our tanks that is disabled, but a huge vehicle is required for the German Tiger, and often German tanks had to be abandoned because huge vehicles were not available. Yes, considering all factors, I believe that even the most prejudiced or the one most difficult to convince will nod toward the Sherman.

The Sherman must give ground to the Tiger when the size of the gun and the thickness of armor is considered. The tanker knows and takes for granted that if his tank is hit by an 88 it will be penetrated. He also knows that the addition of a few tons of armor will not stop an 88. He respects, and always will, the German gun and the thick armor, but he will never swap his tank for those advantages. To build a tank that would stop an 88 shell would be to lose a tank and gain a lumbering steel pillbox with no mobility left. It has been said, practically speaking, that the only thing that will stop an 88 is "cease fire." Similarly, to stop our 76 with high-velocity, armor-piercing ammunition, the enemy will need a mighty heavy tank, indeed.

Once again, let us not forget that the Americans fought an offensive, fast, deceptive, and *winning* war. We crushed our adversary; therefore the tanks which spearheaded the victories must have been good. Tank for tank, toe to toe, we were outclassed. But that was not our way of fighting. For the person still not convinced I suggest that he tabulate the count of American tanks knocked out by German tanks and vice versa, and I am sure that he will discover, perhaps to his amazement, that the scale will swing heavily in our favor.

Not long before the curtain dropped on hostilities in Europe, the American General Pershing tank made its bow. It has a 90-mm gun, weighs forty-six tons, has a different suspension system, and has a low silhouette. It is said that here is a tank that incorporates all the advantages of the Sherman tank, and with its new additions makes it superior to the German Tiger in *every* respect. As far as my personal knowledge goes, I must reserve my opinion until later, for that tank is comparatively untried.

I will say to the persons that have so glibly sold our tank down the river that there is more to it than meets the eye.

CHAPTER TWELVE

PATTON REVISITED

Written by Brig. Gen. Albin F. Irzyk. Reprinted with permission from ARMOR *Magazine, March-April 1995.*

After battling a tenacious, sometimes fanatic enemy; heavy, incessant rains; sleet, snow, cold, and deep and unforgiving mud during November 1944 in Lorraine, the 4th Armored Division in early December had reached Singling in the Maginot Line, only a stone's throw from the German border.

Here, exhausted men and machines were relieved by a fresh 12th Armored Division—a most fortuitous decision by someone in light of following events.

For its rehabilitation in the rear, my 8th Tank Battalion was assigned the town of Domnom-lès-Dieuze, about 15 kilometers west of Fénétrange, and barely 2 kilometers north of the Fénétrange/Dieuze road.

Domnom was a small, dismal, bleak, depressing town. The 8th arrived on yet another gray, rainy, cold, damp, miserable, penetrating day.

The manure piles in front of the half-home, half-barn structures were being soaked by the falling rain, which drained off into the gutters. The town was an altogether disheartening sight and prospect.

How this tiny town could absorb the men and vehicles of a tank battalion was the vexing question. But it has long been accepted that one sign of a good outfit is the rapidity with which it gets dug in. And very soon the units of this outfit had found billets for their men and "spaces" for their vehicles.

It was not long before, all over town, broken tracks were lying on the ground, engine compartments were open, spare parts, tools, cleaning equipment—all the telltale signs of an armored outfit—were strewn around, as men worked furiously to get back into shape.

Late on the afternoon of the third day, I had an urgent message from my combat command, CCB, informing me that I would have yet another visitor, and it would be early the next morning. This was not just any visitor, but the MAN himself, the army commander, Lt. Gen. George S. Patton, Jr.

I was told not to make any special preparations for the visit, to keep the men doing what they had been doing, and to be on hand in the town square at 0900 to greet the general upon his arrival.

I immediately sent word out to the companies about the next day's visitor, and told them to continue their activities, as scheduled.

Of course, the word spread like wildfire, faster even than a hot rumor. The visit of old "Blood and Guts" to THEIR battalion became the exclusive topic of conversation at each of the mess trucks that evening. The comments and banter about the upcoming visit of the "Old Man" were amusing and G.I. "classic."

The next morning, December 11, was definitely not Domnom weather—it was sunny, bright, pleasant, undeniably Patton weather.

I immediately faced a wee bit of a problem. There was really no town square in tiny Domnom-lès-Dieuze. As I glanced about, I noted the small, paved, open area outside the entrance to the village church, where the town folks gathered before Mass. Since the church was about in the middle of the main street, this spot would just have to serve as the town square. It is here that I positioned myself well before 0900.

As I waited, I glanced all about me. Everywhere I looked, the men were hard at work—every bit as busy as they had been the day before. There was one big difference: periodically, a man here, one there would lift his head expectantly with a quick, furtive glance in my direction—then back to work. Things seemed perfectly normal—but they weren't. There was an air of great expectancy—an undercurrent of excitement—totally invisible, but very much there.

Still one more time, I glanced at my watch. The hand had reached the five-minute mark after nine. Suddenly, I was startled to hear a loud scre-e-e-e-e-ch way down the street, where the road from the main highway makes a sharp 90-degree turn into Domnom.

A jeep was trying to negotiate that sharp turn at high speed. It careened on two wheels, then righted itself, and without slackening speed, continued to streak toward me. A figure was standing in the jeep beside the driver, clutching the top of the windshield. Since he approached from the west, the early morning sun hit him squarely—like a huge spotlight zeroing in. But he was not dazzled; he did the dazzling. As he approached me, he reflected the sun—he actually sparkled. As he got closer—I knew the reason. I saw stars: three on the front of the shiny, highly lacquered helmet liner, three stars on each wing of his collar, three stars on each shoulder of his "Ike Jacket," three stars on his riding crop, three stars on the red, metal bumper plate, three stars on the small, gold-fringed pennant, which had been waving furiously from its holder on the bumper—there must have been 24 stars, at least. This was vintage Patton—the showman, the headline-grabber, the press favorite, the flamboyant army general—but, also, the army commander esteemed and held in awe by his men.

As it reached me, the jeep screeched loudly again—this time as it came to a sharp, abrupt stop. I saluted smartly. Behind me three huge farm animals the size of Clydesdales, previously unnoticed by me because of the excitement, who had been drinking at a trough, backed away, apparently startled by the noisy arrival. They turned and began lumbering up the street.

With a wide, crooked grin, exposing some bad-looking teeth, General Patton returned my salute and announced loudly, "Ha, ha—I see that I've started a cavalry charge." With that he hopped out of his jeep and moved briskly up the street with me in tow and about a half step behind. He stopped at every vehicle, at every cluster of soldiers, and had something to say to each—a question, a word of encouragement, of appreciation, a compliment, a wisecrack, a good-natured dig. In an instant he had established total and complete rapport with these men. They were literally eating it up. He was a master at it. His stops were brief, and he kept moving. But in 30 minutes or so, he had "touched" virtually every man in that battalion. Those who were located in the back buildings or side streets had darted up for at least a "peek." His jeep had slowly followed him up to the far end of the street. Now he had it turned around. He slapped me on the shoulder, and exclaimed loudly, "Keep up the great work!"

Then he hopped up onto his jeep, grabbed the windshield again, and as the jeep started moving, returned my salute. The vehicle quickly accelerated and headed back in the direction from which it came and at the same speed. He stood ramrod straight, clutching the windshield with one hand, waving to the troops on both sides with the other— perhaps unconsciously emulating and reenacting the triumphant roll-bys of the Roman conquerors, about whom he had read so much, and with whom he empathized. The troops, of course, stood rooted to the ground, transfixed, bug-eyed. Then, with another screeching 90-degree turn, he was gone.

I was amazed at the tremendous impact that one man can have on a body of men. After his visit, troopers of the 8th worked furiously all day, as if with renewed energy, almost like the elves in the workshop after being visited by Santa, who had vigorously nodded his approbation. The men, as they worked, talked about nothing else all day, and as time passed the tales began to grow—some would eventually expand to legendary size, somewhat like the proverbial fish story.

The visit made the men almost ecstatic. There was no question now but that the army commander knew who they were, what they were doing, and what they had achieved, and had indicated his appreciation and approval of their efforts. There is almost nothing in the world like pride, and they were handed a big dose this day.

The visit became even sweeter when they learned that the only units of the 4th Armored visited by General Patton were CCB headquarters and the 8th.

The man who had visited them, although he had an abundance of color, was not merely a showboat. He had tremendous substance. He would soon prove that convincingly, for little did he know on this day that he and the battalion he had visited would in just one week have a great rendezvous with destiny.

A week later, on December 18, units of the Third Army had orders to attack east. I had sent billeting parties forward to set up billets for use after the 8th Tank Battalion's approach march the next day, to be followed by the attack into Germany.

At 1700, the move to the east was cancelled. At 2300, the 8th was ordered to be prepared to move at once—to the NORTH! At 0050 on the 19th, the I.P. was crossed, and the tanks and men and the commander he had visited on the 11th were leading his army on the long, treacherous, momentous, historic move to Bastogne (elements of that battalion, after traveling over 160 miles, would be IN and OUT of Bastogne the next day, the 20th).

For Patton, a truly remarkable achievement! He had his army poised and prepared to move east to cross the border and attack into Germany. In a matter of hours, he turned many thousands of men and thousands of vehicles ninety degrees from east to north—to move NOT into Germany, but into Belgium, instead.

Years later, President Nixon, a great Patton admirer, would claim that that was the greatest mass movement of men in the shortest period of time in the history of warfare.

Now, let's "fast forward." The war is over—it has been over for three months. The fighting Third Army is now an occupation army. Its combat commander is now military governor of Bavaria.

The 8th Tank Battalion is still in Third Army. I am the kreis (County) commander of Kreis Vilsbiburg, east of Munich.

Late on the afternoon of August 9, I am called by division head-quarters with unusual instructions. I am to take with me a lieutenant who has served as a combat tank platoon leader, a captain who has served as a combat tank company commander, and to report to General Patton the next day to discuss tank operations.

Of course, not knowing what to expect or what questions might be asked, I worked feverishly all evening trying to prepare myself for the visit.

The next day, we drove to Third Army headquarters at Bad Tolz, south of Munich in a beautiful sector of Bavaria.

At 1300, I reported to Gen. Hobart (Hap) Gay, General Patton's chief of staff. General Gay greeted me most warmly, and had a staff officer usher us to the meeting place.

We entered through the back door of what appeared to be a small briefing room. There were folding chairs in rows. Scattered in the rear of the room were staff officers, apparently gathered to witness what was to take place.

We were directed to seats in the front row. Stretching in front of us, almost the width of the room, was a wooden table.

Just moments after we had been seated, a door opened behind the table, and in strode General Patton, leading his dog, Willie, on a leash, accompanied by General Gay and the aide. As General Patton moved into the room, I inwardly gasped in surprise. The figure entering the room was far different from the sparkling, flamboyant, star-bedecked individual who had visited my battalion at Domnom-lès-Dieuze—just before our trek to the Bulge.

This was a subdued, aging gentleman—older-appearing than his 60 years.

He had aged perceptibly in the intervening months. I was struck by two pones on his chest, which appeared to be heaving slightly as he breathed. He paused momentarily, smiled his crooked smile, warmly greeted us, and told us to be seated. He was carrying a blue-lined tablet and a couple of pencils.

He sat down behind the table and immediately began asking questions and making notes on his tablet as he received answers. The thrust of his questions and the discussion were about how his tankers had gone about knocking out German tanks—how the lieutenant, the tank platoon leader, had employed and utilized his five tanks, the tank company commander his 17 tanks, and I my 70 plus tanks. This, of course, required a broad discussion of tank operations and tank tactics.

Time passed quickly. The discussion—questions and answers—flowed smoothly. In no time, it seemed, the shadows outside the windows began to lengthen. The afternoon was over. With that, General Patton rose, warmly thanked us for coming, and strode out of the room.

The instant the door had closed behind him, I realized that I had just been treated to a rare, incomparable, unforgettable experience.

This General Patton had been quiet, patient, kindly, gentle, warm, thoughtful, serious, deeply interested, and low key.

The session just completed reminded me of an aging college professor conducting a seminar for a small group of selected students. There was not a trace or whisper of flamboyance or bravado or a dominant personality.

I was now aware that I had been with and witnessed at close hand two Pattons—the Actor and the Man—the Actor at Domnom-lès-Dieuze and the Man at Bad Tolz. And today I had spent the afternoon in the company of a General Patton that most of the world had never seen—would never see—and did not know. This man on this day did not fit the pattern, could not step into the mold that he, himself, and the world had fashioned for him. For me, it was a most extraordinary, never-to-be-forgotten experience.

I would often wonder, but would never know, the fundamental reason for this meeting—why this great armor officer, this already famous army commander, would spend an afternoon discussing small unit tank tactics.

I wondered if it were, perhaps, to satisfy some curiosity. He was a fabulously successful army commander—widely credited with being an armor genius—whose skillful use of tanks had resulted in wide sweeps and rapid advances—whose tanks had brought mobility, maneuver, and movement to the battlefield, thus appreciably shortening the war. In many circles, he was already conceded to be the greatest FIELD commander this country had ever had.

Yet, he knew full well that his successes would not have been achieved had it not been for those individual tanks out front. When references were made to Patton's tanks, they were really talking about my tanks and those of the other two tank battalions in the 4th Armored Division, as well as the tanks in his other armored divisions.

So it was about those individual tanks out front that the discussion this day ranged. Those individual tanks were really his army's building blocks. And how those building blocks operated against the enemy determined the success of his army. If the tanks were held up, stopped, that huge Goliath—Third Army—was stopped. Conversely, as they moved, so moved his army.

So perhaps on this day, General Patton had simply wanted to study and talk about the actions of his building blocks, which had helped make his army so successful and him a world famous military leader. Certainly, he had mapped the strategy, and with his sixth sense, his great battle sense, he sometimes asked the impossible. And we implemented that strategy and often did the impossible. Or, perhaps, he was gathering material for another of his issues of "Lessons Learned" or "After-Action Reports." Or he may have been gathering background for a book.

I would never know the real reason. But I DID know that on this afternoon I had had a profoundly moving, unique, rich, rewarding, never-to-be-forgotten experience.

To my great surprise and dismay I would learn that, not long after my visit to Bad Tolz, because of what his seniors considered intemperate, injudicious, and inappropriate remarks about the Russians and Germans, General Patton was relieved of command of his beloved Third Army, and assigned to head a "paper" army.

Incredibly, merely four months after my session with General Patton at Bad Tolz, that great soldier was dead! BUT astonishingly, over half a century later, that figure is vivid, vibrant, and still lives.

CHAPTER THIRTEEN

WHEN THE COLD WAR ALMOST BECAME HOT

Written by Brig. Gen. Albin F. Irzyk. Reprinted with permission from Army *magazine, July 2004.*

Many words have been written, documentaries produced and books published about the Cuban Missile Crisis of October, 1962. Yet an extremely dangerous situation not nearly as well known but of critical import prevailed not in Cuba, but in Europe a year earlier, in 1961. As in 1962, a direct and troubling face-off occurred between the United States and the Soviet Union. It became known as the Berlin Crisis. That situation came to a head and reached a crisis point in August of that year. It became by far the tensest period of the Cold War up until then. The Russians and Americans could have come as close to World War III as they did a year later. Despite the seriousness of the situation, relatively little is known about the details of that historic episode, and comparatively speaking, little has been written about it.

Before discussing that troubling and dangerous situation, some background information is appropriate. Early in the month of August, as it had for more than a decade, my command, the 14th Armored Cavalry Regiment, was broadly deployed along the East-West German border, better known as the Iron Curtain. The 14th was a light, fast, mobile armored force of more than 4,500 men that was a combined arms team. It was equipped with tanks, jeeps, mortars, helicopters and fixed-wing aircraft. Its regimental headquarters was located at Fulda, little more than 8 miles from the border and about 60 miles northeast of Frankfurt. Elements of the regiment were spread widely along the border with a squadron to the north, one in the center and another to the south, and an attached squadron even further to the south.

The 14th shouldered tremendous responsibilities, for the missions assigned to it were critically important. The regiment had two main missions. First, it was responsible for conducting ground and aerial surveillance of more than 165 miles of that border—the Iron Curtain. Second, it was the NATO trip wire.

The border over which we had to conduct surveillance separated the west from the east—U.S. troops from those of the Soviet Union. The border markings consisted of small stones imbedded in the ground that went north and south in a very irregular pattern. Since they lay along open terrain, through woods, gullies and ridges, they were difficult to follow and identify. To make the border more distinctive, more readily recognized, prominent five-foot-high, red-topped, white wooden poles were installed.

For the Soviets the purpose of the border was not only to separate us from them, but by erecting an impenetrable barrier it also would prevent East Germans from fleeing to the West for sanctuary. (Over the years, many East Germans were killed or captured attempting to penetrate that barrier.) There were several elements to the barrier located just inside the east zone. The Soviets installed observation towers at strategic locations that were always manned and included automatic weapons capable of producing deadly and withering fire along the border to the north and south of the towers. In addition, they installed a steel mesh fence (iron curtain), barbed wire, mines and mortars, and maintained a regularly ploughed strip about five meters wide (ostensibly to show footprints if East Germans had attempted to flee). For the Soviets, it was a protective barrier from both the West and East.

We performed our surveillance missions on the ground with jeep patrols and in the air with helicopters and fixed-wing aircraft. The jeep patrols rode the border day and night, during all types of weather—

rain, sleet, bitter freezing winter days, hot stifling summer days. Sundays, Thanksgiving and Christmas were merely duty days.

Because many places along the border were inaccessible to jeeps, troopers frequently had to dismount and walk or crawl to appropriate vantage points. It was here that large numbers of U.S. and Soviet soldiers were lined up close to one another, literally face-to-face. It was not unusual to find a trooper peering out, only to find opposite him a Russian peering in.

Augmenting the jeep patrols, observation posts were also used for border surveillance. These were placed at strategic locations that provided a particularly good look into the east and were well concealed. Such outposts were often manned for some hours and provided an opportunity for more lengthy and detailed observation. Both the jeep patrols and the placement of observation posts had an irregular pattern and any kind of set schedule or routine was avoided. The responsibilities of the troopers of the 14th were demanding, dangerous, critical and sensitive. Their operations were as close as one could get to combat without actually being in it.

One permanent observation post was established early on and remained in place until the end of border duty. It would be known as O.P. Alpha (Observation Post Alpha). It provided the best and most breathtaking view of the Fulda Gap. From O.P. Alpha one could look for miles in all directions, particularly to the hills and mountains to the east, but most impressively one almost believed that if he reached down he could touch the broad, beautiful valley that flowed from the east right into the center of the 14th's positions.

The eyes that penetrated most deeply into the Soviet sector were located in the helicopters and fixed-wing aircraft that flew the border. Only inclement weather coming from the hills and mountains to the east prevented daily aerial patrols. Those were conducted by extremely skilled pilots. The border was difficult to follow as it zigzagged through all types of terrain, often with sharp deviations. Because of this challenge, before they were cleared to fly the border, pilots had to complete a thorough and detailed period of instruction and orientation. They flew the border time and time again, accompanied by an instructor, before they were permitted to fly it alone. The pilots fully realized that if they strayed across the border to the east side, they could receive hostile fire and create an international incident. Each helicopter and plane flew with an observer. As the pilot kept his eyes intently on the course he was flying, the observer's eyes stared widely and deeply to the east. The purpose of the ground and aerial patrols was to detect any unusual movement or activity across the border and to note any suspicious physical changes that had been made.

For the 14th Armored Cavalry Regiment to be called the NATO trip wire was not hyperbole but a truism. The regiment's mission placed it firmly and directly astride the famous, fabled, historic Fulda Gap. It was at this point that the east butted farthest into West Germany. This was the ancient invasion corridor, which had served as the strategic east-west passage for six centuries. In 1961, it was still the likely invasion route into Western Europe for Soviet Bloc forces. This is the frontier where it would happen. The Fulda Gap is a series of river valleys running north and south with distinct hill masses and several open passes running through the hills that create the Gap and that wind like a huge serpent, twisting here and there to avoid rivers and forests. The gap broadens into an exceedingly wide ten-mile-long valley north of a town called Rasdorf. This valley is capable of accommodating vast numbers of mechanized and motorized vehicles. Dominant hills— known as the Three Sisters—create a natural line of defense. From O.P. Alpha near Rasdorf, the panorama that unfolds is truly spectacular.

The troopers of the 14th had no illusions about the criticality and importance of their trip-wire mission and its ramifications. Every man in the regiment was fully aware that if the Soviets decided to attack and send their hordes across the border, we would be the first of the U.S. and Allied forces to be fired upon—thus, the trip wire. It would immediately signal to the United States and the world that the West and East were at war.

Because ours was a small and relatively light force, it was a foregone conclusion that we had absolutely no chance of stopping such an onslaught and would rapidly be overrun. Realistically, our mission was to delay their advance and gain time by fighting fiercely, imaginatively, courageously—even to the last man. By slowing the enemy and gaining time, it would enable heavier forces behind us, the first of which was the 3rd Armored Division, to close up, pick up, and join in the fight.

At that time Gen. Lauris Norstad, commander of NATO forces, had under his command 22 divisions with several that were badly understrength. Conversely, the Russians had a massive ground force. According to NATO intelligence estimates, the Soviet Bloc could field 60 powerful divisions almost immediately and 130 within a month. That is an absolutely staggering statistic. Thus, at least on paper, it would have been no contest.

To prepare for the eventuality and execution of our mission, we at the 14th had painstakingly examined, over a period of time, virtually every foot of terrain along and behind the border. From such extensive reconnaissance efforts we selected the absolutely best defensive positions, designated specific units that would occupy and fight from those positions and determined the fastest, quickest and best routes to them. As part of their training, units moved frequently to their positions until every man was as familiar with them as with the back of his hand.

A real test occurred once a month. We were alerted by 7th Army headquarters to move to our tactical positions with a simple call to the regimental duty officer. The alert would come on any day of the month and at any hour—day or night. The most demanding test came when the alert was called during the early hours of the night—1:00 AM to 2:00 AM. Upon receiving the call, the duty officer had to get the word immediately to the far-flung squadrons and separate companies and receive an acknowledgment. At every location, lights went on, alarms sounded, troopers were routed out of beds in barracks, homes and apartments. There was furious and frenzied activity. Every individual, wherever located, would immediately dress in his combat gear, which

was always ready. Troopers on foot at a gallop or in cars would race to the motor pools. In no time engines were running and gear was being stowed. Each unit reported to regiment when it was assembled and moving to its positions. It reported again when it was fully deployed and occupying those positions. The moment the last unit was in place, the regiment notified 7th Army. That headquarters timed the exercise from the moment the regimental duty officer had acknowledged the call until the final regimental report was received. That concluded the alert.

Those monthly alerts were realistic, superb exercises and tests. During each alert, the regiment tried to improve on its previous times, always hoping to set a new record. This self-imposed competition contributed greatly to constantly maintaining its fighting edge.

Regardless of whether it was day or night in cities such as Fulda, Bad Hersfeld or Bad Kissingen, the windows of German homes would be wide open and its occupants would be leaning out of those windows, as the tanks, jeeps and mortars raced to their defensive positions and again when the troops returned.

Dependents—wives and children—were very much a part of the regiment. Because they lived in such close proximity to the border, they were every bit as much at risk as their soldier husbands and fathers. Plans and procedures for them were in effect in case they had to flee on short notice. Every family had to have its survival provisions ready. These consisted of footlockers in basements containing food, liquids, clothing, medicine, flashlights and sanitary products—items essential to survive for a time in the event they were hastily displaced. Randomly, regimental military personnel inspected homes to ensure that their evacuation stores were ready and adequate for that family. Automobiles were required to always have their gas tanks at least half full. Plans for the evacuation of noncombatants were kept up-to-date and were occasionally rehearsed. All dependents knew how and where to go. The wives were jocularly referred to as the "border belles."

Because of the criticality and sensitivity of the role the 14th was performing, members of the regiment had an unusual and heightened interest and awareness of national and international events. By August the troopers of the 14th were well aware that 1961 had already been a very eventful year and had all the earmarks of becoming even more eventful. On January 20, a young John F. Kennedy was inaugurated as our 35th president. He quickly received his baptism of fire as our commander in chief. On April 19, the ill-fated, disastrous operation known as the Bay of Pigs occurred. Shortly after that, the president manfully took personal responsibility for the abortive invasion of Cuba.

In early June, he had his first big test on the world's diplomatic stage in Vienna. He met face-to-face with America's prime Cold War adversary, Nikita Khrushchev. On June 3 at the American Embassy, and extending into June 4 at the Soviet Embassy, over two lunches, the two leaders had 11 hours of what turned out to be a contentious, bitter, verbal duel.

Khrushchev had been pictured in American newspaper stories as colorful, impetuous, unpredictable—even irrational—a kind of buffoon. Kennedy quickly found such a characterization extremely faulty. What Kennedy confronted was instead, an impressive, formidable adversary not to be trifled with. This Soviet leader was extremely well informed, had a broad and deep knowledge of history and was a skilled debater who could thrust forth with telling points and present logical and powerful arguments.

For Kennedy, discussions with that man were the "hardest work in the world." Try as hard as he might, Kennedy just could not find an "area of accommodation." At one point during the discussions, Khrushchev leaned hard on Kennedy, declared that he had decided to sign a peace treaty with East Germany by December and stated that his decision was firm and absolutely irrevocable. (So much for accommodation.) To that declaration Kennedy responded, "If that is true, it is going to be a cold winter."

As their meeting was drawing to a close, the subject discussed was Berlin and the words about it were dark and bleak. The atmosphere during those closing moments was gloomy, depressing and discouraging. What troubled Kennedy greatly was the realization that Khrushchev really meant what he said when he had boasted that he intended to bury us.

As the two antagonists walked from their meeting to the front door of the embassy, they did not speak. The atmosphere was frigid. There were no smiles, back slapping or hearty handshakes. Their final act together was just that— an act, a brief pause for a hasty photograph and an equally hasty and perfunctory handshake.

Kennedy without a doubt was greatly depressed by his first encounter with the enigmatic Khrushchev, and because of the Soviet leader's uncompromising attitude, Kennedy believed that U.S. and Soviet relations were profoundly grave. There were indications that Khrushchev left Vienna still believing that Kennedy was weak and inexperienced.

Subsequent to the Vienna meeting, the Soviet leader continued to maintain his very belligerent posture. Later in June, Kennedy also flexed his muscles by rejecting some demands made by Khrushchev. A noticeable hardening of the Soviet line continued into early July. On July 8, the Soviet leader suspended planned troop reductions.

By July 25, the Berlin situation had grown to such proportions and intensity that President Kennedy decided that he had to talk to the American people once again. That evening at 10 PM he addressed the nation and stressed the need for partial mobilization and psychological preparation for a Berlin showdown. He asked Congress for an additional $3.25 billion of appropriations for the current fiscal year for the armed forces and an increase in the army's total strength from 875,000 to approximately one million. He declared, "We are clear about what must be done—and we intend to do it." He continued by adding, "I hear it said that West Berlin is militarily untenable. And so was Bastogne. And so, in fact, was Stalingrad. Any dangerous spot is tenable, if men—brave men—will make it so."

He closed by saying, "We have previously indicated our readiness to remove any actual irritant in West Berlin, but freedom of that city is not negotiable . . . . The world is not deceived by the communist attempt to label Berlin as a hotbed of war . . . . We seek peace—but we shall not surrender."

As the days passed, the situation in Berlin grew from troublesome to tense and then to chaotic. It was reported that the fear of their future had 1,500 East Germans a day fleeing across the border with another 1,000 being pulled off commuter trains and jailed by communist police. John J. McCloy, Kennedy's disarmament advisor, returned to the United States from a meeting with Khrushchev, reported that the Soviet leader was in a totally belligerent mood and seemed absolutely intent on extracting what he called the "rotten tooth" of Berlin.

Fear that the East Germans would close the only Berlin border caused immense consternation; the escapees became a flood, and then it happened. On Sunday, August 13, East German communist leader Walter Ulbricht began building a wall along the border. Work on this grotesque, incongruous enterprise began at 2 AM. Large numbers of cargo trucks dumped every imaginable item that could form a barrier—concrete pillars, stone blocks, barbed wire—and the tools, picks and shovels to install them. By dawn the city was scarred and seared by a truly ugly wall that had seemed to erupt instantly out of nowhere.

It was not too many hours later, before noon, that I received information that East Germans were at work in East Berlin just inside their border constructing a barrier that would soon be recognized worldwide as the Berlin Wall.

To us on the border, that was a totally unexpected, incredible development, and we instantly recognized that the actions in Berlin were presenting an uncertain, critical and potentially explosive situation. I immediately dispatched the information to all elements of the regiment.

I instructed all commanders to be prepared on a moment's notice to drop whatever was on their schedules and on my order to move without delay to their deployment positions. My immediate and great concern and my big question was—what action would our forces in Berlin take to try to stop or dismantle the construction? Such a confrontation, without question, could easily lead to very serious consequences. We at the regiment began holding our breaths waiting for an answer to our question. The answer was not long in coming, and that answer was—nothing.

The American response was silence. It appeared that no one in Washington provided advice or suggested any immediate action or move. Even West Berlin Mayor Willy Brandt had no idea what to do right then. Military commanders never seriously considered knocking down the wall. They were well aware that it was being installed on rightful communist territory, which they legally occupied, and that if we moved against the wall, we would be invading that territory and inviting serious trouble. It presented a real political and military dilemma. We soon learned that President Kennedy finally decided that our nation would do nothing about the wall.

We on the border were left hanging. We were convinced that the situation was anything but over, and we believed instinctively that something more was going to happen, so we went about our tasks with a most uneasy feeling, still holding our breath and waiting for the shoe that would surely drop. We, of course, had been fully aware that tensions had been progressively building since Khrushchev and Kennedy had met in Vienna. The recent actions in Berlin had greatly exacerbated those tensions. We remained in an animated state for about three days and then I received the startling information from a staff officer at corps headquarters that a belligerent Khrushchev was threatening to close U.S. ground access to Berlin. If this threat were carried out, it would be a momentous, earthshaking development. The only way U.S. ground elements could move from West Germany through East Germany to Berlin was through an established, single 110-mile corridor. That passage was the Helmstedt-Berlin Autobahn. Helmstedt, the jumping-off place, sat on the border separating the British zone from the Soviet zone. It was located between two large cities—Braunschweig to the northwest in the British zone and Magdeburg to the southeast in the Soviet zone. With passage along this axis closed, the United States would be left with but two choices, both of which were dangerous and potentially cataclysmic: to use military muscle to try to force open the passage or, in order to avoid such a major confrontation, to be reconciled to initiating an airlift as Truman had in 1948-49.

With that news it appeared that the shoe had, indeed, dropped. I spent only a moment speculating. My wartime army commander, Gen. George S. Patton, Jr., had preached, "Do something, now!" Without hesitation I ordered the elements of my regiment to move at once to their operational positions. As our vehicles moved through the streets of the German cities, the inhabitants, as always, were hanging out of their windows. This time their faces showed puzzlement, anxiety and even fear. Somehow, intuitively, they recognized that this was not a normal alert, that something important was afoot. Before we departed, our families were also alerted to be ready in the event we were forced to implement the plan for the evacuation of noncombatants.

I reported to corps headquarters that my regiment had moved and was in its forward positions. I quickly learned that with tension there had also been some confusion. I was now informed that Khrushchev had not made an overt threat to close the Helmstedt-Berlin corridor and that thus far there had been no interference with access. A moment later, however, I learned that I had made the right call. I was provided with surprising and astonishing news—the kind that is totally unexpected. President Kennedy had made a critical decision, but one fraught with danger. He had decided that he would send a U.S. battle group, consisting of about 1,500 American soldiers, to Berlin along the Helmstedt-Berlin Autobahn.

It appears that the president had grown weary of Khrushchev's belligerency and bombast. In a sense he would be calling Khrushchev's hand. He was completely within his rights. With the wall going up and with the residents of Berlin living in an intensified atmosphere of uncertainty and fear, he was ready to demonstrate dramatically that there were rights that he considered basic to Berlin; access from West Germany to the city was vital, and under no circumstances would those rights be given up or stolen away.

Kennedy was well aware that this would be a real test of communist threats, and specifically, a head-on test of the crucial rights of access. Such a deliberate move, he recognized, could be viewed at least as an unnecessary irritant, or more important, as a veiled threat. He was under no illusions. He knew that if our troops were halted or interfered with, it meant that the absolute and sacred right of access was being denied to us and shooting could be the result.

From then on, because of the vital and critical importance of our mission, I began to receive regular reports from higher headquarters, which enabled me to be on top of the news as it was breaking. I soon learned that because troops in the forward positions and already facing the communists could not be spared. Thus the troops selected for the Berlin mission were those stationed in the western part of the U.S. zone. Making the journey would be the 1,500 men of the 1st Battle Group, 18th Infantry of the 8th Infantry Division stationed in Mannheim. That city was nearly 400 miles away from the entry point at Helmstedt. The unit, however, was right on an autobahn, would be able to move out immediately and could ride an autobahn all the way to Helmstedt. On Friday, August 18, we were notified that Gen. Bruce C. Clarke, commander of U.S. Army troops in Europe, had selected Colonel Glover S. Johns, Jr. to lead the American battle group along that 110 miles of communist territory between West Germany and West Berlin. Colonel Johns was selected, undoubtedly, because he had a fine record as a field commander during World War II. He was the author of a book, *The Clay Pigeons of St. Lô*, about his experiences. He seemed an excellent choice to lead such a sensitive expedition.

Now the only question that remained was—when? It was not long before we began receiving the answer to that question. We learned that Colonel Johns received verbal orders late on Friday evening. By 5:30 AM on Saturday morning, his troops had received an orientation about the mission, had been fed breakfast and were ready to roll the 400 miles of their approach march. General Clarke was on hand as the force moved out. He sent Lt. Gen. Frederic J. Brown, V Corps and my direct commander, to Helmstedt in his command train, which was fitted with the latest communications equipment and would enable General Brown to send periodic reports about the moving column. The march to the jumping-off point was long and time-consuming. By this operation the United States was telegraphing its next move. This gave the Russians considerable time to chew on it, and if they were contemplating some kind of action, this surely provided a tempting challenge for them. If they waited and did nothing as the battle group moved from Mannhein to Helmstedt that would surely be a good omen. Initial concerns were ultimately allayed, for the battle group reached Helmstedt without incident and bivouacked for the night at an airfield.

Everything was now on a hair-trigger alert. Clarke could communicate with Norstad in an instant, if he needed a response from him or the president. All forces in Europe had been alerted and instructions issued to them. Norstad was prepared to implement plans for air and ground support regardless of how limited or extensive.

Then came the news that brought goose pimples and butterflies in our stomachs. The battle group would kick off at 6:00 AM, Sunday, August 20, for the 110-mile test ride to Berlin.

On the border, in our deployed positions, tension that had been increasing by the hour now reached an unbelievable pitch. It became so tight and crisp that it virtually crackled. We were holding our breaths. It was not inconceivable that we might soon be in a firefight, so we were leaning well forward in our foxholes. We tried to visualize the possibilities and probabilities. The convoy could proceed to Berlin without any attempt to stop it. The convoy could be stopped by a physical roadblock covered by military troops and ordered to return to the west, or it could be fired upon by Russian forces, perhaps including tanks. If either of these two provocations occurred, what would be the actions of the U.S. forces? What orders had Colonel Johns received from the president? If he had been told that his mission was to get to West Berlin and to shoot it out if necessary, World War III could well be hanging in the balance. If U.S. forces returned the fire, the Russians, with massive troops nearby and at the ready, could escalate the situation by moving to the west in strength.

We learned later that President Kennedy and his immediate staff were even more concerned than we were, if that was possible. It was said that back at the White House "tension hung in the corridors like a ground mist before sunup." One member of that staff later declared, "It was a much greater crisis than people know. Talking to President Kennedy then was like talking to a statue." There was a feeling there, as on the border, that the mission could escalate into shooting. An advisor declared, "If a single day can be pointed to when the president felt the nation was entering the danger zone, it is August 20 when the troops raced those 110 miles into West Berlin." It was Kennedy's most anxious moment during the prolonged Berlin Crisis.

The first news was good news. We learned that the lead elements left Helmstedt and moved out onto the autobahn without incident heading for the Berlin Gate. Unit after unit followed unhampered. We received periodic reports that all was well, and as they ate up the miles without incident, tension eased immeasurably. Then came the electrifying news that we had breathlessly awaited. The lead elements had just entered West Berlin.

We learned somewhat later that the operation had been carefully planned, scheduled and timed so that Vice President Lyndon B. Johnson and Gen. Lucius D. Clay, President Kennedy's direct representatives, would be on hand to show the flag to the Berliners, to greet Colonel Johns and his troops and to remain until every man had moved safely into West Berlin. For Vice President Johnson it was a momentous day as thousands upon thousands of West Berliners greeted him and the U.S. battle group. Johnson cried out, "This is the time for confidence, for poise and for faith—faith in ourselves. It is also a time for faith in your Allies, everywhere throughout the world. This island does not stand alone." President Kennedy had graphically and decisively accomplished his mission of raising the spirits of the residents of Berlin and had brought them reassurance, confidence, optimism and even great excitement. Most important, he had courageously showed Khrushchev the hand that he was playing.

The world heaved a great sigh of relief. On the border, when the 14th Armored Cavalry Regiment received the news that it was all over, there was a collective gush of breath; it was as though the helium escaped simultaneously from a thousand balloons. We were like the rubber band that had snapped and was lying wrinkled and listless. The tension that had been so tight for so long had in an instant completely vanished. We were literally weak with relief.

A now unfettered, jubilant but whipped and completely wrung-out group of 14th Armored Cavalry Regiment troopers disengaged from their forward positions and in record time were heading back home. An unbelievable week with endless possibilities, many of them truly alarming, ended on an absolutely upbeat note. As always, the Germans were hanging out of their windows, but this time they cheered the returning warriors. They were keenly aware of the tense situation that had prevailed to the east and knew full well that they had been very vulnerable and that had events taken a different course, they too, would have had to contend with the boots, wheels and tracks of Soviet hordes.

Fortunately, that would never happen.

CHAPTER FOURTEEN

A Saga Of The United States Constabulary

Written by Lt. Col. Albin F. Irzyk. Reprinted with permission from Military
Review: *A Monthly Review of Military Literature from the Command and
General Staff School at Fort Leavenworth, KS, Volume XXVI, Number 12,
March 1947. Originally titled as "Mobility, Vigilance and Justice, A Saga
of the United States Constabulary."*

V ery quietly and unobtrusively a new force took control of the
policing of the United States zone of occupation in Germany
on July 1, 1946. There was no fuss nor fanfare as a brand new
military organization became operational. Rather, the transition was effected smoothly, thoroughly and efficiently. The impact of this change,
however, was felt at once in the entire zone. Yellow flashes of color,
characteristic of the new unit, became conspicuous all along the zonal
boundaries and frontiers separating the U.S. zone from the zones of the
French, Russians, and British and from the countries of Czechoslovakia
and Austria. New and brightly outfitted soldiers in their freshly painted
vehicles were quickly noticed, as well, along the roads and in the towns.
The Germans, displaced persons, and American troops immediately became aware of something new.

Just what is the Constabulary, what is it set up to do and how is it
going about doing its job?

Late in 1945, redeployment had become virtually a torrent.
The American Army of Occupation in Germany was shrinking at an
alarming rate. The occupation, which had only begun a few months

previously, had already reached a critical stage. With each passing day there was more and more to do and, ironically, less and less with which to do it. Obviously something had to be "snatched out of the hat" to save what might become a disastrous situation. It was a foregone conclusion by now that the size of the American army in Germany would be inadequate to conform to the original idea of occupation. Therefore, it was only natural at such a realization to change the plan. It was decided that an answer to the dilemma might be the organization of a small, highly trained, mobile unit that could police Germany on much the same basis as some of our better state police forces in the United States.

Such was the beginning of the United States Constabulary. Could this unit control Germany and at the same time keep to a minimum the number of troops needed to occupy the nation, and thus assist the army in meeting the extremely difficult requirements demanded of it? That answer is now being prepared for the history books.

Late in 1945, the United States Constabulary as such was merely a series of ideas. Early in 1946, those ideas had climbed onto paper. By February, the organization and plans had been approved. To those who had just completed weeks of arduous, grueling work the starting line had just been reached. The words and figures and numbers were to be given life. The previously secret plans were now disclosed, and the persons and units that were to become part of the new organization dug in at once and began to give their creation flesh and blood and a heart.

The 1st Armored Division and the 4th Armored Division, both of which had had long periods of service, had won lasting fame during long, hard months of combat and had only a few months previously been designated as probable permanent occupational divisions, furnished the nucleus for the Constabulary. All ten operational battalions (three tank, three infantry, three field artillery and the reconnaissance squadron) of the 4th Armored Division became Constabulary Squadrons. The division's headquarters and headquarters company became Headquarters and Headquarters Troop of the 1st Constabulary Brigade, the division's Combat Command "A" became the 2nd Constabulary Brigade Headquarters and Combat "B" became the Headquarters of the 3rd Brigade. Similarly, battalions of the 1st Armored Division became Constabulary Squadrons and the combat commands changed to Constabulary Regiments. The balance of the units and manpower were supplied by cavalry reconnaissance squadrons and tank destroyer battalions, most of whom had outstanding combat records. Thus, the beginning was auspicious, for the backbone of the Constabulary was already rich with history and tradition.

Almost immediately, however, the units were whittled down to the bone. All officers and men who would leave for home via the redeployment pipeline prior to June 30, 1946 were immediately transferred to other units. By the time the shuffle of troops was completed, each organization of the new Constabulary force was down to a bare cadre size. There were few officers, men or vehicles. Despite such a severe handicap, the units, by the middle of March, began to take shape. An intensive and extensive training program utilizing the highest standards possible was embarked upon, and almost at once, signs of definite progress were noticeable. Constabulary headquarters, outgrowth of VI Corps, began growing and functioning. This headquarters dealt with each of its squadrons directly and separately, but soon the squadrons were being integrated into regiments and later regiments into brigades. Slowly and gradually at first, this embryo of a completely new military unit, of an experimental force used to control a defeated nation took shape, found its legs, and began to take its first unsteady steps. On July 1, little more than three months later, the unit was full grown and working.

To those on the scene the transformation has been well nigh unbelievable. By its first working day, the Constabulary was a highly trained, well equipped, smartly uniformed, confident and capable organization that already had acquired a high morale, esprit de corps and a healthy cockiness. All this when the American army had reached its lowest ebb in a long, long time and when practically all experienced personnel had since left for home.

Today the eyes of the multitude are upon the Constabulary. The military world, especially, is receiving its recent acquisition with much interest, for the Constabulary is unlike any other military organization. As an experiment in the policing of an occupied nation, the Constabulary has the attention of much of the world focused upon it.

ORGANIZATION

The United States Constabulary numbers today approximately 34,526 officers and men. This large command, headed by Major General Harmon, has a chief of staff and a deputy chief of staff. Its general staff consists of a G-1, G-2, G-3, G-4, provost marshal and a public safety officer. Except for a few variations, it has much the same special staff sections as are normally found in a division headquarters but more especially a corps headquarters. As more and more problems are confronted, more sections are being added, and as a result, the headquarters is still being expanded.

Within the headquarters, in addition to the headquarters and headquarters troop, are special troops consisting of a signal squadron, a band, a school squadron, a military police company, a car platoon, an intelligence detachment, a counter-intelligence corps unit and a representation from the criminal investigation division. Attached to the Constabulary is a special service company and an ordnance medium maintenance company, and in support is an Air Liaison Squadron.

The Constabulary, except for its headquarters and supporting troops, is divided into three Constabulary brigades, the 1st, 2nd, and 3rd Brigades. Each brigade has a headquarters and headquarters troop and its staff generally parallels the Constabulary headquarters staff except to a smaller degree. A brigadier general commands each of the three brigades.

Under each brigade are three Constabulary regiments. Each has a headquarters troop consisting among other things of a horse platoon with thirty horses and a motorcycle platoon with twenty-five motorcycles. A service troop and a tank troop equipped with the latest light tanks complete the regimental headquarters organization.

Three Constabulary squadrons are an integral part of each regiment. A Constabulary squadron has six troops: a headquarters troop, three mechanized troops and two motorized troops. Mechanized troops have already proved themselves more suitable for constabulary operations, and because of this factor, the motorized troops have recently been furnished with additional vehicles in order to make them as mobile and as effective as the mechanized troops. Except for the tanks that are a part of regimental headquarters, all the operational vehicles are either "jeeps," M-8, or M-20 armored cars. A quick glance will show that the operational units of the Constabulary consist of twenty-seven squadrons, nine regiments and three brigades.

Since the Constabulary covers virtually the entire U.S. zone of occupation, its units, of necessity, are widely scattered. Brigade headquarters are located at each of the three *Land* (state) capitals. The 1st Brigade is located in Wiesbaden, capital of Greater Hesse; the 2nd Brigade is at Munich, capital of Bavaria; while the 3rd Brigade is at Stuttgart, capital of Baden-Wurttemberg. Brigade areas conform generally to *Land* boundaries while squadron boundaries usually follow *Kreis* (small German county) boundaries. Each squadron, however, controls several *Kreise*.

Mission

The mission of the United States Constabulary, as stated in the formal, direct and businesslike tone of its directive, is to "maintain general military and civil security; assist in the accomplishment of the objectives of the United States government in the occupied U.S. zone of Germany (exclusive of the Berlin District and Bremen Enclave), by means of an active patrol system prepared to take prompt and effective action to forestall and suppress riots, rebellions, and acts prejudicial to the security of the U.S. occupational policies, and forces; and maintain effective military control of the borders encompassing the U.S. zone."

OPERATIONS

To accomplish its assigned mission the Constabulary mans border posts on the inter-zonal boundaries separating the U.S. zone from the zones of the French, Russians and British and on the frontiers separating the U.S. zone from Czechoslovakia and Austria. Intensified patrolling is done within a 1,000-yard band along the boundaries and borders by foot, horse and vehicular patrols. To give further security in depth, intensified patrolling is performed by vehicular patrols within a band extending 10 miles from the boundaries. Additional vehicular patrols operate constantly throughout the entire area covering hundreds of thousands of miles each week. The patrols periodically cover every road and check every town, village, and hamlet.

Although border control and area patrols constitute two of the major types of operations, the mission of the Constabulary requires a host of others, all of vast importance. In order to discourage and suppress speeding, which has caused so many fatalities in Germany, a network of effective speed traps is operated with spot punishment meted out to offenders by roving summary court officers. Some of the most outstanding examples of the Constabulary in action have been its "search and seizure" operations. Such acts commonly referred to as "swoop raids" are leveled at areas or points where known or suspected illegal activities exist.

After much careful planning, the raiding force usually hits its objective at first light when the persons affected by the raid are still in their last moments of slumber. Surprise is essential to success and usually is obtained.

Still other functions of the Constabulary are the setting up of checkpoints and roadblocks, operating railroad checkpoints and operation of Constabulary stations.

Checkpoints and roadblocks are brief affairs that constitute an extremely effective "spot check." The checkpoints are set up without warning for approximately a half hour at crossroads and on roads. The purpose is to examine the credentials of every traveler that passes that point while the checkers are at work. The principle here is again surprise, and after the post has been operated a short time, and by the time the word is beginning to get out, the checkpoint moves to a new location.

Railroad checkpoints differ from road checkpoints in that they are of a permanent nature and are operated just inside a border. They check every train that is entering the American zone or departing from it. Both passengers and baggage come under the scrutiny of the troopers.

Constabulary stations are a recent development. They are merely a Constabulary office manned permanently by six or eight men in or near an area that is considered troublesome yet which has no Constabulary troops stationed in it. The station will provide Germans and American troops alike with a source to contact when giving or securing information or in the event of an emergency. (The Germans have long since ceased calling the Constabulary, "Harmon's Gestapo," for they realize that the Constabulary is interested only in the protection of the law abiding and the apprehension and prosecution of transgressors.)

EXPERIMENTATION

Continually experimenting, the Constabulary, on July 1 for example, took over border control from infantry units which it relieved, and troopers continued operating as all units before them had done. The border until that time had been controlled by static posts which in most cases covered roads. The posts gained the desired results only in the immediate area of the post. Prospective border violators quickly learned the locations of the posts and simply detoured them and invariably found an open spot to use in their crossing, for soldiers on post were tied closely to the restricted area of their post. (It is an impossibility to completely "close" the border.) Three weeks of experience quickly proved that static posts on the border were not the answer to most effective control of that border. The plan was changed at once to make provisions for foot, horse, and vehicular patrols that operated parallel to the border and in depth. The patrols are dispatched at irregular intervals over changing routes. Static posts have not been entirely abandoned but are still maintained in key places and on main roads. As a result, border violators never know when they will come upon a Constabulary patrol with troopers on the alert for just such individuals. The line of demarcation where border control ends and area security begins is difficult to decide, for many border violators are picked up well into the interior by vigilant patrolmen.

The Constabulary has experimented with all methods of operation in its constant quest for the "approved solution." It has tried performing its tasks with virtually all its troops employed and conversely, it has operated with a good sized force in reserve so that a policy of frequent rotation could be used in order to keep a program of review training constantly in effect, and to prevent the heavily extended troops from growing stale.

The risk of loss in administrative control in favor of added operational effectiveness was taken and small units of platoon size were placed in widely scattered areas in an effort to cut down on "backtracking" of patrols, and to have Constabulary personnel available in all localities. Sometime before, the experiment in effect was the concentration of all non-operational troops in one locality, in an effort to strengthen administrative control. This, of course, weakened in a certain extent the operational effectiveness. Gaining valuable knowledge by its intelligent experimentation, the Constabulary is presently operating under a plan that combines the best features of all the plans that they have tried to date. The end is not in sight, however, as it is contemplated that at least one more shift will be made.

THE CONSTABULARY UNIVERSITY

Much credit for the success of the Constabulary to date must, of necessity, go to Sonthofen. Sonthofen, as all men of the Constabulary know, is the Constabulary University, the institution that gives selected Constabulary Officers and men their Constabulary Bachelor's Degree.

The school sits on the crest of a small hill overlooking the town of Sonthofen approximately ninety miles southwest of Munich. Constabulary students today study in the same classrooms where not too long ago the cream of Hitler Youth trained. Sonthofen School, originally a preparatory school for the National Socialistic Ordensburg, was constructed in 1937 under the direction of Dr. Robert Ley and Baldur von Schirach, cost $26 million, but was never completed. This school is surrounded by the Algeau Alps, and provides its classes with every imaginable facility. Each month Sonthofen turns out just under a thousand trained officers and men. The Constabulary's field grade officers take an abbreviated course lasting five days. Company grade officers and enlisted men are provided with a fully packed four weeks course that General McNarney has said, "surpasses any previous military conditioning program." The school's curriculum consists of four courses: a basic course for officers and enlisted men and three specialized and technical courses for enlisted men—the communications course, the investigator's course and the desk and records course.

Each month, special trains start at the extreme ends of the U.S. zone and converge upon Sonthofen, picking up students all along the way. After they reach the school, the students are presented with a course of study that has rarely been equaled in army training. Courses are thoroughly planned, effectively organized and are expertly and interestingly presented by as competent a staff of military educators as could have been assembled. Subjects include not only the normal military subjects such as maintenance, driver training, leadership, weapons, map reading and tactics, but include a host of subjects called "Constabulary Subjects." These include: passes and permits; technique and mechanics of arrest; operation of desk and records section; interrogation, confession and statements; evidence; rules, collection, preservation; traffic control and accidents and many others. The trooper's education is completed with the study of general subjects of vital interest such as: History of Germany; Potsdam Conference; Military Government; U.N.R.R.A. and Displaced Persons; International Relations; and German Courts,

Laws and Political Parties. As can be seen, the education provided by the Constabulary School is varied and complete. The training must equip the school's graduates to be able to meet the great demands made upon them.

SCOPE OF OPERATIONS

The scope of the Constabulary efforts is tremendous. Its requirements keep it constantly sprinting with all the speed it is able to muster. An illustration to indicate the magnitude of the Constabulary effort is the vehicular and pedestrian bridge and the railroad bridge that cross from the city of Mainz in the French zone to the American zone. On the former the papers and credentials of 25,000 persons were checked on a single day, while on the latter it is customary, on an average day, to check the passes and baggage of 12,000 individuals. By multiplying those two routine instances by many score, one is able to gain some realization of the tremendous responsibility of the Constabulary today.

The men of the Constabulary are not burdened with static commitments such as the guarding of prisoner of war camps, civilian internee enclosures and other vital installations. Such tasks are taken over by the few infantry units that still remain. It is the job of the Constabulary, however, to contact periodically (as often as once every three days) the town mayors of all towns, military government detachments and headquarters of U.S. troop units in the Constabulary areas of responsibility. It is hoped that such close liaison will provide the Constabulary with all the information it requires in order to perform its mission. One of the especially bright features of Constabulary operations is its utilization of German police. Cooperation between the two is good and is becoming progressively better. In very many instances the troops are working side by side with Germans with the latter giving valuable service.

One will quickly agree that the operations just discussed are quite a mouthful. What manner of men are they that are accomplishing or attempting to accomplish such an extensive task?

Youth and Inexperience

Today, the United States Constabulary consists primarily of young, inexperienced men. Most of them have had only a short period of overseas service, and their total time in the army is extremely short, as well. Although approximately 73 percent of the troopers are regular army men, one does not often see men with decorations or overseas stripes in the Constabulary. Many of the regular army men enlisted for a year or eighteen months, and already the enlistment is nearly completed for a large number of them. Many are already in the process of departing for home.

What is perhaps the most outstanding characteristic of the Constabulary is its youth. The average age of the Constabulary trooper is 22, which would indicate that a very high percentage are 18 and 19 years of age.

Since most men who today are assigned to the Constabulary have such little service, they must receive immediate training and indoctrination. Thus, the training of new men is a constant, important part of the Constabulary program.

It has long been assumed that top-notch noncommissioned officers are the backbone of the army. "Old army non-coms" are conspicuous by their absence in the Constabulary as in the rest of the army overseas today, which places a tremendous burden upon the officers and upon the young enlisted men who must assume important jobs without the experience or training necessary to handle them adequately. Similarly, technical specialists who make an army operate and function are sadly lacking. This has caused a critical situation. Radio operators, radio repairmen, mechanics, typists, and the hundred and one other specialists that pump blood into the heart of an army are an extremely scarce commodity, indeed.

Yet, the Constabulary today is doing an outstanding piece of work as is attested by the many units and agencies that are in a position to observe or work with it. The Constabulary troopers have an air about

them and a record of accomplishment that already sets them apart from most other military units.

Uniform

In order to distinguish the Constabulary and to add luster to its appearance the troopers are uniquely uniformed. Yellow is the Constabulary trademark. The troopers' helmet liners have two bright yellow stripes around them with the Constabulary patch on the front, they wear yellow scarves when on duty and in special formation, and even the vehicles hold their own, for they, too, are hugged by wide, yellow stripes. Sam Browne belts, new leather boots and visored caps are soon to be issued to all men in order to make the trooper as natty a soldier as there is today.

Lightning Bolt

The Constabulary like a young child is ever restless, never satisfied. Filled with the determination to do the best job possible, it constantly keeps its eyes and ears cocked for new ideas and new improvements. During a few months of operations it has profited tremendously by experience. Operational exigencies have found wanting the framework upon which the Constabulary was built. As a result, a program is presently underway to attempt to make changes in Tables of Organization and Equipment so that the Constabulary will be so equipped and so organized as to be able to accomplish ever better the task before it.

Thus, the unit with its well-hidden nervousness and perhaps misgivings with which it started is now well established. Still feeling its growing pains and sometimes overzealous in its eagerness to make good, the Constabulary is making now and again an inevitable mistake. No one doubts but that the Constabulary is definitely here to stay. And today all over the U.S. zone of Germany law violators are more skittish, less confident, and less eager to take a chance; law-abiding German civilians are breathing more easily; American and German drivers alike invariably ease up on their accelerators as a Constabulary patrol passes;

and the Constabulary is again showing the world that an American can soldier without being pushed by a war.

And thus in Europe today the flash of the "Lightning Bolt" no longer portends a storm, but is greeted as a good omen; the words "Mobility, Vigilance, Justice" are no longer simply words or even an expression, slogan or motto, but now represent a distinct policy, a manner of operating, a characterization of the performance of the United States Constabulary.

CHAPTER FIFTEEN

MOBILITY, VIGILANCE AND JUSTICE

*Written by Brig. Gen. Albin F. Irzyk. Reprinted with
permission from* Army *magazine, January 2003.*

I n the grand scheme of things two events that took place in June
were relatively minor in nature, but to a group of aging Cold War
warriors, who still often refer to themselves as the Circle C Cow-
boys, the ceremonies were historic, memorable and a long time in coming.

On June 1 at Fort Riley, Kansas, Maj. Gen. Thomas F. Metz,
commanding general, 24th Infantry Division (Mechanized) and Fort
Riley, chose the day of his post open house to open the United States
Constabulary Museum. He and I cut the ceremonial ribbon. Three
weeks later, on June 21, before dozens of former Constabulary troopers
and their families, the museum was dedicated. This time the ribbon
was cut by the museum committee of Bill Tevington, Ray Thomas and
myself. In his remarks, on that occasion, General Metz said that he was
immensely pleased that he was able to play an important role in helping to keep the United States Constabulary from slipping through the
cracks into oblivion. The great significance of these events at Fort Riley
was that there was finally something tangible, a legacy, to prove that
there had, indeed, been an organization in our army called the U.S.
Constabulary.

The day after the ceremony, an active duty major, a friend of the
family, said to me, "I know that you are here for a Constabulary event,
but just what is the Constabulary?"

Fifty-seven years before, Lt. Gen. Joseph McNarney, American military commander in Europe, said to Maj. Gen. Ernest N. Harmon, "Harmon, you are going to be the head of the Constabulary." Harmon's blurted response was, "What's that?" Today, there is virtually no one in our nation or in our army aware that such an organization actually existed. The United States Constabulary was a special organization created specifically for service in the occupation of Germany.

When World War II ended, the victorious nations jointly assumed the occupation of Germany by dividing it into four zones of occupation: the Russian, British, French and United States. In its zone of occupation, the United States Army was faced with difficult and unprecedented challenges. There was no functioning border and no municipal, state or national police forces.

There were no governing bodies of any kind—no burgomeisters, Kreis commanders or Lander leaders in control. Further aggravating the situation, the beaten country was flooded with thousands of refugees and displaced persons desperately looking for food and shelter. As could be expected, crime was rampant.

It was the tactical units put into place right after the war that prevented total chaos. One of those elements was the 4th Armored Division.

That division had distinguished itself by spearheading the advance of Gen. George Patton's Third Army across Europe. As the war was ending, it was told that it would be a permanent occupation division. After V-E Day, the battalions of the division were spread throughout its occupation zone and were bringing law and order to the communities, and assisting the demoralized German population in getting their lives back together.

During the early weeks of the occupation, I moved successively from tank battalion commander to chief of staff of the division, and had a pivotal role in what was soon to develop. At division headquarters we were busily involved in carrying out our assigned mission, when, without any warning, we were hit by a combination hurricane, cyclone and tornado. We were told that the division would be summarily deactivated and would be a division no more. This was staggering, unbelievable news. (So much for "permanent" and "division.")

What came next was even more astonishing. The division was directed to proceed with utmost urgency to divest itself of all the items that had made it a fearsome power during the war—its tanks, halftracks and armored artillery, as well as heavy engineer and ordnance vehicles and equipment. We were informed that the elements of our division would become the nucleus of a brand new organization.

Senior officials had apparently determined that, to have a successful occupation, the United States required an entirely different military force that would have to be created almost from scratch. That force had to be lighter, faster and more mobile—able to move quickly and cover lots of ground. It would be akin to mechanized cavalry. It would have a strength of about 38 thousand, and its missions would be incredibly challenging and demanding. It would have to control the population of a defeated and occupied territory by maintaining general security in the U.S. occupied zone of Germany. That meant that it would be maintaining order in an area equivalent to the size of Pennsylvania. That region was home to 16 million Germans, and had over a half million refugees, as well as thousands of U.S. troops within its sector. The new unit would operate under a banner that proclaimed its credo, its motto—Mobility, Vigilance and Justice.

In the reorganization, the 4th Armored Division Headquarters would become Headquarters, First Constabulary Brigade; its Combat Command "A," Headquarters, Second Brigade; Combat Command "B," Headquarters, Third Brigade. There would be three regiments in each brigade. Each regiment would have three battalion-sized units called squadrons (after the cavalry) with troops instead of companies. Thus, in the three brigades there would be a total of 27 squadrons.

All battalions of the 4th Armored Division, regardless of what they had been before, became squadrons and were scattered throughout the three brigades. There were not enough battalions in the 4th to flesh out all the regiments, so battalions from the 1st Armored Division and separate tank, field artillery, tank destroyer and antiaircraft battalions were gathered throughout the theater and integrated with those of the 4th Armored.

There was a tenth regiment, designated the 4th Constabulary Regiment. Although it was organized like the other nine, it had a different command structure. The regimental headquarters, with two squadrons, was located in Austria. It came under the operational command and control of the area commander in Austria. A third squadron, the 16th Constabulary Squadron, was loosely under the 4th Regiment's umbrella, but it was located and operated in Berlin under the Berlin Command. It considered itself the 16th Constabulary Squadron (Separate).

VI Corps Headquarters provided the resources for the Constabulary headquarters.

As all this reorganizing was taking place, each unit had to shuck its TO&E (tables of organization and equipment) and acquire the new Constabulary TO&E.

Among the more significant changes were the replacement of medium tanks, half-tracks and howitzers with light tanks, M8 armored cars, motorcycles, large numbers of jeeps and even horses.

While units were being transformed, so were the individuals who would no longer be only soldiers, but Constabulary troopers. Each individual faced a psychological challenge. He would no longer be in a tactical unit, was no longer a warrior, a fighter. He had to turn his back on his specialty—tanker, infantryman or artilleryman—and train hard in his new role—that of soldier/policeman.

Almost at once and everywhere, it seemed—on every vehicle, every sign and on the shoulders and helmet liners of every trooper—appeared the then famous Constabulary patch. It was a bright yellow circle with a narrow blue border; centered on the yellow was a large, bold, blue "C" through which thrust a red lightning bolt. These three distinctive colors represented the cavalry, infantry and artillery. The most prominent color, however, was cavalry yellow. In addition to the

patch, helmet liners were encircled by yellow stripes. All vehicles had large circle "C's," and the larger the vehicle the larger the "C." They also were encircled by broad, yellow stripes. Men and vehicles were so colorful and so distinctive that they were easily and readily recognized. They made a most significant and startling splash when they first appeared in the German cities, towns and countryside.

The selection of Maj. Gen. Ernest N. Harmon to be the first commanding general and organizer of the U.S. Constabulary was a stroke of genius. He was just finishing his assignment with the XXII Corps in Czechoslovakia. He had broad combat experience, was a most successful armored division commander, had a colorful personality and was a demanding and no-nonsense disciplinarian. He was absolutely the right man for the job. He assumed command in early January, 1946. He was given what appeared to be an impossible mission. That mission was to have the Constabulary operational in six months, a most ambitious undertaking. On July 1, 1946, it was operational—off and running— from concept to reality in six months, a staggering achievement.

The big question mark, what appeared to be the Achilles heel of the organization, was the individual Constabulary trooper. During the period the Constabulary was being organized and after it began its operations, there was great personnel turmoil in Europe. The warriors of World War II were returning home in droves. During the first two months of its operations, the Constabulary lost 14 thousand men, close to half of its authorized strength. Their replacements were 18-, 19-, 20-year-old troopers and young officers, all with limited military service and experience. These would become the backbone of the Constabulary. Upon their shoulders would rest the fate of the Constabulary mission.

They faced a situation that had never existed before and were confronted with unbelievable, demanding challenges. They had no preparation for their jobs. There were no field manuals to study, no precedents. They were given tremendous responsibilities and very little direction or supervision. The entire effort was peculiarly dependent upon the good judgment and sensitivity of the individual trooper. Their operations covered lots of ground and took them far and wide in small groups, long distances from their headquarters and very often only two to a jeep. They operated an active system of motorized patrols that carried them regularly to virtually every corner of their area of responsibility.

The troopers controlled the borders, established temporary and permanent roadblocks, conducted small and large scale raids and involved themselves deeply in the suppression of black marketing and all types of crime. They possessed the power of arrest, search and seizure. Most important, they established and maintained an ideal and secure environment for the military government to do its critical work.

As they carried out their duties, these young, impressionable, often naïve, Americans were confronted with every temptation known to man. They were exposed to a society which for them was beyond comprehension. An ingenious black market flourished. The offering of substantial bribes was commonplace. Germany was filled with desperate people eager and willing to pay high prices for permission to cross borders illegally and to escape detection in the black market.

Yet these young Americans successfully resisted those temptations and did not succumb to the heavy pressures often applied to them. My service was during the first year and a half, the formative months of the Constabulary. During that period, I was not aware of a single serious incident involving a Constabulary trooper—truly remarkable under the circumstances. We had defeated Germany; we were the victors, the conquerors. In previous centuries, conquerors were known to pillage, loot, rape and burn. The Constabulary troopers, however, were anything but swaggering, overbearing, chest-thumping conquerors.

They performed in a responsible manner, and toward the defeated, demoralized Germans they were sensitive, caring and compassionate. When the Germans saw the yellow colors and the Circle "C," they did not recoil in fear and run and hide. Rather, they watched the approach of the Constabulary troopers with gratitude and respect, even admiration, for they knew the young men were there to help.

The United States Constabulary existed as an organization and served for the brief period of six and a half years. After that, it was no more. Why such an unbelievably short time? Was it a failure? The answer: anything but. This was a great success story. After six and a half years, the United States Constabulary had accomplished the United States Army's mission of ensuring the success of the American occupation of Germany. After that relatively short period of time, our leaders decided that Germany was in control of its own destiny and the Constabulary was no longer required.

Our leaders at home had recognized the tremendous value of the U.S. Constabulary. It was acknowledged in the Congressional Record of the 81st Congress as "probably the keenest, most vigilant eye we possess—ready to live up to [its] mission." Live up to its mission it did. As we look at Europe and see the Germany of today, great credit has to be given to the U.S. Constabulary for helping that country pick itself up off its knees and giving it a jump start to become the great nation it has become.

The establishment and opening of its museum is a unique Constabulary achievement. Its members have been well aware that museums are traditionally established by organizations with decades of service in order to depict long periods of history. The Constabulary's history extended a mere six and a half years, and its existence ceased 50 years ago. Its significance, however, cannot be measured on a calendar.

The aging Constabulary veterans are justifiably proud of what they and their organization accomplished. This museum preserves their legacy, which had been rapidly disappearing from sight. As an offshoot of the cavalry, it is appropriate that the museum should be at Fort Riley, the "Home of Cavalry."

CHAPTER SIXTEEN

THEY, TOO, WERE HEROES

*Written by Brig. Gen. Albin F. Irzyk. Reprinted with
permission from* Army *magazine, December 1982.*

As part of a five-day weekend "National Salute to Vietnam Veterans" in November, 1982, it took volunteers in the Washington Cathedral 48 hours and 29 minutes over a three-day period to read the 57,939 names of Americans killed and missing in Vietnam. Finally, some attention was being paid and recognition given to those who served and those who died in that war. High time!

These days, it is difficult to find a single soul who now will say one good word about what we did or tried to do in Vietnam. The way we have neglected the memories of those who left their lives in Vietnam, and the manner in which we have treated those who served and returned—the so-called "Vietnam Vet"—is shameful and, indeed, a national disgrace.

Writers, politicians, extremists and many people of good intention refer to Vietnam as "our defeat," "the war we lost," and they want no part of it. About the Vietnam War there is almost total ignorance. Tightly closed minds, simmering emotions and sterile pens still prevail.

In contrast, the Civil War and World Wars I and II have been described in exhaustive detail, in endless volumes. Stories have been told over and over from every possible angle. They have been examined, analyzed, dissected, grilled, stewed and fried. Any suddenly discovered nuance immediately brings forth a rash of new words.

Because we do not want to hear about the Vietnam War, we have no use for the Vietnam Vet. We did not welcome him home, did not honor him as we have the veterans of all previous wars. No, we simply filed him away. He slunk home, quickly got rid of his uniform and now rarely admits, even to friends and associates, that he served in Vietnam.

He rarely joins veteran organizations. He hardly ever participates with other veterans at formations on Memorial Day, the Fourth of July or Veterans Day. In our society he is not admired, respected or honored as are other veterans; rather, he is looked upon with suspicion and even disdain. He is a kind of military nonperson, an outcast. The great tragedy is that our nation really does not know the individual who served in Vietnam, what he was asked to do there and, even more tragically, it does not care to know.

Today we live in an era of images. It is the image that counts. What is the image that America has of the Vietnam Vet? The picture that comes across is that he is a drug user and he learned to use them in Vietnam. While there, he fired artillery shells indiscriminately and burned friendly villages; he killed innocent women and children in the process of hunting down members of the North Vietnamese army and the Vietcong; he fragged officers and noncommissioned officers. Since he has been home, he has let his hair and beard grow, he has become a bum and lately, in small groups, he has been agitating for and demanding the restoration of counseling and "rap" centers, which he needs to keep himself going.

That is the image which seems to prevail. To reinforce that image we have recently been getting the "real, true, hot dope" from Hollywood. From the movie capital has come an outpouring of extremely bad movies about Vietnam. The veteran in the movies is depicted on the one hand as a ruthless killer and on the other as a patsy of the Pentagon. He has returned home, and is now pictured in a broken and disordered state both emotionally and behaviorally. He cannot hold a job; his movements are spastic; and because of a guilt complex and constant nightmares, he is apt to go berserk at any time and start shooting in all directions.

The real disgrace is that the Hollywood version is not too far from the generally accepted picture of the Vietnam Vet held by our society. "Wrong, wrong," I shout, in a voice as loud as I can muster. "That image is dead wrong!"

As an extension of the "salute" in Washington, I wish to paint a picture of the Vietnam veteran that is truly different from the one which is generally perceived but one which is much more accurate. I have great respect and admiration for the Vietnam veteran and what he did.

In my eyes the individual who served in Vietnam stands every bit as tall and is every bit as great a hero and should be honored every bit as much as any man who served in our armed forces at any time since the Revolutionary War. As it turned out, he just happened to choose the wrong war.

I believe I am an expert on the American who served in Vietnam. I am much more qualified to talk about this person than newspaper writers, T.V. commentators and, above all, moviemakers. Having spent two years in Vietnam, I was in the thick of the Tet Offensive in Saigon in 1968 and, during my second year, I spent over 600 combat hours in a helicopter directing and supervising military operations of the tactical elements of an infantry division. I talked to and lived with the troops in Vietnam. I directed and ordered them into battle—the men who are now Vietnam veterans.

The servicemen in Vietnam were kids, only 18, 19, 20 years old, in some cases just 17. They had not quite finished high school or had just barely graduated. They were, in most cases, draftees—drafted to serve two years. They did not run off to Canada or Sweden; rather, they reported as ordered, were inducted, put on their uniforms and served.

They received eight weeks of basic military training, then eight weeks of advanced individual training—a grand total of 16 weeks, only four months, of military training. After this training, they were not assigned to a unit. They did not participate in platoon, company, battalion, regimental or division training as we did during World War II. They did not train in the desert, on Tennessee maneuvers, or on the Salisbury Plains of England as we did, over a period of many months. No!

Sixteen weeks only, then off to war. They were put on a commercial jet aircraft, not a troop ship with their unit, not a Military Air Transport Service (MATS) plane with their buddies. No, they found themselves with a planeload of strangers and were served in-flight meals by uniformed airplane stewardesses. That is how *they* went to war.

Did they leave a country at war, a country totally mobilized, totally dedicated to the completion of that war, where the Reserve and National Guard and all able-bodied men were fully mobilized, where war production was in full swing with even "Rosie the Riveter" leaving her family to help; with gas, sugar and women's stockings rationed; with everyone aware of, concerned about, totally involved in the war effort, as it was when I left during World War II? Oh, no!

When they left, there was hardly anyone really aware that there was a war going on. There were virtually no visible effects on the country; certainly no rationing and, uncomprehendingly, not even the mobilization of the National Guard and Reserve. It was a country which apparently "could care less," except for those who protested, demonstrated and criticized. But, basically, it was "business as usual." That is what those kids left behind, when they went to war.

Their war was 24 hours, half a world, away by jet. They left the most sophisticated, civilized society in the world: hot and cold running water, cars, Burger Kings, Mom's hot apple pie—and landed in a country that was poor, backward, unsophisticated, and primitive, a wild, jungle, swamp country whose name they had not even heard of until a short time before. So that is where they were going to fight.

But when they landed, they did not really know why they were there, nor did they know what they were fighting for. Apparently, no one had tried or been able to explain it to them. Small wonder. Geo-politicians, editors, senators, university presidents, T.V. commenta-tors—men far more learned, intelligent, sophisticated, experienced, educated than those kids—debated vociferously, bitterly, endlessly on this subject. Opinions covered every shade of the spectrum. There were violent disagreements. So, how were these young kids to know?

Despite all this, *they* did not debate. They went, fought, perhaps were wounded, and, if they survived, were on a jet returning home 12 months to the day after they arrived. For them it was a one-year war.

In retrospect, we asked a multitude from these kids. When they landed in Vietnam, they were less prepared mentally, militarily, educa-tionally, intellectually, psychologically than any men this country had ever sent to war. After landing, they were given a four-day orientation at a base camp, and the next thing they knew they were with a bunch of strangers wallowing around in the swamps and jungles of Vietnam, chasing and fighting the enemy in what is called the toughest testing ground of man—the field of combat. They were commanded by ser-geants, lieutenants and captains with just a few months more service who were only a year or two older than they.

Because of the one-year tour, necessitated by the draft, their outfit changed completely during their 12 months with it. Individuals were constantly arriving and leaving. Their outfit was never set. They con-tinually had different battalion commanders, company commanders, platoon leaders and squad leaders. Such an unsettling turnover was fur-ther intensified and aggravated by combat casualties.

I would challenge General Motors to build cars, General Electric to produce toasters and even the corner supermarket to keep operating if they lost top executive, middle management and the work force *in toto* every 12 months. Yet, that was the challenge met by every unit in Vietnam.

I have seen young men soaked and chilled for 40 straight days and nights with never a dry thread, while constantly patrolling and fighting during the monsoon season. Their only touch with reality was the occasional helicopter which was able to find them to drop off rations—cold, canned food—and ammunition.

I have monitored a young man with three others like him, a group of four, as they moved deep into enemy-infested jungle, equipped only with a map, compass, pack radio, ammunition and some food. Amazingly, they found the intersection of two footpaths in that deep jungle. There the group set up an ambush and remained completely silent for four to five days, or until the ambush was triggered. Those "kids," perhaps only recently Little Leaguers, were matching wits with fanatics, more animal than men, in their native, natural and completely advantageous habitats.

I have visited a combat trooper in the hospital shortly after a battle, where he humbly but proudly accepted the medal which I pinned on him. His uppermost thought, which he quickly mentioned, was his hope that his wounds would heal quickly so that he could return to his buddies and his outfit as soon as possible. Regardless of his own condition, he was also quick to point out how far worse the man in the next bed was, and how courageously he was taking it.

Before I went to Vietnam, I heard senior commanders say, "I have commanded troops in World War II, Korea and now Vietnam. These troops are as great as I have ever had."

I went to Vietnam with my tongue in my cheek. I returned a believer. The Vietnam soldier had a tremendous attitude. He looked one in the eye, answered questions directly, was intelligent, capable, but, above all, he was brave and he really soldiered.

While I was in Vietnam, patriotic people like Woody Hayes, after his Rose Bowl victory, Ricardo Montalban, Gypsy Rose Lee, Martha Raye, T.V., movie and sports stars visited our unit and ate with us. They invariably said in surprise, "I came over here thinking I could do these young men some good. I have done *them* no good, but they have done *me* a tremendous amount of good. They are an inspiration. I am so proud of them."

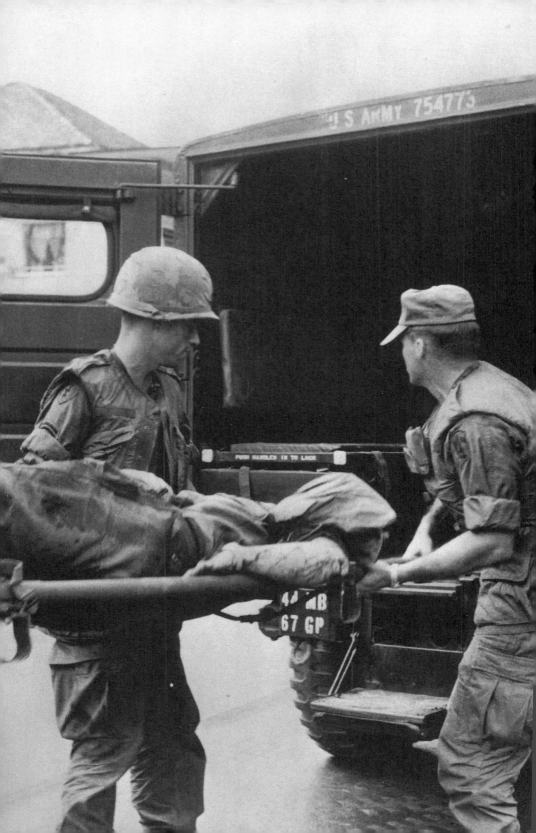

These young men did not ask to go to Vietnam. They were ordered there because of decisions made by our civilian authority. Once there they fought; many were wounded and many died. For those who survived it was a one-year war. For the very many who were drafted, they entered the service, were trained, fought a war and were back to the society from whence they came, all in two years.

That is the real picture of the Vietnam Vet, the man *I* have known, and observed closely, with whom I served and whom I admire and greatly respect. He was given an unpopular, unpleasant, dirty job to do, and he did it and did it well.

In paying this personal, special tribute to the soldier who served in Vietnam, I wish to apologize for my very many fellow citizens who remain completely unaware of his performance of duty and for their callous, uncaring, ungrateful way of shunting him aside without even a small measure of the recognition he so richly deserves.

The Vietnam Vet is all about us. He is the lawyer, accountant, clerk and gas station manager. He is the responsible citizen raising a fine family. But we do not recognize him. He has no obvious identification like a nametag, and he chooses not to mention that part of his past. But the real reason we do not recognize him is that he does not conform to the image our society has prescribed for him.

It is time for America to wake up, to recognize that the Vietnam veterans, and particularly the 57,939 who left their lives in Vietnam, stand every bit as tall, are every bit as great a group of heroes, and should be honored every bit as much as any group of men who fought and died for this country at any time since we fought that first War for Independence.

CHAPTER SEVENTEEN

SAIGON AT TET, THE EMBASSY BATTLE

Written by Brig. Gen. Albin F. Irzyk. Reprinted from
Unsung Heroes, Saving Saigon, *Ivy House Publishing Group, 2008.*

Just three months earlier, the $2.6 million Embassy Compound had been completed and opened on Thong Nhut Street. Its six-story chancery building loomed over Saigon like an impregnable fortress. The building was a white reinforced concrete complex. It was encased in a massive concrete sunscreen that overlapped shatterproof Plexiglas windows, and was protected by a sturdy ten-foot high concrete wall.

It was a constant reminder to all who saw it of the power and prestige of America. It was a massive structure. But its symbolism was even more enormous. It goes without saying that the Embassy was, for the Communists, an absolutely huge target, the prime target in Saigon, and without a doubt in all of Vietnam as well. Seizing the U.S. Embassy quickly was a vital, critical mission for the Communists. They astutely recognized the tremendous symbolic and psychological effect that the triumph of hoisting and flying the Communist flag over the U.S. Embassy within minutes of their push into Saigon would have. There would be worldwide reverberations. Consequently, during the very first minutes of the Communist assault on Saigon, the American Embassy was the prime target of the initial, important installations to be attacked and seized.

It was a small force of sappers—only twenty individuals—who had the mission, did the attacking. The sappers belonged to a very special breed. They were little people who were devious, dangerous, lethal. They were able to slither under coiled barbed wire protecting American firebases without disturbing Claymore mines, and wreak havoc within the firebase. Their missions, which they willingly accepted, were habitually suicide missions. Thus, their selection for the Embassy assault, they recognized, could be a suicide mission, and they were well prepared for it.

Twenty men, at first blush, would appear to be a very small force entrusted with such a valuable and formidable objective. However, as we are well aware, the sappers expected little or no resistance from ARVN forces. The Vietnamese police force, responsible for the exterior security of the Embassy, was a corrupt organization, and anything but courageous, so they were definitely not a threat. Understandably, the sappers believed that they had nothing to fear from the Vietnamese. That left them to deal with the members of the U.S. Marine Security Detachment (MSD) assigned to the Embassy, who were responsible for its security. However, that was a very small force, which was lightly armed.

On the other hand, twenty men, banded together, moving aggressively about the tight confines of the Embassy grounds, would quickly become a crowd. That small crowd, armed with AK-47s, B-40 Rocket Propelled Grenades (RPGs), and satchel charges, would quickly become a small, extremely potent army.

Sometime after midnight, and before the VC opened its attack on Saigon, the sappers met with their two team leaders. Those individuals outlined the plan and issued instructions. It was a simple operation. The sappers were to scale the wall and seize control of the chancery. No withdrawal plan was mentioned.

The meeting took place only five blocks from the Embassy at a greasy car repair shop and garage at 59 Phan Than Gian Street. At the appointed time those twenty VC sappers climbed into a small Peugeot

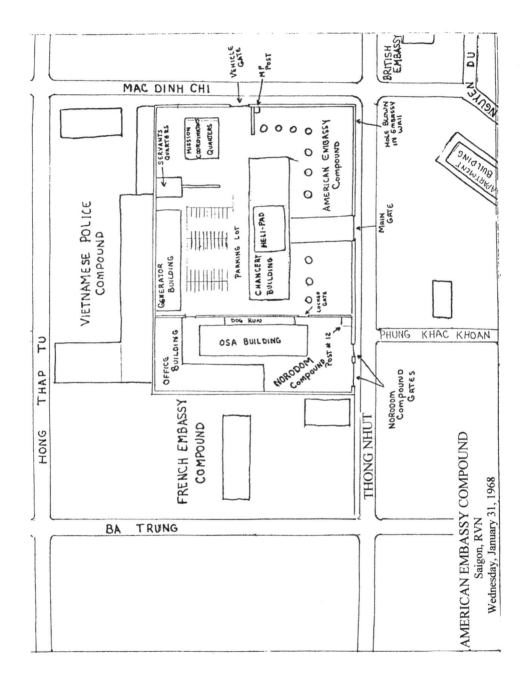

MAP 7. AMERICAN EMBASSY COMPOUND, SAIGON

truck and a taxicab for the short ride to their objective, the U.S. Embassy. They wore black pajamas and shirts, much like ordinary civilians, and red armbands. This Embassy team came from the elite 250-man-strong C10 Sapper Battalion, whose headquarters was near the Michelin rubber plantation north of Saigon. Some of these individuals had been born in Saigon and were familiar with the streets of the crowded city, had worked there as taxi and pedicab drivers. Others arrived on busses packed with holiday travelers two days before the Tet attack, and went to safe houses—some next door to the repair shop. It was at this location where their weapons and explosives had been smuggled in over the previous weeks in rented trucks loaded with rice, tomatoes, and firewood, and stashed.

The Embassy sappers rendezvoused with their team leaders at the repair shop and the cached weapons were broken out of their containers. Their assault on the Embassy would be only a part of the sapper battalion's assignment, which was to spearhead the attack on Saigon followed closely by eleven battalions of VC, totaling about four thousand troops.

The battalion's mission that morning, in addition to seizing the U.S. Embassy, was to gain control of the Presidential Palace, the national broadcasting studio, the South Vietnamese Naval Headquarters, the Vietnamese Joint General Staff headquarters at the Tan Son Nhut Airbase, and the Philippine Embassy. All of these were to be held by the sappers for forty-eight hours until the VC battalions pouring into the city would relieve them.

Immediately after the word was out that the U.S. Embassy was being assaulted, shockwaves quickly circled the globe. The astonishing news was grave, frightening, and caused great consternation for much of America. Heretofore, the folks at home did not appear unduly upset, and were taking the war pretty much in stride. It was difficult to follow engagements that were taking place half a world away. They found that the attacks, the battles, and the places in Vietnam were unpronounceable; the type of war and locations were, for them, quite vague. So for most Americans, the fight at the Embassy was at last something very real. That engagement was the first tangible battle of the Vietnam War, which they understood, as it was simple, and clear. Yes, it was a dramatic eye-opener.

The U.S. Embassy, Saigon, Vietnam
The early morning hours of January 31, 1968

Like members of the Headquarters Area Command (HAC) and its 716th Military Police Battalion, the U.S. Marine Security Guard Detachment (MSG) was at a heightened alert and readiness. Capt. Robert J. O'Brien, the officer in charge of the MSG detachments, had met with Mr. Leo Campsey, the State Department regional security officer, at 1600 the previous afternoon, and was informed of the possibility of a sapper attack in the Saigon area. In response to this information Captain O'Brien directed that a second guard would be posted at all one-man posts, and that a rooftop watch be established at the new chancery building at the U.S. Embassy.

At 0100 hours Marine Sgt. Raymond P. Schuepfer and L.Cpl. James P. Wilson assumed their duties at Guard Post #12 in the Norodom Compound, across the interior wall separating it from the chancery building. Additionally, Sergeant Schuepfer had been designated as the walking, roving patrol, responsible for checking the area on an hourly basis.

At 0200 hours Marine Sgt. Ronald W. Harper, who had assumed duties at the important and very critical Guard Post #1, which was the lobby and front desk of the chancery building, along with Corporal Zahuranic, decided to go to the roof of the building to relieve the previously posted Sgt. Rudy A. Soto for a short break.

While on the roof, Sergeant Harper looked out in all directions, in and around the Embassy. He spotted nothing unusual, and all appeared normal and quiet. Sergeant Soto completed his break at 0215 hours, and returned to his post on the roof. With that Sergeant Harper moved out and began his descent to his post in the lobby.

Shortly after, at 0238, Sergeant Harper again left Post #1 to see if his guards at Post #12 in the Norodom Compound needed coffee. As he approached the post, he met Sergeant Schuepfer, who was returning from his patrol of the compound, and reported that all was quiet. As Sergeant Harper was pouring a cup of coffee, he glanced toward the office building and observed a Vietnamese man standing nearby. As Harper was about to ask if the individual was an Embassy guard or driver, the man raised a weapon and automatic fire came spewing forth. As he recoiled in surprise, Sergeant Harper heard, from a different direction, a deafening explosion that must have come from someplace very close. He dropped his cup and rushed from the guard shack at the dead run, heading for his own post. There was no sign of the armed Vietnamese, who had somehow disappeared. As he ran, Sergeant Harper was completely unaware of the action taking place not much more than a stone's throw away.

Two Military Policemen occupied a post at the side gate of the Embassy on Mac Dinh Chi. The front main gate facing Thong Nhut had been secured for the night, but the side gate remained unlocked. At this time a small truck and taxi with their lights off moved silently along Mac Dinh Chi. They moved past a Vietnamese police station and an officer-occupied checkpoint. However, there was absolutely no reaction from the Vietnamese police. Upon reaching Thong Nhut, the sappers turned right on that street. As they did, fire from an AK-47 came out of their taxi aimed at the two MPs standing at their post at the side gate. The vehicles continued slowly down the road and were out of sight. The moment the vehicles stopped, the sappers were out, and instantly began unloading their RPGs and satchel charges from the vehicles.

The two MPs had earlier been issued steel helmets and flak-jackets and had them on when they occupied their post. They were Specialist Four Charles L. Daniel and Private First Class William E. Sebast of the 527th MP Company, which had been attached to the 716th MP Battalion. At the sound of the first AK-47 shots, without hesitation both MPs dashed inside the Embassy Compound, slammed the steel barred door with a loud clang, and locked it with the heavy chain and padlock.

Events were now moving swiftly. It was now 0247. Less than ten minutes earlier, Sergeant Harper had been at Post #12 checking to see if his guards needed coffee.

Specialist Four Daniel's next action was to grab his guard post radio, which, of course, was on the MP network. He shouted, "WACO, WACO, this is the American Embassy!" and added, "Signal 300," which was the brief code for enemy attack. (This report is what my driver, Sergeant Williams, heard in his quarters behind mine, as he always had his MP radio on. The moment he heard the report he began to dress furiously.) Daniel had barely finished his message when he and Sebast were literally rocked back on their heels and deafened by the noise of a powerful explosion. As soon as they were able to settle themselves, they saw that sappers had blown a hole in the southeast corner of the ten-foot wall. (It was this explosion that had rudely awakened me at my quarters only a few blocks away. My watch read 0247.) The hole initially was relatively small, but so were the sappers. The hole was large enough for the tiny sappers to wiggle and crawl through.

Daniel and Sebast immediately grabbed their M-16s, swung their weapons so that the muzzles pointed straight toward the hole, and sprayed it with multiple rounds from their guns. The two sappers already through the hole were instantly killed. Firing AK-47s ahead of them, the VC continued to penetrate the hole while others scaled the wall. Soon they were pouring out a very heavy volume of AK-47 fire. Most unfortunately, regrettably, and tragically, Daniel and Sebast were overwhelmed, and never had a chance. Daniel was shot in the face and Sebast in the chest, and both died instantly. Their crumbled bodies were soon covered with concrete fragments and dust, as the barrage of AK-47 fire splintered the wall behind them. As the dead MPs lay facedown on the ground, the sappers began fanning out over the Embassy grounds.

At a dead run, after leaving Post #12, Sergeant Harper reached the front door of the chancery and quickly darted inside. He, at that point, was unaware of the events that had unfolded around the corner near the vehicle gate; that the explosion he had heard had blasted a hole in the Embassy wall. Once inside the chancery, he immediately locked the main door. As he was doing that, two sappers positioned themselves behind a circular concrete planter. One quickly aimed his RPG at the front door of the chancery. Just as Sergeant Harper turned away from the door, a B-40 rocket exploded against that six-inch teakwood main door, sending shrapnel into the lobby. One bit of shrapnel entered Harper's leg. Corporal Zahuranic was not as fortunate. He had been sitting at the receptionist desk talking to Mr. E. Allen Wendt, the Embassy Duty Officer. Zahuranic received a serious shrapnel wound to the head resulting in severe bleeding from his head and ear. He also suffered a broken leg.

As Sergeant Harper was applying first aid to the unconscious Zahuranic, a second B-40 rocket was fired, penetrated the granite slab bearing the seal of the United States, and exploded near the receptionist desk. Neither Harper nor Zahuranic was further injured by that blast.

As earlier mentioned, Sergeant Soto was positioned on the roof of the chancery. He had heard an explosion coming from the direction of the Presidential Palace. He immediately moved along the roof to the edge so as to be able to see better. As he looked down, he saw Vietnamese running toward the Embassy, and after they reached the high wall he watched in horror as a blast opened a hole in that wall at the corner of Mac Dinh Chi and Thong Nhut. Almost immediately, he heard automatic fire, and picked out the first defenders of the Embassy Compound: Daniel and Sebast holding their ground and pouring accurate fire at the break in the wall, killing two sappers before being cut down themselves. Their courageous and valiant stand provided the split second timing that Sergeant Harper had required to rush to the front entrance of the chancery and to secure its main door. Unquestionably, the VC would have rushed into the building if it were not for Daniel and Sebast's gallant action.

It was ironic and tragic that Sergeant Soto was able to observe all this action, but was unable to help the besieged MPs. He was armed only with a shotgun and .38 pistol. With his shotgun he attempted to provide supporting fire, but his shotgun jammed twice while he was chambering a round. His .38 was way out of range and, thus, was useless.

The noise at the Embassy was heard five blocks away at the Security Guard billet, a converted hotel known as the Marine House. Captain O'Brien, the officer in charge of the Marine security guards, had only recently returned from a tour of his detachment's posts. Now he, accompanied by a sergeant, rushed to his radio-equipped sedan, and headed right for the Embassy. Three other Marines followed in an International Scout. The Marine Security Guards wore their regular utilities (fatigues) and caps. They were not able to convert to infantry as the MPs had and, thus, did not wear steel helmets or flak jackets. At the intersection of Mac Dinh Chi and Hong Thap Tu was a Vietnamese checkpoint. For the very first time that evening they finally "showed themselves" by pointing in the direction of the Embassy, and shouting, "VC! VC!"

Captain O'Brien had his little team dismount from their vehicles, and advance on foot to the locked vehicle gate, right next to the Daniel/Sebast post where it all began. When he reached the locked gate, in hushed tones he tried to make contact with the two MPs. Puzzled, he, of course, received no response.

At that moment Captain O'Brien was unaware that a very real war had begun. Within seconds of one another, men on both sides had been killed in action near where he was now standing. Daniel and Sebast and the two sappers, if not the first, were certainly among the earliest casualties of that war in Saigon. And as Captain O'Brien would soon learn, two of his Marines had already been wounded at that most critically important location, Post #1.

Alerted by his movement, six sappers inside the compound spun toward the Marines on the outside, and suddenly O'Brien was face to face with that war. Now there was an eyeball-to-eyeball confrontation. O'Brien's only weapon was a pistol, so he shouted to one of his sergeants who had a Beretta, and who instantly shoved the muzzle of his submachine gun through the barred gate and without hesitation sent forth a burst. He scored a hit, for he watched as a sapper fell to the ground. That was the first Marine-inflicted casualty. The remaining sappers retaliated by sending forth a heavy volume of fire, which forced the lightly armed Marines back across the street. There they tried to take cover behind trees, and futilely fired their pistols. This was no contest—small arms fire versus automatic weapons fire from the enemy.

Marine S.Sgt. Leroy J. Banks was also awakened by the explosions at the Embassy. He dressed quickly and rushed to the front gate of the Marine House, where he assumed command of the reaction force that had assembled there.

He moved out with his reaction force within minutes of Captain O'Brien, and headed for the front side of the Embassy. As they advanced, Banks split his little force into two teams—one to move along the roadway trees and the other to follow him along the front wall of the Embassy.

From the already alarmingly busy MP net, Lieutenant Colonel George, the Provost Marshal, was quickly aware of the attack upon the Embassy. His first action was to direct the 716th Military Police Battalion to respond to the attack by sending a reaction force to the Embassy. As part of his instructions, he reminded the force to dismount a block away, and to check out the situation on foot.

It was Sergeant Leslie R. Trent, the Charge of Quarters, 527th Military Police Company, who rushed to Sergeant Rivera's room in the International Hotel, and told him to get his reaction force moving as the American Embassy was under attack. Since they had slept in their fatigues, it took Rivera only a matter of minutes to form his team. At the same time, what little information was available was being passed on to Lt. Frank Ribich by his battalion commander, Lieutenant Colonel Rowe. It would be Ribich who would take charge of the reaction force. Sergeant Rivera had, in the meantime, moved his men to the alert vehicles.

As this was taking place, back at the Embassy, Sergeant Bank's reaction force, upon nearing the Norodom Compound, came under heavy automatic fire. Banks yelled to Sergeant Schuepfer, who was inside, to unlock the gate. Banks was told that that there were already sappers inside the main Embassy Compound. Banks immediately decided to let his men, who were under the cover of the tree line, remain there while his fire team moved up along the wall to the main gate, where they could fire through the wrought-iron gate into the compound. As they moved along the wall toward the compound, a hand grenade was tossed over the wall, hitting Sgt. James W. Jimerson on the leg. He reacted instantly, kicked the grenade into the road, and yelled to his buddies, "Hit the deck!" which they did. That saved them, for although the grenade exploded, none were injured. Almost instantly, the group came under heavy sniper fire and another tossed grenade came over the wall. They were forced to retrace their steps to the Norodom gate. This time Sergeant Banks and his reaction team were able to move inside through the gate, which Sergeant Schuepfer had unlocked for them.

Back at the International Hotel, Lieutenant Ribich joined Sergeant Rivera, and they loaded their reaction force into the waiting vehicles. These consisted of a three-quarter-ton truck and a jeep. Each member of the force was armed with a .45 caliber pistol with three magazines of .45 caliber ammunition, and an M-16 rifle with a hundred rounds of ammunition. Once loaded, the reaction force departed for the John F. Kennedy Circle, where they would dismount and walk the rest of the way to the Embassy.

Sergeant Schuepfer, accompanied by Corporal Huss, as part of his patrol duties was checking to ensure that the rear entrance to the Norodom Compound was secure. Corporal Huss, upon moving to the nearby rear parking lot, immediately spotted a suspicious looking individual. He held his fire to be sure that the individual was not an Embassy employee. That he was not was immediately confirmed. The intruder, carrying an AK-47, walked into a lighted spot. Now, without hesitation, Corporal Huss fired his .38 caliber revolver, his only weapon, and hit the VC's lower body seriously enough to knock him down. Although apparently badly wounded, the sapper was able to crawl away and under vehicles in the parking lot. Because Corporal Huss had expended all his ammunition, he considered it unwise to attempt to capture the sapper by crawling after him.

Corporal Ryan, a member of Sergeant Bank's force, had assumed a position near the Norodom gate. He could see a jeep rapidly approaching the main gate. He recognized it as an MP patrol vehicle that had apparently been prowling the streets of Saigon. The patrol radio must have flashed the news of the enemy attack at the Embassy. With that, the two-man patrol must have sped to the Embassy to check on the situation there. The two passengers in the jeep were Sgt. Jonnie B. Thomas and Specialist Fourth Class Owen E. Mebust. The moment the jeep stopped, Sergeant Thomas hopped out on the passenger side and turned to walk to the rear. He had barely moved when he was shot in the back by a sniper. He stumbled and then collapsed. Corporal Ryan yelled for the driver to take cover. Specialist Fourth Class Mebust must not have heard Ryan, or disregarded the warning in his eagerness to help his wounded buddy. Once out of the vehicle, he ran around it to get to Thomas. Upon reaching Thomas and realizing that he was dead, Mebust reached for his radio microphone to send a distress call but never made it, as he too was instantly killed, this time by a burst of automatic fire.

The Military Police reaction force arrived at John F. Kennedy Circle, about two blocks south of the Embassy, at 0315. Lieutenant Ribich and Sergeant Rivera had the men dismount, and the group was quickly divided into two teams. Since they were not aware of the exact situation, it was considered prudent to advance to the Embassy on foot. Within four hundred feet of the Norodom Compound the reaction force came under intense automatic fire, which forced them to take cover. However, they continued to advance. As they neared the compound, Lieutenant Ribich could not help but notice Sergeant Thomas' and Specialist Mebust's jeep, and then their bodies. There was absolutely no evidence to show how the jeep's two passengers had been killed. This was puzzling, for the sappers were inside the compound, and the two MPs died outside of it.

It was now 0337. Lieutenant Ribich, after assessing the situation, concluded that Thomas and Mebust had been mowed down by fire from outside the compound. His force continued to receive automatic fire, and Lieutenant Ribich now knew without a doubt that the fire was not only coming from the outside of the Embassy, but from a source almost directly opposite the main gate. That culprit was easily identified. It had to be the eight-story apartment building that dominated the east side of Thong Nhut and the main gate, as well. Here, unquestionably, was where the sniper and automatic fire originated. Realizing this, Lieutenant Ribich immediately ordered Sergeant Rivera to move his fire team and to assault the building and secure it. Sergeant Rivera, even with his small force, knew that he would have to start at the top and work down. So he and his men rushed the building and continued on to the top. As they ascended the building, they found no signs of snipers or other armed individuals who obviously had quickly vacated the premises. In a minimum amount of time they reached the top of the building and moved out onto the roof, where they spotted four armed individuals. Sergeant Rivera spat out an order, and they instantly dropped their weapons. A quick examination of their identification cards surprisingly revealed that they were American civilians. They were ordered to return immediately to their rooms. It would turn out that the apartment building was the residence of a wide miscellany of individuals.

As his force cleared the building floor by floor, Rivera ordered all the residents to remain in their rooms. When his search was complete, his team secured all entrances to the building, so as to deny to the VC further entry into the building.

Thus ended a somewhat small, puzzling aspect of the Embassy battle. The mission of the twenty sappers was to get into the Embassy Compound, and to take control of it. Now it became evident that they had allies in the person of the sniper or snipers, and the shooters of the automatic weapons. One has to wonder if the sappers knew that they had allies outside. This development had to be the work of a clever planner who had looked ahead. He must have known of the apartment building and its dominance over the main entrance to the Embassy. He also must have calculated that once the attack on the Embassy commenced, men and vehicles would be drawn to the main gate on Thong Nhut, and would be lucrative targets for shooters positioned in the apartment building. So he had at least one sniper and one individual armed with an automatic weapon stashed inside the building, awaiting the commencement of the Tet attack.

Now with the threat eliminated, that flank was secure. Lieutenant Ribich was also, at last, able to move his men into the Norodom Compound. Once inside, he sought out and located Staff Sergeant Banks, who was the ranking Marine guard inside.

As events would subsequently unfold, the meeting between Lieutenant Ribich and Staff Sergeant Banks would prove to be a portentous one.

As has been mentioned, every U.S. Embassy located in the wide variety of countries around the world has assigned to it a Marine Security Guard Detachment, whose responsibility is to provide security for that Embassy. The size of those detachments varies considerably. They are based primarily on the size and importance of the country, and the political and diplomatic factors then prevailing.

Because of the uniqueness of the situation in Vietnam and Saigon, the Marine detachment was a sizeable one. It was expected that its personnel had drafted contingency plans for such things as nuisance and terrorist attacks, side-by shootings, demonstrations, and protest gatherings. The State Department planners, however, in their wildest imaginings could not have visualized or foreseen such a formidable at-

tack on the Embassy as part of the unbelievable widespread Tet offensive on the city of Saigon.

As mentioned, responsibility for the security of the Embassy rested upon the shoulders of the U.S. Marines. Headquarters Area Command had in Saigon and environs 450 installations for which it was responsible, but the U.S. Embassy was not one of them. The State Department assumed responsibility for their Embassy. HAC's MPs routinely patrolled the streets around it, and the MPs had a presence in the Embassy Compound, but it was limited to a two-man post. The Marines were in charge. It was their fight. However, this one was much too big for them. They could not do it alone. And so in this very grave emergency, HAC's MPs joined forces with them.

Now what was unfolding was a totally unexpected, unplanned-for contingency. The Marines and the HAC MPs certainly had never expected to be called upon to work together under such a drastic, dramatic circumstance. But there they were, operating together within the tight confines of the Embassy Compound. At night, in the dimly lit compound, they were confronting scattered, suicidal, heavily armed, diminutive individuals. The Marines and MPs would also be scattered and operating singly or in pairs. Friend and foe could easily get mixed up at such close quarters, inviting confusion and the alarming possibility of Marines and MPs firing upon one another.

Enter two individuals junior in rank who alertly, astutely, and quickly recognized that such just could not happen. The moment Lieutenant Ribich met Staff Sergeant Banks, he quickly described the deployment of Sergeant Rivera's small force. Then these two individuals made a critical decision that would have a profound impact on the entire remaining Embassy battle. They recognized that both the Marine and MP chain of command had to be kept intact, while at the same time both sides had to be completely aware of what the other was confronting. So two individuals set up an extremely simple, informal, ad hoc joint command. This makeshift action proved to be critically effective during the entire subsequent battle, and assisted greatly in bringing about the successful conclusion of the battle with no friendly fire casualties.

Following his meeting with Staff Sergeant Banks, Lieutenant Ribich contacted Sergeant Harper at the main desk to receive a report on the chancery situation. He especially had to know, and thus asked, if any sappers had gained entrance into the chancery. Sergeant Harper confirmed that none had gotten inside. With all the confusion then prevailing no one could possibly recognize or realize how critical were the words, "None have gotten inside." What those words, unbelievably, also meant was, "None will get inside. Thus, the chancery is secure."

How could that be? It could be because the sappers had an absolutely golden but fleeting window of opportunity to seize the chancery. It was theirs on a silver platter. Yes, when the sappers invaded the Embassy grounds, the chancery was theirs for the taking. There was nothing in their way. It was defenseless. Yet, they blew it!

They had just killed the only two visible military men, MPs Daniel and Sebast. The only other armed military personnel in the entire Embassy Compound at the time were Sergeant Schuepfer and Lance Corporal Wilson, who were manning Post #12 in the Norodom Compound. This was some distance from the main door of the chancery, and was separated from it by an interior wall and locked gates. Sergeant Harper and Corporal Zahuranic were stationed at Post #1, which was in the chancery behind the main door in the lobby. Sergeant Soto was positioned on the roof of the chancery. That was the total military strength.

Included in the population of the Embassy Compound were civilians and noncombatants. At that time they consisted of the following: Mr. E. Allen Wendt, a USAID economics expert, who was serving as Embassy Night Duty Officer on the fourth floor of the chancery, two Vietnamese employees—a night watchman and a teletype operator on the ground floor—a code clerk and an army communications operator, the CIA Night Duty Officer, and two of his men on the 4th floor.

Two others were Col. George D. Jacobson, U.S. Army (Ret.) and M.Sgt. Robert A. Josephson, U.S. Army (Ret.), who served as associates to the ambassador. Jacobson's title was Mission Coordinator, and he lived in the French villa in the north corner of the compound behind the chancery. This was Josephson's last night in Vietnam, and he was the houseguest of Jacobson. Both were unarmed, and neither could contribute in any way to the defense of the Embassy.

As related, almost immediately after they gained entry into the Embassy grounds, sappers positioned themselves in front of the main door and quickly fired two RPGs, one after another. These splintered the main door and sent fragments into the lobby. These wounded Harper superficially and Zahuranic seriously. A tossed grenade also somehow reached the lobby.

At this point Sergeant Harper believed that it was all over. He steeled himself for the expected onslaught. With Zahuranic out of action, he was alone, but prepared to go down fighting. He knew full well from the already damaged door that two more RPGs, or four at the most, would completely shatter the door, leaving it wide open for immediate entry by a small horde of sappers, who would quickly take control of all floors of the chancery.

But amazingly, incomprehensibly, as he waited breathlessly for the next moment, which would be his last, the blow never came. No more RPGs, no sappers came slashing through his door. Moments at first, then minutes, began to pass. He continued to hear voices, and then he heard RPGs fired, but they were random shots at the upper floors. The massive, coordinated attack, much to his astonishment and huge relief, never came.

What happened? After the initial two RPGs damaged the chancery door, the sappers did the unthinkable. They did not follow up, but instead moved away. There was nothing, absolutely nothing to stop them. Incredibly, they stopped themselves. Astonishingly, it appears that after their two RPG shots, they may not have been aware of the damage they had done, and were waiting for someone to tell them what next to do. It was readily apparent that there was no someone; they were without a leader, no sergeant or lieutenant to direct, coordinate, and lead their efforts.

The only plausible explanation, but possibly the correct one, as later events would indicate, *is that the first two sappers who slipped through the blasted hole in the wall surely must have been the two team leaders.* When they died at the hands of Daniel and Sebast, the success of the operation died with them. The remaining leaderless sappers obviously did not realize that all they had to do was to join together in front of the main door of the chancery, fire a small barrage of RPGs to reduce the door to splinters, charge in and take control of the entire building. It seemed like such a simple, obvious operation. Yet, it did not happen. One of battle's rare, precious gems is surprise. This is fragile, fleeting, but also very powerful. When one has it, it must be used suddenly, quickly, without hesitation, for once it's gone it can never be recalled. The sappers had surprise in the palm of their hands for a brief period, but let the unforgiving opportunity get away, squandered.

The remaining sappers, without a leader, were now an uncoordinated group of individuals. Without question their team leaders, during their briefing, had stressed the importance of that particular building, but the sappers were not sophisticated enough to realize the tremendous psychological impact it would have worldwide if it were in their hands. They were simple but very dedicated, capable soldiers. They knew that withdrawing from the Embassy Compound was not an option. Thus, they would fight to the finish in that relatively small box.

Although the chancery had not been captured and appeared secure, the real Embassy battle was just beginning. It would be a series of dangerous, bloody, dirty little skirmishes. The battle itself would be as "unclassic," unconventional, as one could possibly be. The "battlefield" was a tiny walled-in area with a small variety of buildings, parked cars, interior wall and gates.

The contrast between the two combatants could not be more remarkable. On one side there were the sappers, now apparently leaderless. They wore civilian attire, but were heavily armed. They were dangerous, tenacious, had been well trained on how to kill. Moreover, they were now desperate, suicidal, for they knew that they would not leave that battlefield alive. Accordingly, they would seek and destroy, take down with them as many as they possibly could.

Arriving on this battlefield after the sappers had infiltrated and deployed were MP and Marine reaction forces. Although these elements were well aware that they would be fighting sappers, they had absolutely no idea of how many, or where they were hiding. The MPs and Marines were not nearly as heavily armed as their foe. Their mission, likewise, was seek and destroy—eliminate the sappers from the Embassy grounds.

The Embassy battle would be a series of small, isolated, uncoordinated actions—a war of attrition. Each side would seek targets of opportunity, and try to snuff them out. There would be duels between individuals.

The battle would end when the last sapper was killed or captured.

* * *

It was those individual confrontations and events that together brought total victory to the Embassy battle.

At this point in the battle, the sappers were in control of and roaming about the Embassy compound. The main gate had been locked early, before there was any sign of sappers. The side (vehicle) gate had been left unlocked and open until the sappers appeared and fired on Daniel and Sebast, who immediately closed and locked the gate. Thus, the only way for the sappers to gain entrance to the Embassy grounds was by crawling through the blasted hole and by scaling the ten-foot wall, both of which they did.

As for the MP and Marine reaction forces and reinforcements to come, the only options open for entry into the Embassy Compound were scaling the wall or blasting open the locked gate. Scaling the wall was briefly considered and quickly discarded. It was dark but there was visibility. Figures could be spotted. Upon reaching the top, individuals scaling the wall would be briefly silhouetted and extremely vulnerable. Gathering at the main gate to blast open the lock was also not feasible at this particular time. So the U.S. elements had used the only way readily open to them to enter the Embassy complex, which was through the Norodom Compound gate that had been opened from the inside.

Separating the sappers and the Embassy Compound from the Norodom Compound was an interior wall. For elements of the reaction forces to gain entrance into the Embassy Compound, they had to do it from the Norodom Compound, through an unlocked gate. Thus, most of the engagements in the remaining battle would take place in the rear of the chancery.

Corporal Huss and Lance Corporal Caudle had moved out into the Embassy Compound into an area near the rear parking lot. Deciding to run for the door to the generator building, Caudle received fire from automatic weapons. When he reached the generator building, Caudle rushed through the door and hit the floor as the building was being peppered. Corporal Huss was able to spot the sappers doing the firing. Since he had only a .38 revolver, which did not come close to providing him with the firepower that he needed, he returned to Staff Sergeant Banks in Norodom for more and better weapons. After Huss had left, Caudle emerged from the building only to have a sapper hiding behind a tree in the parking lot open fire at him. He jumped back inside the building, and again plopped down on the floor. It was not a bit too soon, for at the next moment a burst of fire, including an exploding rocket, hit the wall.

Corporal Huss provided Lieutenant Ribich and Staff Sergeant Banks with a quick, brief situation report. Banks immediately headed out with Sergeant Jimerson, Sergeant Spersrud, Corporal Marshall and two MPs for the generator building. Two minutes after Staff Sergeant Banks had departed at about 0400, an MP patrol, which had responded to an Embassy distress call, reported to Lieutenant Ribich. This patrol was equipped with an M-60 machine gun. Since the MPs and Marines were seriously outgunned by the sappers, Lieutenant Ribich instructed the MPs to follow him. They moved out at a dead run around the Office of the Special Assistant (OSA) building to the generator building. Ribich immediately placed the machine gun in the doorway and began firing at suspected locations of sappers among vehicles in the parking lot. Ribich returned to the Norodom Compound, leaving Banks in charge.

Sergeant Jimerson kept darting outside to try to draw fire and provide targets for the M-60 machine gun. Lance Corporal Caudle, who had been the first one in the building, was now absorbed into the team.

Staff Sergeant Banks decided to move his team, one at a time, through the open doorway into the parking lot. Sergeant Jimerson—who was armed with a Beretta, which gave him more and better firepower than a pistol—jumped out first, so as to be able to lay down a base of fire for the others. As he stepped through the doorway, he spotted two sappers running across the parking lot and fired all twenty of his rounds, knocking down both of them.

As he turned back to the doorway, he was the target of a great burst of fire and a rocket, which exploded close to the door and to him. He received a small wound to his left hand. Still a bit dazed by the concussion, the continuing fire found him again. He received a second wound to his right leg. It was now perfectly obvious to Staff Sergeant Banks that they were badly outgunned by the sappers, who had selected good positions and were now entrenched in the parking lot. A further advance or attack was out of the question. So he decided to withdraw temporarily to the front of the Norodom Compound with part of his force. He would leave two military policemen with the M-60 machine gun and two members of the team to hold their position and cover the area.

While the two MPs were administering first aid to him and preparing him for movement, Sergeant Jimerson shouted that a rocket was coming in, and immediately the two MPs jumped on him to cover his body. The rocket exploded, spraying the area with shrapnel and wounding one of the MPs in his left arm. The protection provided by the flak jackets worn by the MPs prevented Jimerson from being wounded again. There is no question that Jimerson showed great daring and courage and certainly distinguished himself during this brief engagement with the sappers.

At about this time Corporal Marshall and Corporal Ryan, inside the Norodom Compound, climbed to the top of the OSA Building, which afforded them an excellent field of fire into the Embassy Compound. Ryan followed Marshall as they climbed up. Not long after he positioned himself, Marshall noticed that fire from the M-60 seemed to be forcing sappers to leave their positions and move about. Corporal Ryan, armed with a Beretta and about two hundred rounds of ammunition, suddenly noticed that three sappers had moved into range in front of their position. He immediately opened fire. The sappers instantly realized that they had moved too far, and that men on the roof were firing at them. Without hesitation they stopped, turned, and raced toward the safety of the main entrance. Corporal Ryan, aiming at the fleeing sappers, fired another burst, and amazingly all three sappers went down. Then Marshall observed a sapper crawling from behind a planter near the chancery, fired several rounds at him, and apparently killed him.

Although two more sappers were spotted, before they could fire on them, Corporal Ryan himself was wounded in the head, left arm, and left leg by a rocket that hit the OSA Building. Wounded in the face by shrapnel from that round, Corporal Ryan was assisted down from the roof by Corporal Marshall, and handed over to several Military Policemen on the ground. Marshall returned to his position on the roof with Ryan's Beretta and about one hundred rounds of ammunition. Ryan was moved close to the front, and he requested that an MP put a field dressing over his wound. Fearing that a piece of shrapnel protruding from his head might kill him if moved, Lieutenant Ribich instructed them to leave the wound alone. As Ryan was evacuated, Corporal Wilson climbed up to the roof to assist Marshall.

About this time, Staff Sergeant Banks, using the phone in the guard shack, contacted Sergeant Harper in the chancery lobby. He was vastly relieved to learn that Sergeant Harper and the chancery main door had not been assaulted in any way since their initial confrontation. Harper declared that he was well aware of sapper movements on the Embassy grounds, but, amazingly, they had left him alone. Banks then explained to Harper that a decision had been made to wait until daybreak for the big assault on the Embassy Compound, and assured Harper that they would get to him at the earliest opportunity.

About 0418 the Military Police desk received a request from Lieutenant Ribich for a substantial and varied supply of additional ammunition. Lieutenant Colonel George contacted Sergeant Kuldas, who was his traffic chief, and gave him the important mission. Sergeant Kuldas without hesitation departed for the ammunition bunker, dug out the various types that were needed, and in no time personally delivered the shipment to the Embassy.

Capt. James T. Chester, Commander of "B" Company, 716th Military Police Battalion, departed from the International Hotel at 0430 with a fifty-man reaction force. After arriving within one block of the Embassy, Captain Chester, along with Lieutenant Ribich, who had joined him, Sergeant First Class Williams, and two Military Policemen, moved on to the Norodom Compound.

Fire from that compound into the Embassy Compound seemed to be effective in pinning down the sappers. Nevertheless, Captain Chester and Lieutenant Ribich wanted to be sure that all avenues of escape were closed to the sappers, and that they would remain trapped in the embassy compound. Accordingly, they decided at about 0500 to position Chester's force along the street in front of the chancery.

Meanwhile, Corporal Marshall and Corporal Wilson, who had been positioned for some time on top of the OSA Building, spotted a sapper behind a tree and fired in his direction. The sapper returned fire, hitting Cpl. James C. Marshall in the neck. He fell to the roof. Corporal Wilson rushed to his aid and found that the shot had killed Marshall. The fire toward the roof now became heavy. Apparently the sappers had discovered that was where much of their grief had come from. With that, Wilson yelled to the MPs to get off the roof.

At that hot bed of activity, the generator building, action continued. Three Marine reinforcements, Sgts. David R. Bothwell, Richard L. Johnson, and Joseph S. Wolff, left the Marine House, scaled a back shed, and joined Sergeant Reed, who was already in the area. The four of them quickly moved to the rear of the generator building. The moment that they were settled, they began pouring a steady volume of fire at the sappers who had taken cover behind cars in the parking lot. Sergeant Bothwell spotted and killed two sappers who were at the far corner of the chancery building. In retaliation, sappers behind a pillar near the chancery began firing at the team on top of the generator building. As the sappers moved to better firing positions, Sergeant Johnson opened fire with his Beretta, forcing them to move for cover, which provided an opportunity for Sergeant Reed to kill a member of the group. The remaining two sappers, now without cover, stopped and began firing again and so did Sergeant Johnson. One of his bursts hit the leading sapper, who went down but managed to get back up, and both rushed around to the shelter afforded them on the opposite side of the building. The team had been firing furiously and now found themselves short of ammunition. This was a good time for one of its members, Sergeant Wolff, to undertake the risky but necessary trip back to the Norodom Compound for a quick re-supply.

In the Norodom Compound, Lieutenant Ribich was in contact with the Military Police radio net control station, WACO, and was told that Lieutenant Colonel George had declared that it was now time for the assault on the Embassy Compound and the elimination of the remaining sappers. Ribich gave the order to move out at 0700, which would be daylight. Shortly after, he was told to move his kickoff fifteen minutes earlier, to 0645. Once the order "Go!" was given, the Embassy battle would soon come to a close.

The battle had not by any means followed a predictable pattern. It had been weird, no continuity, no common thread of any kind through it, and with totally unexpected twists and turns. The sappers had roamed the grounds firing away at anything they saw moving. The Marines and MPs did their best to pick off the sappers one by one.

Both sides were formidable adversaries. The sappers were predictably fanatical, resourceful, and had used the great firepower of their AK-47s to full advantage. For a small band, their ferocious fight had a great impact.

The Marines and MPs, likewise, had acquitted themselves superbly. They were considerably under-gunned, but were tenacious and successful in picking off sappers.

But now, with the assault about to kick off, it would finally be over for the sappers still remaining. They had weathered an intense, demanding, stressful and costly night. And at this point they had just about "shot their wad." Now they were facing a force that would outnumber and simply overpower them. However, they would still have a couple of surprises up their sleeves. Like pesky varmints, there was still "no quit" in them, and they would continue to lead a surprisingly merry chase until they went down fighting.

From the outset of their attack on the Embassy, it had been expected that the chancery would be the focal point, the centerpiece, of the Embassy battle, and it would be where the battle would begin and where it would end. Amazingly, after two RPG shots and a tossed grenade at the main entrance, the chancery would "never be heard from again." The Embassy battle would end in the most unlikely place, in the most unlikely way. The final minutes would be almost unbelievable.

The moment the word "Go!" was sent out, Specialist Fourth Class Healey and Sergeant Shook drove a jeep right to the main gate and shot the lock off, but much to their surprise and chagrin they could not force the gate open. Big, burly Sergeant Kuldas and several MPs added weight to the vehicle, and pushed it against the gate. The best that they could do was to force it open enough to allow the members of the attacking force to enter the compound one at a time.

Healey was the first man through. After him, the following troops fanned out like a wide sweeper across the grounds, with their weapons at the ready and with their safeties off. The first sapper reaction was almost instantaneous. As Healey was moving along in front of the door to the chancery, he detected a movement to his left, turned and watched in horror as a sapper tossed a grenade at him, which landed at his feet. Healey instantly shot and killed him. But seconds had elapsed, and Healey steeled himself for the grenade that was ready to explode at the very next second and probably kill him. Much to his great surprise and astonishing reprieve, the grenade at his feet was a dud. He had been spared.

While some of the Military Policemen were moving along the wall and across the compound, engaging the sappers in the front part of the compound, Sergeant Rivera's force of military policemen, along with Marines, entered the parking lot from the Norodom Compound. As they were moving along the parking lot, Sergeant Kuldas, Corporal Moyer, and Specialist Fourth Class Singer noticed bloodstains on the Embassy Compound side of the wall that separated it from the Norodom Compound. Footprints on the wall indicated that it was highly likely that a sapper had scaled the wall. Kuldas and Singer moved back into the Norodom Compound, and proceeded to move along the walkway that separated it from the OSA Building and the wall. They continued to follow the bloody tracks and came upon the dog run, where they surprisingly spotted an abandoned AK-47 and more blood in the middle of the run. It appeared incongruous, but the sapper seemed to have been attacked by a dog. In a sudden state of panic, he must have dropped his gun and made a run for the safety of the OSA Building. Sure enough, Sergeant Kuldas found bloodstains at a doorway to the office building. He entered the building and found a blood trail on the hallway floor, which he followed to the door of the map room, which he found was locked from the inside. With that he shouted for someone inside to open the door. With no response forthcoming, he blasted the door. As the door flew open, there stood the someone, a frightened, shaking, unarmed sapper with his hands straight up in surrender.

This turned out to be quite a story. Some days after the end of the Embassy battle, the February 9, 1968 issue of *Life Magazine* carried a full front page picture showing a sapper with a bloodstained face, two very bloody arms, and a shirt covered with blood, his arms stiffly straight up in surrender. He is standing between the powerfully built Sergeant Kuldas, who towers above him, and a younger, robust, tough-looking MP. By contrast what is seen is a tiny, youthful, bewildered, innocent appearing individual, but until captured, he was a potent, lethal, dangerous weapon. Of the twenty sappers, nineteen were killed, and this was the only one wounded and captured. He was not able to go down fighting like his compatriots, because he had abandoned his AK-47.

Shortly after moving through the steel door separating the Norodom Compound from the parking area, Sergeant Rivera immediately spotted three sappers, took them under fire, and it appeared that he had quickly killed the three. After that, he and his team continued to sweep the parking lot area to ensure that if there were any sappers left there, they were all dead.

Then followed another absolutely bizarre confrontation. It would be an almost hour-long shootout with, of all things, a single, wounded sapper. This was not an ordinary guy. He was frantic, fanatical, an amazingly tenacious, clever, diehard sapper, who turned out to be a one-man army. He provided one more surprising twist in the already utterly strange Embassy battle. No! The final shot would not be fired, the last sapper killed, at or in the chancery. It was in, of all places, the mission coordinator's quarters in the northeast corner of the Embassy Compound. As Sergeant Rivera, with his Military Policemen and Marines, moved along the Embassy wall, word reached them that a wounded sapper, seeking refuge, had just burst into the mission coordinator's quarters.

This was a two-story, white stucco villa. A very uneasy and greatly troubled Colonel Jacobson had spent the night in the upstairs hall of that building. It must have been a frightening night for him to hear firing all around him, not knowing if it was friend or foe, not knowing what was really happening. Worst of all, he had expected sappers to burst into his home at any moment, and he was unarmed and defenseless. He had found a hand grenade in the desk in his bedroom, which he had been clutching. If sappers had come charging up the stairs at him, the one grenade was his only weapon.

Sometime after daylight, he moved from the back hall to the top of the stairs. As he looked down the steps, he was astonished to note bloody spots on the rug at the bottom of the steps. Colonel Jacobson instantly knew that he had company in the villa. Fright began edging toward panic. He still had phone contact outside of the villa and he recognized that if there ever was a time to use it, it was now. He sent out an emergency call about his dangerous predicament. The "word" soon after, somehow, reached Sergeant Rivera. Without hesitation he moved his force right to the villa.

The first effort by the Military Policemen and Marines upon reaching the building was to rush the back door. They were met by a hail of fire from the very alert, dangerous sapper, who drove them back with his powerful AK-47. Sergeant Rivera, without hesitation, slipped his force toward the front door. Once again it was Healey who grabbed the lead, kicked open a door on the front porch and, along with Marine Sergeant Bothwell, charged inside. Someone was waiting, for Sergeant Bothwell immediately received a shot in his thigh. Under fire, Healey quickly dragged the Marine out of the house and onto the porch, and then threw a grenade into the villa. It was not immediately known if the grenade had any effect on the sapper, but the explosion stunned

Colonel Jacobson as he lay on the top step ready to use his one grenade if the sapper climbed the stairs to him.

Captain O'Brien now appeared on the scene and went right to the aid of Bothwell, his wounded Marine. He charged up the porch steps, and started to pull Bothwell to safety, when of all things, a grenade came at them from out of the house. O'Brien reacted instantly and covered his sergeant, only to be wounded himself. It was obvious to all that the sapper, like a cornered rat, was fighting a desperate and clever battle. The situation and the evacuation of Bothwell became even more complicated. While all this was taking place, two teargas grenades were pushed through the bars of a first floor window by MPs. O'Brien quickly slipped a gas mask over Bothwell's face and then over his own. Healey, nearby without a gas mask, clearly felt its early sting.

The very desperate Colonel Jacobson appeared at his bedroom window shouting frantically for a weapon. He was certain that the CS had now swept through the first floor, and would force the sapper upstairs. Once again it was Healey. He stood completely vulnerable on the lawn close to the building, and tossed up to Jacobson a .45 pistol and a gas mask. Once he had them in hand, Colonel Jacobson did not waste a moment getting his gas mask on and selecting a corner defensive position. Now he was a bit more ready for the next development, whatever that might be. The tables had suddenly turned in his favor.

The sapper, without a gas mask, was probably half blind. Going up the stairs now dominated by Colonel Jacobson was the only way to get away from the gas. So as he began his ascent, he also began to fire his AK-47. He climbed the steps as quickly as he could, and fired his powerful weapon back and forth up the stairs. On a much broader scale this might be termed, "reconnaissance by fire." Some of his shots were hitting just over Jacobson's head. Just as he was about to reach the top, he shifted his position a bit. With that, Colonel Jacobson jumped up and fired twice at point-blank range. The sapper never had a chance, and that small, amazing, one-man fighting machine was instantly killed. As he began to tumble down the stairs, Colonel Jacobson grasped his

AK-47. Now he believed that he was much better prepared to greet the sappers who were sure to follow.

However, the movement that he now heard at the bottom of the steps was not more sappers. No, it was Military Policemen. Believing that the sapper was still covering the front door, they smashed open the rear door. The last sapper was dead.

This totally unexpected, incongruous, unbelievable climax to the Embassy fight had ended. The Embassy battle was over.

OBSERVATIONS

It is my firm belief that Specialist Fourth Class Charles L. Daniel and Private First Class William E. Sebast, although never so recognized, remain the great but unsung heroes of the Embassy battle.

As events unfolded and the fight evolved, the enemy attackers became a group of rudderless sappers. It is almost a certainty that the first two sappers through the Embassy wall were the "brains," the leaders of that small group. Had they not been mowed down at the very outset of the battle by Daniel and Sebast, it would have been only moments later that the chancery would have been assaulted and quickly occupied on all floors by the sappers. This did not happen. Daniel and Sebast saved the chancery. Even more importantly, they saved American lives. With a dozen or more sappers, each with an AK-47, holed up and holding on in the chancery, it would have been an absolute major undertaking to regain control of and to clear the chancery. The assault would have been murderous and extremely costly. Entering the tight confines of the building, climbing up the stairs in the face of heavy fire coming down the stairs, could have been total disaster. Bringing in troops by helicopter would not have helped, for the roof and helipad were easily closed off.

To the vast relief of a multitude, the unthinkable never happened. Daniel and Sebast gave up their lives, but saved the day.

Daniel and Sebast: genuine heroes in the Embassy battle.

Contrary to newspaper, magazine, television accounts, and assertions by individuals, and as here already described:

The VC *never*:

Seized the chancery.

Held the chancery.

Captured the chancery.

Entered the chancery.

* * *

The MP log had this entry:

0420 General Westmoreland calls, orders first priority effort to recapture the U.S. Embassy.

At 0420 the MPs and Marines had total control of the Norodom Compound, had fought and killed sappers in the back part of the Embassy Compound, and held control of the chancery. All that was left to secure was a portion at the ground of the front part of the Embassy Compound. At that very moment Captain Chester was departing for the Embassy with his fifty-man reaction force to help do just that.

* * *

Another genuine hero: He was merely a private first class, but Paul V. Healey, during the Embassy Battle, was always in the forefront, the first man out. He demonstrated great initiative, determination, courage, and selflessness. For his actions in the fight he was awarded the Distinguished Service Cross (DSC) for extraordinary heroism.

* * *

Some months after the Tet Offensive, there were still scars on the chancery façade and in its lobby. But there was also something new in that lobby. There had been a plaque erected commemorating the U.S. military men who died defending the Embassy. The words on the plaque read: *In memory of the brave men who died January 31, 1968, defending this Embassy against the Vietcong: Sp4 Charles L. Daniel, MPC; Cpl. James C. Marshall, USMC; Sp4 Owen E. Mebust, MPC; Pfc. William E. Sebast, MPC; Sergeant Jonnie B. Thomas, MPC.*

* * *

Except for the last hour and a half, the Embassy Battle was fought at night with but dim light. For good reason, the main outdoor Embassy lights had never been turned on.

The Embassy fight ended at 0830. The Embassy was officially declared secure at 0915.

During the Embassy Battle five Americans (four MPs and one Marine) were killed and fifteen were wounded.

The moment the fight was over at the Embassy, the military policemen returned to their headquarters to react and respond to the endless demands for their assistance and support in fighting off the VC in various parts of Saigon.

* * *

A Great Irony: In 1975, seven years later, the last Americans evacuated from Vietnam and Saigon took off in helicopters from the helipad on the roof of the chancery of the American Embassy in Saigon. That was the Embassy where personnel of Headquarters Area Command (HAC) fought gallantly and courageously, and were wounded and died, to save it from a vicious Communist assault during an earlier era.

In 1975, almost immediately after the last helicopter had left the roof, the Communists seized, captured, held, and entered the chancery and the Embassy Compound. In essence, our government ceded the U.S. Embassy in Saigon to the Communists.

For us who had diligently and courageously tried to protect it, it was a troubling, disheartening, sobering page in our nation's history.

CHAPTER EIGHTEEN

MY TWO WARS

Written by Brig. Gen. Albin F. Irzyk. Reprinted with permission from Daughters of the American Revolution Magazine, *January 2001.*

In his now famous Valedictory at West Point many years ago, Gen. MacArthur reminded us that old soldiers never die—they simply fade away. What he did not mention was that as they fade away, they are often flooded with memories. These seem to increase as the years behind steadily multiply, while those up ahead rapidly diminish. And those memories invariably bring with them periods of reflection.

Recently, while immersed in such a reflective mood, I found myself, once again, looking back upon two of the most vivid, momentous, vital, critical, significant periods of my life—my two wars, WWII and Vietnam. I had always felt tremendous unease when I thought about them together, and this time, more clearly than ever, I realized how totally and completely different those two wars were. The more I thought about them the more astonished I remained by their marked differences.

I decided that, perhaps, the best way to analyze critically and to make a graphic judgment of those stark, staggering, and remarkable differences was to make a side-by-side comparison. This I did, and when finished, more than ever before, I found it incredible, unbelievable, incomprehensible that one Nation, my Country, could have prosecuted two wars in such a disparate manner. I feel compelled now to share the results of that side-by-side comparison.

The first of my two wars began for me as I, in my tank, landed on Utah Beach on July 14, 1944. I was a young major, the operations officer of a tank battalion, as I began my 10-month war in Europe.

It was early in September, 1967 when I, as a brigadier general, touched down at Tan Son Nhut, Saigon, to begin my two-year war in Vietnam. For a brief, fleeting moment I felt a bit like Pug Henry of the "Winds of War" and the "War of Remembrance," for I was at war once again, and I realized that my two wars were separated by 23 years and two months. But as I proceeded to draw and develop my comparisons, it would become graphically clear that the differences were not measured by 23 years but by eons.

World War II started on September 1, 1939 with Blitzkrieg—the massed German tank invasion of hapless Poland. For the U.S. WWII had a clearly defined beginning—the bombing of Pearl Harbor by the Japanese on December 7, 1941. WWII from Blitzkrieg to the surrender signing by the Japanese on September 2, 1945 would extend for six years and a day, but WWII for the U.S. would last for a lesser period—three years and eight months.

But when did the war begin for us in Vietnam? Was it with the introduction of the first advisors, or was it when we suffered the first casualty from enemy fire, or when? In contrast to WWII there really was no defined beginning. Yet, it would extend for an agonizing, unbelievably long period of years.

The logical place to begin this side-by-side comparison is with LEADERSHIP.

During the entire period of WWII, except for the final four months when the war was already writhing in its final spasms, we had one president, Franklin D. Roosevelt. We, as a nation, were truly and exceptionally blessed, and for that we should consider ourselves particularly fortunate. He was absolutely the right man, in the right place during the right period of our history.

As a leader, he was superb. And *he was the leader*. He was in charge. He made the necessary decisions; the difficult, critical ones. It was his hand on the throttle, throughout. His valued right hand and implementer of many of his decisions was Gen. George C. Marshall. Together they were an incomparable, invaluable tandem. Yes, there was a strong supporting cast: Winston Churchill, Harry Hopkins, Secretary Stimson, General Eisenhower, General MacArthur, Admirals Nimitz, Leahy, King, the combined British and American Staffs. But it was Roosevelt all the way—a dynamic, decisive, bold, courageous, visionary, flexible leader.

And in Europe, my theater, we had a single, overall commander, Gen. Dwight D. Eisenhower. From Washington to the battlefield, the chain of command was simple, clear. And once the political, strategic decisions were made, Roosevelt, except for an occasional interaction, let the military fight the war.

How staggeringly different in Vietnam. In office during our involvement there was not one president but five: Eisenhower, Kennedy, Johnson, Nixon, Ford. Our participation with that country dated as far back as 1954. It was during that year that we had the Geneva Accords that led to the partitioning of Vietnam, as well as the birth of the Southeast Asia Treaty Organization (SEATO). But it was during President Kennedy's time that many of the initial decisions were made that would forever haunt us. And it was not until the Ford Administration some fourteen years later that the direct involvement (but not the nightmare) would end.

And during that entire period, where was the Rooseveltian leadership: the clear-cut, attainable objectives, the visionary, decisive decisions; the simplicity and clarity of the chain of command?

After Kennedy, we had Johnson, Nixon, Ford. In addition to our multiple presidencies, we had a stage full of performers, a veritable galaxy of advisors, many of whom David Halberstam would ultimately place under his umbrella of "The Best and The Brightest."

During those years, we had three main military field commanders: Generals Harkins, Westmoreland, and towards the end—Abrams; five ambassadors: Nolting, Lodge, Taylor, Bunker, Martin. There was

Gen. Earle Wheeler, chairman of the Joint Chiefs of Staff, and Gen. Maxwell Taylor, President Kennedy's favorite advisor, who floated in and out of that Country. A genius from the Ford Motor Company was brought in to be the secretary of defense, and he brought with him over thirty younger and lesser geniuses, who would soon be labeled the "Whiz Kids," and who quickly came to believe that moniker. Very soon after, they were lording it over, belittling, and even ignoring the senior, experienced, proven military leaders with whom they worked. This was unsettling as was the knowledge that they were soon applying Systems Analysis to Military Operations.

Beyond all of these was a vast multitude of additional advisors—many extremely well known, virtually all with most impressive academic (often Ivy League), political, and "think tank" credentials. Among these were such as Secretary of State Rusk and the Bundy brothers, McGeorge and William. Included, also, was a group of renowned elder statesmen labeled "the wise men." Collectively these individuals represented some of the best brains our nation could muster, and all of these to a greater or lesser extent had a finger in the Vietnam pie, and to a greater or lesser degree must accept and share the blame for the consequences of their actions and advice.

But it was McNamara who was in charge, who "ran the show." He was the Field Marshall. He was the one the president listened to; the one who rejected and ignored the advice and opinions of the service chiefs, who admittedly were not always responsive and reliable. It was McNamara, not the military, who developed the Strategic Concept (such as it was) and the doctrine of graduated pressure.

And, tragically, the military was not given its head to fight the war. Civilians (McNamara) tightly held the reins, and all too frequently made the military decisions—too many of which seriously handicapped the military. Distressing and demoralizing to the military were reports that President Johnson even spent time in the White House Situation Room helping to select bombing targets.

And then as time passed McNamara would begin to have "doubts" about the war over which he had had such a tremendous influence, and would be succeeded by that wise, venerable advisor to Presidents, Clark Clifford.

From leadership we move to MISSION and CONDUCT of the wars. In WWII the strategic mission was clear and simple—to defeat those superpowers, Germany and Japan, and the lesser one, Italy—a big mouthful, indeed. Then Pres. Roosevelt, our bold leader, told the enemy and the world just where he stood and exactly what he wanted. As early as January, 1943 at the Casablanca Conference, he defined precisely the rules by which we would wage the rest of the war. From that conference came the words, "firm intention of the U.S. and the British Empire to continue the war relentlessly, until we have brought about the 'Unconditional Surrender' of Germany and Japan." How more clear, simple, and forthright (and demoralizing to the enemy) could a strategic mission be? From that time on it would become a "no holds barred" war.

The mission in Europe, where I fought, was, likewise, clear and simple to understand. It was, first, to seize a toehold on the continent, to push out from the bridgehead, and advance to the East destroying forces in the way, and to conquer Germany. In the process we would employ every tactic and relentlessly every weapon at our disposal to include the bombing of Germany's major cities—nothing was "off limits."

General Patton typified the simplicity and clarity of operations. His army operated under "mission type" orders. The best example: when an armored division commander shortly after the Normandy breakout seized a major objective well ahead of schedule, he reported this to General Patton and asked for further orders. General Patton is reputed to have answered, "Go East and go like Hell!"

The mission in Vietnam was nowhere nearly as clearly defined. Our original motives were fundamentally altruistic. Our hearts were in the right place. South Vietnam was threatened by forces north of the 17th Parallel, and like a creeping cancer, the insidious Vietcong from within.

We wanted to help save it. For us there were absolutely no thoughts of aggrandizement—we were not involved to conquer or seize land. On the contrary; we would ultimately and unselfishly expend thousands of lives and billions of dollars. However, also in the back of our minds, we had to admit, was the nagging fear that the loss of South Vietnam might set in motion the "Domino Theory."

But something happened "on the way to the Forum." Yes, our initial motives may have been laudable, but somehow, somewhere they bogged down, began to lose focus. We were not able to get the gears to mesh. We became unsure of what we really wanted, or what to do and how to go about getting it. There was constant confusion in respect to objectives and courses of action to gain those objectives.

We began by advising the South Vietnamese on how and where to fight, then took over the fighting for them, and after we tired of that, we turned the fighting back over to them. And early on their president was not only toppled but assassinated, as we appeared to have turned our backs, or, perhaps, helped with a gentle shove.

Early on we supported the Strategic Hamlet Program. Later, as we became deeply involved tactically, we held for long periods of time defensive positions. There were seek and destroy missions, later, pacification missions. We fought for, seized, cleared, developed, and manned firebases, then left them. We fought for, cleared villages, and left them to be reoccupied by the enemy. We fought for valleys, mountains, and jungle trails. We fought up and down the length of South Vietnam, seemingly aimlessly for over ten years. And most of the time we fought the war on enemy terms. They acted, and we reacted.

It is readily apparent that the mission and conduct of the two wars differed markedly as did the METHOD of fighting which will be discussed next.

In WWII in Europe the defining word was "relentlessly"—"lifted" from the Casablanca Conference. Relentlessly is how we fought the war in Europe. It was all out war as Hitler had already clearly demonstrated. He set the tone with his "Buzz Bomb" attacks on London and the bombing of cities. For us it was attack, attack, and bomb, bomb. When necessary and without compunction, we bombed major German cities—Cologne, Dresden, Berlin, Frankfurt, Regensburg, realizing that it would mean destroying century old structures and killing multitudes of German civilians. Repeat: this was total war.

The military were told what to do, but the "how," basically, was left up to them. There was no "meddling" by a secretary of defense, or a bunch of "Whiz Kids," or by "advisors."

And on the ground gains and successes were clearly measurable by kilometers and miles—so many miles gained yesterday—so many more miles to the German border, to the Rhine, to the German heartland. The military knew what needed to be done, and went about doing it.

How very different in Vietnam. The worst type of war to fight is a Limited War. Vietnam was a Limited War, and the great tragedy is that we applied our own handcuffs by doing most of the limiting to ourselves. Early on our secretary of defense made it clear that we would not invade North Vietnam. There was even talk about erecting some sort of electronic fence along the 17th Parallel. What a boon, bonanza, tremendous advantage to the North Vietnamese. Now they could stop worrying about, preparing for, and could completely disregard an invasion from the South.

The North Vietnamese would attack our forces out of Laos and Cambodia, and our troops would chase them back to the borders, but not *into* those countries. The enemy had a "free ride" to absolutely safe sanctuaries. They could hit with impunity, knowing that when the jig was up, they could flee to safety like the mouse chased by the cat—to its little hole.

There was one major port, Haiphong; one major city, the capital, Hanoi. Yet, we chose not to bomb them. We could have destroyed them in one fell swoop. The B-52 was far superior to the B-17s and the B-24s, the workhorses of WWII. We did not hesitate to bomb the jungles, but we gagged about bombing the cities.

We had in Vietnam, at a given time, forces of over half a million men—army, navy, air force, marines fighting a full-blown war. Yet there was never a declaration of war. However, President Johnson, in an effort to legitimize what we were already doing, seized upon an alleged, veiled provocation by the North Vietnamese as a subterfuge to pressure Congress to pass the Tonkin Resolution, authorizing military action in Vietnam.

As was true of our strategy, tactically—on the ground—there seemed to be no firm goals, no clear objectives. We continually jumped at reports of enemy movement, and often attacked unseen enemy. Rarely did we initiate an action on our own.

And since we were not able to measure success by such tangibles as yards, kilometers, or miles we resorted to unrealistic measuring sticks—of which the most unbelievable, incongruous one was the body count. This would turn out to be a meaningless, inaccurate, distorted, exaggerated, deceitful, fraudulent method of measuring battlefield success. And, unfortunately, it was the "best" one we could come up with.

It was not until late in the war that we finally made swipes at Hanoi and Haiphong, and President Nixon, after much agonizing and soul-searching, eventually authorized a limited invasion of Cambodia.

Now it is appropriate to examine the SOLIDIERS who fought those two wars and the TRAINING they received. By the time of Pearl Harbor the draft was already in effect. But immediately after the bombing in Hawaii, induction stations all over our country were flooded. There were long lines of men who were waiting patiently to volunteer to serve. It seemed that virtually all able-bodied men were prepared to leave occupations, professions, businesses, schools, families to sign up for the duration plus six months—which for many would turn out to be three and four years. There was no evidence of fleeing to avoid service. Everyone, it seemed, wanted IN. Those who were rejected for physical or medical reasons were heartbroken, demoralized. Many would be guilt-ridden, and would spend much time in later years trying to explain why they were not able to serve. The military would become a cross-section of our country—all elements of our society would serve in the ranks of our armed forces.

For over three years I was a member of the 4th Armored Division. That outfit was based at Pine Camp, New York, and trained in the winter snows of upper New York State. Then it was on to Tennessee maneuvers, seven months in the Mojave Desert, six months at Camp Bowie, Texas, and even considerable training time on the Salisbury Plains of England. No unit could have been better-trained, more ready for combat than that division.

During the first day of combat after breaking out of the Normandy bridgehead, men were heard to shout, "Just like maneuvers!" Yes, it seemed that they had done that before, except that the uniforms worn by the enemy were different, and the fire coming in was live. The men of that division had lived together, trained together for many months—were buddies, a team, had bonded tightly. When they traveled, it was together on troop trains, troop ships. During combat, the units remained intact; replacements came to take the places of those killed or wounded.

Once again, how very different in Vietnam. Our servicemen who served in that war were just kids—18, 19, 20 years old, with many just 17. They had not yet finished high school, or had just graduated. Very many were draftees, drafted to serve two years. They reported as ordered, were inducted, put on uniforms, served and fought. They watched as very many of their fellows fled to Canada or Sweden, or hid within the campuses of colleges and universities, and even graduate schools. Let's face it—very few of the affluent or educated fought in Vietnam. And the kids in Vietnam were on an average at least half a dozen years younger than their WWII counterparts, and the vast majority were still single.

They received eight weeks of basic military training, then eight weeks of advanced individual training—a grand total of sixteen weeks, four months of military training. After this training, they were not assigned to a unit. They did not participate in platoon, company, battalion, regimental training. No! Sixteen weeks and off to war.

They were put on a chartered commercial aircraft, not a troop ship with their unit; not a Military Air Transport Service (MATS) plane with their buddies. No. They found themselves with a planeload of strangers, and were served in-flight meals by uniformed stewardesses. That is how they went to war.

Twenty-four hours later they landed half a world away. After landing, they were given a four day orientation at a base camp, and the next thing they knew they were again with a bunch of strangers—this time wallowing around in the swamps and jungles of Vietnam in what has been called the toughest testing ground of man—the field of combat.

When he landed in Vietnam, that individual was less prepared mentally, physically, educationally, emotionally, intellectually, psychologically than any man this country has ever sent to war. Just 24 hours before, he had left the most sophisticated society in the world—hot and cold running water, cars, McDonald's, Mom's hot apple pie. Now he was in the jungles and swamps of Vietnam.

Because of the draft, his would be a one-year war. He would be on a plane again returning home 12 months after arriving in that country. And every man who had been in his unit when he joined it, was already gone. The unit was ever changing; it was never set. Men were constantly coming in and going out—a corporal today, a sergeant tomorrow, a lieutenant next week. The unit would change 100 percent every 12 months. I would challenge General Motors to build cars, General Electric to produce toasters, and even the corner supermarket to keep operating, if they lost top executives, middle management, and the work force every 12 months. Yet, that was the challenge faced by every unit in Vietnam.

Now a word about the HOME FRONT. During WWII the whole country was at war. The populace was totally involved—the war touched everybody. It was a unified nation. War production was at full steam. For the first time women in great numbers joined the work force. It is estimated that over five million women would work for the first time. Their efforts and accomplishments would be symbolized by "Rosie the Riveter."

There was gasoline and sugar rationing, as well as the rationing of women's hosiery. Everyone, in one way or another, was part of the war effort. There was hardly a household without someone in the service. Many wives led nomadic lives as they followed their men from camp to camp.

During the Vietnam War, the picture was totally different. The war seemed to have no visible effect upon the populace. Hardly anyone, apparently, was aware that there was a war going on. Certainly, there was no mobilization of industry, no rationing of any kind. Basically, it was business as usual. America, it appeared, was a country that could care less. EXCEPT—when their fellows were fighting and dying, other young people launched protests and demonstrated. They seized ROTC buildings on college campuses, and set fires to National Guard armories in cities and towns. A vocal, busy, active minority did its very best to try to create divisions within this country.

Vast differences continue to abound—now, a discussion of the ENVIRONMENT and ENEMY that each faced.

During WWII, I fought in France, Belgium, and Germany. These were sophisticated countries much like ours. They, also, had substantial homes, plumbing, extensive roads, railroads, farms. The climate was similar, as they, too, had the four seasons.

And the enemy was much like we. They, also, wore combat uniforms. We had the Sherman tank, they had the Panther and Tiger. We had outstanding artillery, they had the fabulous 88. We had the bazooka, they had the even better Panzerfaust. They were educated, sophisticated. It was like the dueling of two similar, highly trained, motivated,

evenly matched gladiators—trying to outthink, outsmart, out-maneuver, overpower the other. Thankfully, though it was not easy, we won out.

Vietnam, on the other hand, was an unsophisticated, backward, poor, wild, primitive country with swamps, rice paddies, triple canopy jungle—with monsoons when the rain came down almost incessantly for nearly forty days and forty nights. Yes, there were even elephants and tigers.

And the enemy—well, there were really two enemies. The one was an army that wore uniforms, that had the outstanding AK-47, that had excellent rifles, mortars, artillery (some extremely long range) provided by the Russians and Chinese. The other was an army that fought from within, like an insidious cancer. They wore black pajamas and wore straw, conical hats. They were the smiling, friendly, do-anything-for-you good citizens. As barbers, they would cut your hair during the day, and try to cut your throat at night. Both of these armies were devious, treacherous, dangerous. They were absolute masters of their unique, unusual environment and habitat. They definitely had the home court advantage. They installed punji sticks, which if stepped upon, would ruin a foot or leg. They were amazingly imaginative, clever, and ingenious in the construction and placement of booby traps. They were like animals, and dug deep into the earth. Their tunnels ran for miles, were deep enough so that a person could stand upright in them, and some even housed hospitals. Individuals could completely submerge themselves in water, breathing only through a reed. Their tenaciousness was remarkable. A North Vietnamese soldier would walk endless miles through the jungle to deliver two mortar rounds, would turn around and walk back endless miles to pick up two more. That is what our American kids faced, were up against.

As mentioned above, during WWII, it seemed that virtually every able-bodied man in America was in uniform, along with many women. President Roosevelt had no hesitancy or compunction about calling to duty the NATIONAL GUARD and RESERVES—units and individuals. After all, this was the logical, expected thing to do. The National Guard and Reserves were long ago created, organized, designed to join, complement, support, relieve, back-up the regular forces, if those were forced to fight a war. And during WWII they did just that—assumed their rightful role.

But amazingly, incomprehensibly, astonishingly (those words again) during the Vietnam War, neither National Guard or Reserve units were called up. As many as half a million men were serving in Vietnam, but the National Guard and Reserves were still home; their duty at home was in their armories. Apparently LBJ feared to alienate his critics even more, and chose not to make the call. Gen. Harold K. Johnson, the army chief of staff, is reputed to have regretted until the end of his days his failure (and perhaps martyrdom) to stand up to the president on this matter.

A word now about CENSORSHIP. During WWII, television, of course, had not yet made its appearance. Thus, there were no TV cameras in the battle areas. Censorship in Europe was extremely tight. General Eisenhower controlled newspaper reporters virtually with an iron hand. They went only where he authorized them to go, and they were privy only to what he wanted them to know. Consequently, there was little opportunity to stray from factual reporting, and to interpret or slant the news. Thus, the information that the American public received was generally straightforward and basically accurate.

My division was General Patton's spearhead during that historic sweep across the widest part of France. Although operating in the very thick of it, it was 2½ months before the first mention of the division was made in the *Stars and Stripes*.

Every letter written by a serviceman was censored. Recipients on occasion found tiny holes in the letters indicating that names of places had been "scissored."

By the time of Vietnam television had long been with us. Thus, as expected, T.V. cameras aplenty were there together with print reporters. They roamed the battle areas, it seemed, with little restraint. Daily briefings were held for journalists. The information they garnered and were provided kept them "up to the minute."

There is ample evidence and a multitude of examples to indicate that the news from Vietnam was not always objectively, accurately, and professionally reported. All too frequently, it was steered, managed—even exaggerated and distorted. To make matters worse and even more disconcerting, the "news" sent from Vietnam was often "slanted" further by the editors back home before it was published. From this, frequently, emerged not only half-truths but also "untruths."

American families at home, if they chose, could watch on their T.V. screens pictures of the Vietnam battlefields. Often these viewers were fed, along with the T.V. dinners on their laps, pictures of American soldiers fighting and dying.

And what about RETURNING HOME FROM WAR? After WWII in Europe had ended, when the troop ships arrived in New York Harbor, there were welcoming parties, bands, Red Cross ladies with metal pitchers filled with fresh, cold milk, and soon after parades. I returned to New York eleven months after V-E Day. My ship was still met by a band and the Red Cross ladies were still there with their milk. For weeks and months after, the people of our nation in a variety of ways showered their gratitude, praise, and appreciation upon their esteemed and proud veterans.

Was it different for the Vietnam veteran? Of course. If he had not been killed or wounded, he was on a plane returning home almost exactly a year to the day after arriving in that country. He went over as an individual and came home as an individual, again with a group of strangers. Once more it was a commercial aircraft with in-flight meals. When he landed in California, there was no band or Red Cross ladies. After he got off the plane, as soon as he could, he headed for home. More accurately—he slunk home. Along the way, he was insulted, ridiculed, vilified, even spat upon. He took off his uniform as soon as he could, not admitting for a long time that he had been to Vietnam.

When he filled out his job applications, he somehow neglected to mention that he had served in that country. He became a bitter, disillusioned veteran.

At the end of WWII our military was by far the largest, most successful, most powerful ever assembled by this nation. And the proudest—and rightfully so. It had met the challenge and done the job supremely well. Our citizenry fully recognized their accomplishments, and the military was held in the highest of esteem. Everyone who had served was made to feel like a hero, and one of it's best known even became president.

That refrain once again—how very different with Vietnam. Despite extensive difficulties, endless frustrations, handicaps—obstacles and hurdles of many varieties placed in their way—the military, overall, WON in the field. Even Tet of 1968, although deeply marred psychologically, was a definitive military victory. Yet, the military were labeled "losers." Understandably, after the war the military were demoralized. They believed that their political leaders, the media, and even the American public had badly let them down. For years they were held in low esteem by their countrymen, and it took a very long while to begin to "bounce back."

And what are the lasting, vivid final pictures we retain of the end of WWII and of Vietnam?

On May 7, 1945 the Germans surrendered unconditionally, and the following day, May 8, the war in Europe ended.

But it was on September 2, 1945 that a distinguished, high-powered, formally attired Japanese delegation boarded the venerable battleship, USS *Missouri*. Allied fighting men stood or hung from every vantage point. Virtually every inch of available deck space was occupied. The men and their now famous leaders had their eyes glued on the table upon which rested two copies of the surrender documents. They watched almost without breathing as the Japanese signed the surrender documents that officially ended WWII. It was a serious, sober, subdued, unprecedented, yet triumphant event. Electricity was in the

air, and powerful drama, as well. That epochal day will be forever remembered in the history of our nation. It was everything that President
Roosevelt would have wanted and expected.

Thirty years later, at the end of April, 1975, for 19 hours, 81 helicopters would evacuate from Saigon 1,000 Americans and 6,000 Vietnamese. The picture that will remain imprinted indelibly in our minds
is of the last helicopters to leave the roof of the U.S. Embassy. There
is pandemonium, panic, terror. Hordes of stricken, desperate people
fight, battle, claw to seize a seat. Failing that they make a last, frantic,
quixotic attempt at rescue by clutching out to the moving helicopters
as they make their final lift-off from the roof.

And in the swirling dust a disgraceful, disquieting, dismaying image appears—that of total, abject humiliation.

During WWII, we did it right. During Vietnam, we did it
wrong.

What went wrong and why? The question begs more questions.
Where was the leadership, will, zeal, focus, vision, moral courage (to
make the difficult decisions), tenacity (of which the enemy had plenty),
sense of purpose, unity of effort, determination, and much more?

But the one big question that gnaws at, eats my heart and soul:
how could the nation which launched the successful Normandy Invasion, without question the most massive, powerful, concentrated military undertaking in all of military history; could fight throughout the
vast Pacific and defeat that superpower, Japan; could fight in Europe
and defeat that superpower, Germany, and the lesser power, Italy; could
equip and supply our far-flung forces literally worldwide; could provide
supplies and equipment to such Allies as Russia and Great Britain—
how could that same nation be involved for nearly fourteen years with
a tiny, backward, half-baked country, and leave with its tail between its
legs?

As the king in "The King and I" muttered, "It's a puzzlement."

CHAPTER NINETEEN

THE DAY I BECAME A BRAVE RIFLE

*Written by Brig. Gen. Albin F. Irzyk. Reprinted with
permission from* ARMOR *magazine, May-June 2000.*

Gen. Winfield Scott, at the Battle of Chapultepec, was reputed to have exclaimed about the 3rd U.S. Cavalry Regiment, "Brave Rifles, veterans, you have been baptized in fire and blood and have come out steel." Thenceforth, the troopers of the 3rd Cav would be known as the "Brave Rifles."

My baptism of fire came not on the fields of strife, but at peaceful, picturesque Fort Myer, Virginia, where the 3rd U.S. Cavalry Regiment was stationed. It occurred during my first tour as officer of the day. My "blooding" was not in combat, but for a brand-new, pre-war second lieutenant, it proved to be a pressure-packed, challenging, inspiring, exhilarating, exhausting, tempestuous 24 hours.

It all began at a gallop at Guard Mount, and never let up. As I descended the steps of the guardhouse resplendent in polished boots, spurs, breeches, Sam Browne belt, saber, and campaign hat, I was weak-kneed with a pounding heart. My quivering legs somehow got me to my post. As I stood before the perfectly aligned, crisply and immaculately uniformed troopers, my mouth was dry, and my mind suddenly went blank like a quarterback about to call his first play and not remembering one thing out of his play book. My last vestige of confidence vanished when I saw my sergeant of the guard. He was a tiny, wizened, but very tough old soldier with over 20 years of service who allegedly ate second lieutenants with his scrambled eggs for breakfast. I knew his reputation, and had heard him on the parade ground during close order drill shout, "When aye say aysa rite, aye wanna heer dose aysa cleeeek."

But somehow the tough old sergeant and the new lieutenant were carrying it off. Now the ranks were open, and I was passing slowly, carefully, from man to man, checking each weapon, shoes, crispness of the summer-starched khakis, haircuts, shaves, position of the caps, knowledge of general and special orders, confirming that each was, indeed, qualified to stand guard.

At the same time, I was searching for the most perfectly turned-out trooper, who would be designated the colonel's orderly. The chosen soldier would not have to pull guard duty, and his selection was a greatly sought after honor for him and his troop. It was so competitive among troops that troopers were known to have been carried from their orderly rooms to guard mount by their fellows, so that they would not crack or wrinkle the heavily starched trousers at the knee.

I was now down to three. After checking handkerchiefs, undershirts, polish of their brass, and asking ever increasingly difficult military questions, I finally had my man, and guard mount was soon over.

I was now the officer of the day, and for the next hours, I would be in charge of the post, as the colonel's designated representative. I did not have time to reflect upon my newly exalted status or my great responsibilities, for my corporals were now running the prisoners out of the guard house, and lining them up for a rapid roll call. I watched with more than a vested interest, for like a supply sergeant, I was about to sign for them.

As soon as the count was correct and my signature on the dotted line, they were hustled out at a rapid clip for the mess hall, some distance away. They marched in a tight body, and members of my guard circled them like outriders during a cattle round-up, or fighters escorting heavily laden bombers, and every bit as alert.

The moment I saw their plates being filled, I sallied forth directly toward the flagpole, for it was now almost time for retreat. As I arrived, to my great relief I found the detail to be complete and in place—two men to fire the retreat gun, two to lower the colors, and the bugler. I glanced at my watch. I had been warned to start EXACTLY on time—after all, the colonel's quarters were only a stone's throw away, and HE might be watching. My watch said, "Now!"

I nodded to the bugler. With his first notes, I became swept up and deeply moved by the small, simple, yet poignant ritual, which unfolded before me. I was standing on a high bluff looking down upon the whole city of Washington, D.C., which seemed to sprawl tightly around my feet. Behind me the setting sun, like a giant spotlight, bathed the city in the brightest of light. Every detail was so clear and so close that I was tempted to reach out and touch the Lincoln Memorial,

Washington Monument, and the Capitol. The bugler's notes were so strong, so clear, so penetrating that I was sure that the entire city before me was hearing him.

The spectacular setting and simple ceremony were so stirring and absorbing that I had difficulty holding back the shivers. Then came the BOOM of the gun, and the bugler, again, with his beautiful, plaintive, haunting notes—as I saluted and watched the colors being slowly and carefully lowered. That simple, dignified, and beautiful ceremony signified the end—the high point of the soldier's day—and left me with a vivid and absolutely unforgettable picture. From that day on, retreat would always have a special meaning for me.

As soon as the flag was folded and the detail began marching away, I shook myself back to reality, and hastily returned to the guard house. The prisoners were back from their meal. I gave them time to get settled in for the night, then went in to check them.

As I wandered among these basically good-looking troopers, despite their prison garb, caged and lying on hard, uncomfortable bunks because of some transgression, I could not help but be struck by how this depressing sight contrasted so vividly with the truly beautiful one which I had so recently witnessed.

Darkness quickly settled in, and now it was time to carry out yet another one of my gamut of responsibilities. One by one, I visited each of the 14 widely scattered guard posts, and was challenged 14 times by 14 different sentries. I was encouraged and reassured that my guards were alert and familiar with their general and special orders, and that the post was secure.

This had been a long, demanding procedure, and midnight was approaching. Yet, before the task was completed, there was one more post to be inspected; the 15th. This one was the most distant, most unusual, and most special. It was the sentry at the Tomb of the Unknown Soldier, deep in Arlington National Cemetery.

As it had been with the other 14 posts, this one would be on foot—*a la pied*. The day of the jeep had not yet arrived. From the guard house my steps took me past the old, venerable, brick chapel, and through the nearby gate into the cemetery. I took a deep breath, for staring straight ahead of me was total blackness. The bright lights of the post which I was leaving accentuated the darkness which I was facing.

I moved out briskly, for I had a long, long walk ahead of me. The lights of the post had gradually dimmed, and soon disappeared behind me. It was now pitch, inky black, and absolutely still. The only sounds to be heard were the sharp crack of my leather heels as they hit the pavement. Since there were no competing sounds, the noise of my boots was greatly magnified. Each time the heel came down, it was like a spaced, single, pistol shot echoing in the heavy stillness of the night—crack, crack, crack.

As I walked deeper into the cemetery, I began to be flooded with emotions. It was eerie, unreal, spooky, scary. Here I was in a vast cemetery all alone. What had I gotten myself into? Misgivings began to emerge. Who would know it if I turned back right now and forgot the whole thing? I, the only living person among acres and acres of dead. My chest got tighter, my breath shorter—crack, crack, crack. I gritted my teeth, and just knew that I had to ride it out. I resolutely continued on, and began to think positively.

My eyes were now more accustomed to the deep gloom. I could make out, dimly, row upon row of identical white headstones. Visible, too, from time to time were more elaborate markers and monuments. I began to reflect upon who it was that was buried around me and why they were there. Suddenly, abruptly, I realized how very privileged I was. Here, enveloping me, were military heroes from every war in which the United States had ever been engaged, even including some from the Revolutionary War. There were military leaders and military men whose exploits fill endless pages of history books, recipients of the Medal of Honor, individuals known only to family and friends, and, as I would soon note, some known but to God. I was suddenly sobered and awed to realize that I was moving about the greatest collection of heroes in all the world.

I knew that, earlier this day, hundreds of people, busloads of them, had been scattered throughout the cemetery to pay homage to these heroes. Now I had them, all of them, the whole cemetery to myself. I was privileged, indeed.

My heart had stopped pounding, I was swallowing easier, my footsteps quickened—were more purposeful. I was now eating up the yards. Suddenly, it was no longer totally black, for up ahead I noted a faint spot of light.

As I walked, it gradually became larger and brighter, and I knew that I was about to reach my destination. I moved closer and then abruptly stopped. There before me in an island of bright light was pure, powerful drama. A lone sentinel stiff—almost rigid—in crisp, sharp, splendid uniform, was executing an intense, moving ritual. He paced back and forth before the tomb—21 precise steps, an "about face," a shift from "right shoulder to left shoulder arms," a 21-second halt, and 21 more precise steps back. It was truly an awe-inspiring, breath-taking spectacle.

As I emerged out of the darkness into the bright light, I heard a loud, firm, "Halt, who goes there?" Standing at rigid "Attention" with his rifle at "Port Arms" was the guard who had abruptly stopped his pacing and now waited for me to identify myself. After a brief exchange of words, I instructed him to "carry on," and he resumed his brisk, clipped pacing.

My next duty was to inspect the guardroom in the base of the amphitheater. Before entering the room, I turned and drank in once again the poignant, symbolic, floodlit scene. Once again how privileged I was not only to "see" this tribute to that fallen hero and all those he represented, but to be, this night, the sole witness, the only spectator.

Soon I was back in the darkness retracing my steps. Those steps now were buoyant, for I felt exhilarated. What a rich, never-to-be-forgotten experience.

Before I knew it, I was out of the cemetery, and back in the guard-house. After a brief "breather," it was back to work—hitting, again, before dawn, the 14 guard posts.

The long, eventful night had finally ended. The post was once more busy, bustling. I watched as my NCOs married up combinations of a guard and two prisoners, and sent each detail to their work locations.

For the officer of the day, the job was only partially finished. More challenges lay ahead. Promptly at eight o'clock, I stood at post head-quarters in front of the desk of Mr. Whitehouse, the senior warrant officer. I stared at the tall, lean, completely white-headed individual who looked old enough to have served with Teddy Roosevelt. My fate was now in his hands, and I wondered tremulously what that would be. He acknowledged my presence by reaching immediately into a side drawer of his desk. He removed some thin, typewritten, "onion-skin" sheets of paper, and wordlessly handed them to me. I walked out of his office and into the corridor. My heart sank, for I counted six sheets of paper. Each one represented a funeral in Arlington National Cemetery that day. I had "maxed the course," for in those days six was the most that could be handled. It had been impressed upon us that the officer of the day was solely responsible for the funerals on his tour, and that he would ensure that each funeral was completed exactly as prescribed—that there was no second chance, no second time around.

From my fellow lieutenants, I had heard all the "horror stories," undoubtedly highly exaggerated, about the OD who had a funeral without a bugler, another without a firing squad, still another without a chaplain who, himself, was forced to say, "ashes to ashes." The most colorful, of course, was about the OD who was bustling around, and in his great haste had stepped back and into the freshly dug grave.

Now it was my time. I was responsible for six.

When I came out of post headquarters, I spotted a pick-up truck, and knew that for this detail I would have "wheels." I hastened to the office of the superintendent, and was immediately handed a map of the cemetery with circled locations of each grave, numbered in sequence. I jumped back into the truck, and hastily reconnoitered each widely scattered site to determine where it was, and how to get there. I rushed back to the post, and found the first funeral detail already forming. After checking and inspecting it, it was time to go, and the first funeral in Arlington National Cemetery that day was underway.

As soon as the graveside services had been completed, I quickly returned, and there, already forming, was the detail for the next funeral. And so it went all day, back and forth.

It turned out that my six spanned the spectrum from the very simple—chaplain, pallbearers, bugler with few mourners, to the elaborate with full military honors—including caisson, rider-less horse, sizeable honor guard, firing squad, and many mourners. Each was so sad, sober, moving that I became not a spectator but a mourner.

Now, finally, it was time for guard mount once again. There stood not an apprehensive, trembling young lieutenant, but an exhausted, shell-shocked one. I was still in a daze, and wondered if anyone could pack more varied activity into a 24-hour period than I just did.

From somewhere came the words, "old officer of the day." I shook myself and realized that they were directed at me. I was finished, my tour was over; I had survived.

Once again the boots went click, click, click. This time they headed in the direction of my bachelor's quarters and bed. It had been a tumultuous day, an emotional roller coaster. I felt a great sense of achievement, of fulfillment. I now knew that I had won my spurs and earned the appellation—"Brave Rifle."

CHAPTER TWENTY

WHAT MADE THE
4ᵀᴴ ARMORED DIVISION GREAT?

Address by: Brig. Gen. Albin F. Irzyk (Ret.)
29ᵗʰ Annual Convention, 4ᵗʰ Armored Division Association
Pittsburgh, Pennsylvania—1949

M y comrades and your ladies. Tonight you do me a very great honor. However, you have honored me before. You elected me your third president. I followed those two great and distinguished soldiers, Generals Wood and Clarke. I stood before you in Boston in 1948 and accepted that important office, and stood before you again in Philadelphia in 1949 and relinquished that office.

But tonight I am deeply and profoundly touched. For your main speaker at this, the 29ᵗʰ Annual Convention, you have decided to go with one of your own. You could provide me with no greater tribute. I realize only too well that in years past, you have been addressed by a U.S. senator, by a governor, by the chief of staff of the army, and by the general who placed on our division colors the Presidential Unit Citation, and by many other distinguished individuals. So, I am deeply grateful, indeed, for this opportunity and privilege, which you have provided me.

The subject of my address tonight is: "What Made The Fourth Armored Division Great?" You all remember many years ago that a man by the name of Sir Alexander Fleming put a bunch of ingredients together, and he came up with a miracle drug called Penicillin. More recently a man by the name of Jonas Salk put a bunch of ingredients together and came up with a vaccine that revolutionized medicine by preventing polio.

Well, someone—it must have been the Man upstairs—put a bunch of ingredients together and came up with a miracle division, the 4th Armored Division. What were those ingredients?

Well, the 4th Armored had men from New York, Pennsylvania, New Jersey, and Ohio. But, every other division had men from New York, Pennsylvania, New Jersey, and Ohio.

Well, the 4th Armored had Jews, Italians, Poles and Baptists. But, every other division had Jews, Italians, Poles, and Baptists.

Well, the 4th Armored had taxi drivers, garage mechanics, successful businessmen and union laborers. But, every other division had taxi drivers, garage mechanics, successful businessmen and union laborers.

Well, the 4th Armored had tall men, short men, fat men, skinny men—rich men, poor men, professional men. But, every other division had tall men, short men, fat men skinny men—rich men, poor men, professional men.

If all this is so, what then made the 4th Armored different from all the other divisions? What were all the ingredients that made it GREAT?

Frankly, I don't know. This question has not only puzzled me, but has long puzzled other soldiers, historians, and correspondents—and I am sure many of you. All have wondered what combination of ingredients made the miracle division. I really don't think there is a pat answer.

However, there are some ingredients that I do know about—that we had that no other division had—and these I would like to discuss with you.

The first ingredient was TRAINING. We were more superbly trained than any other division. The cold snows of Pine Camp; flexing our muscles and moving, moving on Tennessee maneuvers; the heat and sand of the Mojave Desert; the great firing ranges at Camp Bowie; and the final tuning up on the Salisbury Plains, where we were on

D-Day. What a combination of experiences! On top of that our leaders were imaginative, realistic, and daring with our training. Who else but the 4th would put a company of tanks in a Wadi in California against another company of tanks both firing live .30 caliber machine guns at one another? While everyone else might be satisfied with a moving target that was a wooden frame on a sled—not the 4th. It used a real, honest-to-goodness moving tank at which it fired live .30 calibers. I can recall vividly right after the break-through when we were rolling to Coutances and Avranches—I yelled, "This is just like maneuvers!" The only difference—the big stuff we were firing were not blanks, and the people we were capturing by the hundreds did not wear aggressor uniforms. No division had been exposed to so many different facets of training in such a wide variety of locations—was better trained—was more ready for combat, than we. When we kicked off, we were honed to a razor's edge.

The second ingredient that I am sure of was the requirement to send out CADRES. We moaned at the time, but it was a tremendous blessing. No division sent out more cadres than we. Yes, with those cadres, unfortunately, we had to send out some really top people. But, also, and more important—we used those cadres to weed out. Cadres gave us an opportunity to sift, to cull, to refine, to polish. When we sailed overseas, our barrel was filled with big, red, shiny, juicy, firm apples. There was not a rotten apple in the bunch. They had all been sifted out.

The third ingredient that I am sure of was MAJ. GEN. JOHN SHIRLEY "P" WOOD. In my eyes, and I am sure in yours, he was unquestionably the greatest division commander of World War II and perhaps in all of U.S. warfare. There has never been a division commander before or since who loved every man in his division as he did, and who, in turn, was loved by every man in that division. No other division commander saluted his men before they had a chance to salute him. Yet, I recall when I first reported to Pine Camp, one of the first questions I asked was, "How is our division commander?" I don't remember whom I asked, but he answered, "He's kind of weak." "Why do you say that?" I asked. "Well," he answered, "We recently had a division review, he made a speech, and he ended it by saying, "God bless you men." Weak? Boy, we would soon know better.

At Pine Camp that same General Wood kept us on post, restricted us, made us train all day and attend classes at night. Admit it, there isn't a man here who was at Pine Camp, and that includes me, who didn't bitch and gripe about that. But he knew what was good for us—thank God he knew.

Our General Wood was reprimanded, ridiculed, and rebuked during critiques on Tennessee maneuvers. His superiors told him that he moved too fast and too far. They told him that he just could not do it in combat with the enemy shooting, fighting, and attacking, so why was he doing it in Tennessee? General Wood stood his ground, and quietly told them—we can do it and we will do it.

I recall a wet field in France—our first break after 2½ months of hard fighting. Word came down that General Wood was on his way to visit us and to speak to us. I spent many, many minutes lining up and dressing the battalion. General Wood arrived, jumped up on a platform and in one second he undid all I tried to do. He said, "Gather 'round, men." Then he thanked us for what we had done, told us how humble HE felt in our presence, and then he choked up as he talked. Yes, the 4th Armored had "P" Wood. No other division had a General Wood.

The fourth ingredient that I am sure of is our ARMY COMMANDER, GENERAL PATTON. As we all know, he was daring, imaginative, audacious, visionary. But to be that successful he needed the right tool. He found that tool—the 4th Armored. Patton and the 4th—the perfect combination. Supposing our army commander had been Monty. He would have told us to move three miles and we would have moved three miles in a day. The world would never have known that we could move 20 or 30 miles a day or more.

And because we moved so far and so fast—General Patton didn't have the time and was too far away to prepare for us detailed operation orders. So, he developed for us the mission type order. We received the order by radio or courier delivered overlay. It had a line—line of departure; a broad arrow—axis of advance; a goose egg—the objective. That's all. Oh, yes, he added, "Get going at first light." That's all it took to get that splendid division galloping 30 miles to the right place. And once when we ran out of maps and orders, all he needed to say was, "Go East!"

They say that Patton was the great exponent of the calculated risk. Patton said, "If I have a fifty-fifty chance, I'll take it, for the superb fighting qualities of the 4th Armored Division will give me the one percent necessary." We had the right army commander to pull the best out of us—to send us on impossible missions that we made possible. He dreamed up the missions—we executed them. Thank God we had a Patton and not a Monty.

The fifth ingredient that we had that no other division had was a unique and unquenchable SPIRIT. That spirit was manifested in many, many different ways. We lived it.

Those of you who know me, know that I don't sound off unless I mean it. When I left on Utah Beach the LCT that had taken me across the channel, the British skipper said, "Good luck." I turned to him and said, "You'll be reading about us. Remember—it's the 4th Armored Division." He laughed and said, "Oh, you Yanks are all alike." But I believed it.

I lived with a tank crew. We ate together, slept together, fought together, shared the fruitcakes from home. Yet, when we were out of the tank and I was passing by, they lifted their heads, saluted smartly, and said, "Good afternoon, Sir." Spirit. God what a bunch.

When the Repple Depots ran out of tankers, they sent us infantry replacements. Never saw a tank before. Yet, in three days they were tankers. Spirit. How was the division able to fight for almost a year, turn over at least three times in many slots and without any practice, march perfectly in a division review in Landshut, Germany, when we received our Presidential Unit Citation? Spirit.

This is the 29th Annual Convention. What brings you back year after year, using your vacation time, your vacation money? Some of you have never missed. You come because you want to see again and talk to the man on your right and on your left, because you admire him and love him probably more than your own brother. That is the mystifying and wonderful spirit of the 4th.

The sixth ingredient that we had and which no other division had was a SOUL. The soul of the 4th Armored will march forever and will never die. That soul had elan, aggressiveness, the will to fight, dash, confidence, audacity, and a debonair, reckless but ordered discipline.

The final ingredient that I will mention that the 4th had that no one else had, was PEOPLE—fabulous, extraordinary, unforgettable, wonderful people. We had Pat Heid, who should have been medically evacuated, and who risked his life every day by doctoring himself without anyone knowing it, so he could keep rolling with the 4th.

We had Father Ernst who won a Silver Star, and who in his jeep and with his Mass kit was always just one step away from the action, ready to set up and offer Mass at the briefest lull in the action.

We had Abe Baum and his intrepid gang that drove to Hammelburg.

We had Jimmie Leach who had at least five Purple Hearts that I know of, and still headed for the hottest action.

We had Abe, who was destined to become and did become the number one soldier in the army.

We had Constance Klinga of "C" Company of my own 8th Tank Battalion, who on the July 31, 1944 uttered the cry that became one of the great battle cries of World War II—"They've got us surrounded again, the poor bastards." Who but a 4th Armored soldier would utter an audacious, cocky, reckless, nose-thumbing cry like that?

People—yes, people—the most important ingredient of them all.
What made the 4th Armored Division GREAT?
You and you and you and you! Every damned one of you.
That's who!
Thank you.

CHAPTER TWENTY-ONE

MEMORIAL SERVICE

Remarks by Brig. Gen. Albin F. Irzyk (Ret.)
31st Annual 4th Armored Division Association Convention
Orlando, Florida—July 16,1977

C omrades and your ladies: For me, today, my task is a sobering, difficult, emotional one. This morning, as this association has done for 31 years—we are gathered to honor, to pay tribute to, to pay homage to, to think about, and to remember the 1,519 men who gave their lives fighting for their country and their division. One thousand five hundred and nineteen—almost two battalions worth of men who went to Europe with us—but unlike us, did not return home. Each one of those 1,519 is a genuine, authentic hero.

Those men gave up for their country the most precious commodity God can bestow upon us—an individual, human life. No one has yet had the temerity to try to place a dollar sign on the value of an individual, human life. It is far too precious. It is really priceless.

Each of us is given just one life. There is no second time around. Yet, those men gave up that one life that was given to them. What they did has often been referred to as making the supreme sacrifice. What more can a man give to his country or to his fellow man than that precious, valuable commodity—his own life?

Yes, those are heroes—in the truest, purest sense. They fit the mould of Nathan Hale who said, "I regret that I have but one life to give for my country," or of Joseph Addison who said, "What a pity is it that we can die but once to save our country."

Not only at times like this—at conventions, but at other times over the years—I find myself thinking about those men and wondering about them. Quite a number I knew well. They were my friends, associates. We trained together, lived together, and fought together. Some of them died carrying out missions I had assigned to them.

Many of them I did not know, and it is about those that I wonder most. There were many who were married, had children. They will never celebrate a 30th or 40th wedding anniversary, or attend a high school or college graduation of one of their children. They will never experience the great joy of being a grandfather.

There were many who were recent bridegrooms before sailing overseas. They left young widows. They will never experience the complete fulfillment of that marriage, or the cherished pleasure of raising a fine family. There were many who were very young, still single, who would never complete their educations, and who would never know the deep love of a true, fine woman.

As you so well know, there was no pattern to their dying. Some of the 1,519 were killed at the very outset of the war—at Coutances, Avranches. Some in the middle—at Bastogne. Some at the very end—along the Danube or in Czechoslovakia.

When those men went overseas, every one of them knew the dangers, risks, challenges—knew they might never come back. Yet, they worked hard, fought hard. If they were told to be the lead tank, the front infantry squad, to probe for mines—they went. Every morning when they moved out to attack at first light, they knew it might be their last day. These men had no illusions—any day, any minute, any second—this might be it. But for them, finally did come the day, the hour, the second.

We look up and we see a number—1,519. Merely a number. Yet, that number breaks down into 1,519 individual lives. Each was an individual human being with fears, likes, dislikes, emotions—with a lust for life, with ambition, goals, objectives, and with a great capacity for love.

Yes, I think about them often, and as I think I cannot help but wonder—"There but for the grace of God go I"—and "There but for the grace of God go you." Why was it they and not we?

We ran the same dangers, received the same fire, had the same close calls. Why was it they and not we? During the war for a while, I kept track of my close calls and then lost count. Two I will never forget. At Lorient I thought it was all over, and as a calmness settled over me, I saw my life flash before me. At Chaumont on the way to Bastogne when my tank was hit I felt the presence of God.

Each one of you may recall a close one—perhaps several close ones. So close they could have gone either way. Many of those who were killed never should have been—riding along a supposedly cleared place and hitting a mine, leaving a tank to relieve himself, only to be hit by a stray shell fragment.

Many of us who were constantly in the thick of it were not called. Why? There is no explaining. You remember—we had an expression, "That one had his number on it." What we meant was—that it was something we could not control, that it was predestinated, foreordained. We had to believe that someone, somewhere—someone up above controls the destiny of warriors, and when we were in Europe, he had other plans for us.

Each one of us here today should be truly humbled, truly awed. As we look at that number 1,519, we should say over and over, "There but for the grace of God, go I." Let us never forget it. We should be eternally grateful for every hour, every day that we have been given since WWII, and it now adds up to 32 years. A bonus of 32 years. Thirty-two years that we have had with our families, with our careers—32 more years than those 1,519 had. We must be forever grateful to God for singling us out, for choosing us to finish the war safely, to return home.

And with heads bowed and tears in our eyes, we should express gratitude, love and appreciation to those 1,519 for staying in Europe, so that we could come home, so that we could enjoy a convention like this.

If there is a heaven, and I firmly believe there is, I can't help but feel that all 1,519 are up there in that heaven, that they are looking down upon us today, that they are sharing this convention with us, glorying in the role they played in making the 4th Armored—great!

And I suspect that they are touched—with perhaps a tear or two sliding slowly down their cheeks, knowing that after all these years, their comrades down on earth remember them, honor them, cherish them, and are deeply grateful to them.

As they look down, and as I look up, I wish to say to them a simple, humble thank you. And as I enjoy this convention, I will be thinking of them, remembering them, and sharing it with them.

This morning we should also honor and remember those members of the 4th who fought valiantly, came home, became members of this fine association, and have since passed on, thereby thinning our ranks even more.

At this memorial service each of you has reflected on the past, and each of you has his own personal, private thoughts. I suggest that we all bow our heads for a moment of silence and meditation and to honor and to pay tribute to the 1,519 men from this division who died in Europe, and to those association members who have left our ranks for greener pastures.

I would like to close with a quotation from the New Testament: "Greater love hath no man than this, that a man lay down his life for his friends."

PHOTO LOG

Pg 32-33   Before the river, the canal had to be negotiated. © Brig. Gen. Albin F. Irzyk (Ret.)

Pg 34-35   Lt. Bill Marshall watches as his tank tows the second tank of his platoon. © Brig. Gen. Albin F. Irzyk (Ret.) (as captioned in *WWII Magazine*)

Pg 64   Author and son standing on the bridge over the Eichel River that was seized intact. © Brig. Gen. Albin F. Irzyk (Ret.)

Pg 65   Author and Gerard Bazin, French historian, at railroad under-pass, which if damaged would have trapped the 8th Tank Battalion and prevented the seizure of the Eichel River Bridge. © Brig. Gen. Albin F. Irzyk (Ret.)

Pg 96   Generals Wood and Patton. © Patton Museum, Fort Knox Kentucky

Pg 134-135 A clear view of the road into Chaumont and north to Grandru. The battlegrounds for two days of heavy combat. © Brig. Gen. Albin F. Irzyk (Ret.)

Pg 148-149 The beech tree in winter and the author. © Brig. Gen. Albin F. Irzyk (Ret.)

Pg 154   Peaceful and war torn Chaumont. Two different looks at the beech tree. © Brig. Gen. Albin F. Irzyk (Ret.)

Pg 160-161 The author at the rebuilt Urmitz Bridge. It is fully operational with heavy railroad traffic. © Brig. Gen. Albin F. Irzyk (Ret.)

Map Index